Worrier state

Manchester University Press

GOVERNING INTIMACIES IN THE GLOBAL SOUTH

Series editors: Srila Roy, Associate Professor of Sociology, University of the Witwatersrand, Johannesburg; Nicky Falkof, Associate Professor of Media Studies, University of the Witwatersrand, Johannesburg

About the series

Governing Intimacies in the Global South deploys the categories of intimacy and governance to offer novel insights into the subjects, politics, cultures and experiences of the global south. The series showcases work that speaks to the affective and intimate worlds of communities located in Asia, Africa and Latin America while remaining attuned to governmental, social and other regulatory frames that undergird these worlds.

It seeks to bridge the gap between developmental analyses of the 'rest of the world', which theorise macro structures to the exclusion of the intimate, and historical and ethnographic records of micro-settings, allowing these to speak to larger structural conditions and constraints. Emphasising the postcolonial making of gender, sexuality and race as categories of meaning and power, this series views the relation between intimacy and governance from a position of theorising from the south, contributing to a reimagining of the idea of global south itself.

Worrier state

Risk, anxiety and moral panic in South Africa

Nicky Falkof

MANCHESTER UNIVERSITY PRESS

Copyright © Nicky Falkof 2022

The right of Nicky Falkof to be identified as the
author of this work has been asserted by them in
accordance with the Copyright, Designs and Patents
Act 1988.

Published by Manchester University Press
Oxford Road, Manchester M13 9PL

www.manchesteruniversitypress.co.uk

British Library Cataloguing-in-Publication Data
A catalogue record for this book is available from
the British Library

ISBN 978 1 5261 6402 5 hardback
ISBN 978 1 5261 7188 7 paperback

First published 2022
Paperback published 2023

The publisher has no responsibility for the
persistence or accuracy of URLs for any external or
third-party internet websites referred to in this book,
and does not guarantee that any content on such
websites is, or will remain, accurate or appropriate.

Typeset
by Cheshire Typesetting Ltd, Cuddington, Cheshire

For Joe

Contents

Acknowledgements

As anyone who's spent time with me in the last few years will know, this book has had a complicated and sometimes painful gestation. I am deeply indebted to the many thoughtful people in my life who remain willing to thrash through sometimes incoherent ideas with me, particularly those who sit around multiple kitchen tables in multiple cities with multiple cups of tea helping me make sense of suspicions, hints and fragments. I have not named you all here, but this project, like everything I do, would not be what it is without the patience, warmth and humour of my friends. It is also, to some extent, a book about my city, Johannesburg: seductive and traumatising in equal measures, exhausting but always surprising, sometimes hard to love but always hard to leave.

Thanks to Martin J. Murray for his invaluable comments and willingness to read the entire manuscript. For their perceptive feedback on drafts of the various chapters, thanks to Carli Coetzee, Srila Roy, Katlego Disemelo, Roshan Dadoo, Richard Ballard, Iginio Gagliardone. As well as reading a chapter and suggesting the title, Mehita Iqani helped to develop the initial idea for this project (and so many others). The idea for Chapter 3 was suggested by Bev Goldman and developed in conversation with Sandile Maphanga and Zanele Mthombeni. Chapter 5 emerged with the help of Chloe Hutchinson during a lengthy visit to Brighton. Thanks to Katlego Disemelo and Sean Thurtell for assistance with translations. For reading suggestions, productive arguments, publishing advice and general comradery, thanks to Sara Orning, Urvashi Butalia, Busi Dlamini, Cobus van Staden, Antonia Steyn, Tiffany Willoughby-Herard, Sarah Nuttall, Kirk Sides, Dina Ligaga, Simon van Schalkwyk, Jennifer Malec, Max Bolt, Zoe Groves, Tim Wright, Shireen Hassim, Roshan Cader, David Hornsby and my colleagues in the Wits Media Studies department. It has been a real pleasure to work with Manchester University Press, particularly my editor Tom Dark, who offered enthusiastic support at a complicated moment. Thanks to Themba Khumalo for allowing me to use his magnificent artwork on the cover. This book has been greatly enriched by the input of Nkululeko Sibiya, Mpho Moloto, Meso Qhobela and Gilda Vamussa, outstanding young scholars who acted as research assistants at various stages of the project. Thanks too to students in the Wits Media Studies third year class New Media and Society and the Honours class Critical Media Analysis for allowing me to bring my research into their seminar time and for offering enthusiastic and creative engagement with the issues presented in this book. Sections of Chapter 3 were originally published as an article in *Feminist Media Studies*; my thanks to the journal for permission to reuse this material. I am indebted to the luminous scholarship of Sara Ahmed, Grace Musila, Gabeba Baderoon and Zygmunt Bauman, among many others, and so grateful for the perceptive comments of anonymous reviewers, whose insight and generosity have significantly improved this project. Weaknesses and oversights that remain are entirely my own.

This book is based on research emerging from a long-term project that has been funded by a Friedel Sellschop award from the University of the Witwatersrand, a Thuthuka Early Career Fellowship from the National Research Foundation of South Africa and a fellowship from the African Humanities Program of the American Council of Learned Sciences. Thanks to Valerie Killian and Kathleen Ripamonti for patiently and cheerfully helping to administer everything. The very first parts of this work were initiated during an ACLS-funded visiting fellowship at the University of Dar-es-Salaam. The conclusion was written during a fellowship at Sussex University, and the manuscript was revised during a fellowship at the Institute of Geography at the Universidad Nacional Autonóma de Mexico, sadly cut short by the arrival of the coronavirus pandemic. So many thanks to my hosts at these institutions, Lightness Sungulla, Malcolm James and Federico Fernández Christlieb. Final revisions were completed during a writing retreat on the Durban South Coast, funded by the Governing Intimacies project (Andrew W. Mellon/Wits University). Chapter 5 was written during a residency at the Rockefeller Bellagio Center in Lake Como, Italy. Warmest thanks to Pilar Palacio and her team, and to my fellow residents (particularly Maureen Kelly, Timmy Bouley, Amitava Kumar, Mona Ali, Cathy Lee Crane, Patrick Ally) for one of the most enriching experiences of my career, and also for some excellent boating. Bellagio is a haven for writers. There is nothing else quite like it, and I remain deeply grateful for the trans-formative weeks I spent there.

A number of events in the last decade have showcased the variety of contemporary work on cultures of fear, particularly in Africa. Some of these have taken place at the Wits Institute for Social and Economic Research (WiSER), based at my home institution. In early 2017 a group of mostly US scholars held an event there titled 'The Politics of Dread'. Later that year a colleague and I hosted a workshop called 'Urban Anxieties in the Global South', and in early 2018 two Wits anthropologists put together a conference called 'On Suspicion and the Contemporary'. In 2016 I presented work drawn from this book at a conference at Sussex University in the UK on the topic of 'Cultures of Risk'. In 2017 I did the same at CRASSH, at Cambridge University, where the event was named 'Anxiety In and About Africa'. The thoughtful scholarship that went into creating these varying approaches to fear, anxiety, dread, risk and suspicion has been hugely valuable in developing my thinking on these questions. It is also significant that so many people from so many fields, but many with an overarching interest in Africa or South Africa, have begun to draw on related concepts and terminology to develop our understandings of how modern life looks and works from within these places. Clearly these are approaches whose time has come.

Sections of this book have been presented at various conferences and seminars since 2014. My particular thanks to the organisers and attendees of the 'Encontro Binacional Estudos do Consumo, Brasil – Africa do Sol' at ESPM in Brazil, in 2014; 'Promises of Monsters' at University of Stavanger, Norway, in 2016; the African Studies seminar series at University College London, UK, in 2018; 'Middle Class Urbanisms' in Maputo, Mozambique, in 2018; the decoloniality seminar series at Rutgers University, US, in 2019; the English department seminar series at Stellenbosch University, SA, in 2019; and the race, ethnicity and postcolonial studies seminar at Sussex University, UK, in 2019.

As with all things, I would not be able to write (or think, or live) without the emotional and often practical sustenance of my friends and family in Johannesburg, Brighton, London and elsewhere. I am unusually fortunate to have communities of loved ones – too many to list here – in so many places. For their fortitude during the writing of this book, I owe special thanks to my immediate family in Joburg and London; to Kirsten Evans, for facilitating my double life; to all the Brightonians who have fed, hosted and listened to me since the big exit; to the pimpos, for food, love and Joburg nuance; to John Trengove and Tammy Sassoon, who remember everything; to Lucy Draper-Clarke and Hayley Gewer, for holding space for anxious writers; and to Richard Parry, for reminding me of the value of ambivalence.

This book is dedicated to Joe Walsh, who is the best person.

A note on referencing and racial language

Texts that provide theoretical, critical or factual material are cited using the Harvard author–date system and collected in the bibliography, while texts that are the objects of the chapters' analysis are collected in four appendices that can be found at the end of the book. Some of the material cited in this book is originally in Afrikaans, isiZulu and isiXhosa. Where necessary, quotes have been translated and original text included in the endnotes.

Throughout this book I use the racial designations 'black', 'white', 'Indian' and 'coloured'. These are everyday terms in South African legal, media and popular discourse, where they are not generally capitalised. I use them here as they are very much part of common parlance and it would be almost impossible to write about this deeply racialised country without them.

Nonetheless it is important to state aloud that whatever their utility, these words have their history in colonial and apartheid racial classifications that were developed for particular ideological purposes; that 'race' as a series of categories is never fixed or final; and that the concept itself is a flawed and reductive way to define human life. In speaking critically about race, we hope to eventually find our way out of it.

Introduction

In a bright summer month in 2012, equipped with new degrees and new ideas, I returned to South Africa after years of living abroad. My homecoming was joyful but also disconcerting. Friends, family and acquaintances seemed concerned that my time in the UK had robbed me of my street-smart reflexes and I was soon inundated with advice on how to survive in my home country. Living safely in South Africa, it seemed, required an insider's access to sometimes arcane, sometimes counter-intuitive knowledge. Talk of crime, risk, danger, security and social decay peppered these conversations, some of which were full of indignant confusion that I would sacrifice a 'safe' life in England for the risky, unsettling realities of home.

I was told that it was important to pick a safe neighbourhood to live in and to rent a property that had adequate security, in the form of bars, electric fences, motion sensor beams and armed guards who would arrive at the touch of a panic button. It was not just criminal outsiders who posed a problem: I should also be wary of untrustworthy landlords, housemates and domestic workers, as well as neighbours and their employees who may be watching my home. I had to be careful opening doors to strangers and should check the credentials of municipal workers before allowing them to enter. Mysterious symbols chalked on walls meant that a house had been earmarked for a break-in, while 'everybody knew' that you just could not go to or through certain areas of the city. I was to sign up for private medical insurance immediately in case 'something happened', as I would also be unsafe – albeit in different ways – at a public hospital. I should watch out for scams at banks or through my cellphone. Strangers, as a rule, were not to be trusted.

Getting around was particularly fraught with danger. I was absolutely not to walk anywhere after dark and should avoid walking
alone during the day. Commuting by bicycle or using public buses
and minibus taxis was out of the question for a middle-class white
woman. I should only use private taxis if I was already familiar with
a driver. My best option would be to buy a car, after which I must
watch out for drunk drivers, potholes and bad roads. When driving
at night I was to make sure never to pause at a traffic light or stop
sign as these were prime targets for hijackers and smash-and-grab
thieves. I was also, however, never to go through a traffic light or
stop sign as minibus taxis were notoriously aggressive, careless of
laws and likely to smash into me given half a chance. Moving was
risky; so was staying still.[1]

Many of these dramatic tales of risk and threat were racialised,
sometimes overtly. White acquaintances, and much of the media
and political discourse that was aimed at them/us, made it clear
that black men in particular presented a threat to my safety. These
theories were offered as self-evident truths in the face of a silenc-
ing 'political correctness' that further endangered people – that is,
people like 'us' – by forbidding us from acknowledging the sources
of peril. They were claims to pragmatism, positioned in opposition
to a perceived policing of speech that may offend the delicate sen-
sibilities of 'liberal' whites but that nonetheless 'needed to be said'.
Such arguments, usually casually made, were distressing and enrag-
ing, not least in their assumption that, as a white person, I would
automatically agree with them. And yet despite my commitment to
anti-racism, despite my desire to perceive myself as a 'good' white
who is not like 'those others' (Thompson 2003), I too felt, and still
feel, anxious in some parts of the city. I have found myself clutching
my handbag more tightly or locking the doors of my car in response
to seeing certain kinds of people on the street: usually black, always
male. While I am painfully conscious of the racial nature of these
emotions and the centuries-long historical injustice that underpins
them, I nonetheless cannot deny that I feel them, even as my ethical/
conscious self pulls back in disgust. My determination to move
lightly through the streets of Johannesburg has been compromised
by these deep and ambivalent fears, by my sense of outsiderness in
the inner city, by the seemingly endless conversations about crime

and danger that characterise South African 'white talk' (Steyn 2004) and by the affective overload of the 'fortress architecture' in the suburbs where I live (Murray 2011). As much as I tried to resist it, my experience of returning home was fraught with the complexities of negotiating a fear that is social as much as personal. Coming back to South Africa has made it clear that my politics cannot unsettle the parts of my identity I am uncomfortable with; rather, as Robyn Weigman would have it, I must face the possibility that 'white antiracism is itself a symptomatic feature of white self- and social mastery, not its political or epistemological displacement' (2012, p. 140).

These anxieties about security and identity, along with many others, have been echoed and expanded upon by colleagues and students, by politicians, community leaders and social media celebrities, by vulnerable workers and cautious foreigners, and appear in multiple forms within the traditional and digital media that I encounter. It is clearly not just wealthy whites who are worried. Criminals, dangerous drivers, homeless people, corrupt police, bad hospitals and abusive employers are all objects of collective concern. People worry daily about the economy, the safety of their bodies and possessions, the condition of roads and other infrastructure, failing institutions and unreliable politicians, apparently uncontrolled influxes of people from elsewhere in Africa, experiences or accusations of racism, tainted food, HIV and other diseases, skills shortages, job shortages, the education system and a host of other concerns, most of which have been dramatically exacerbated by the COVID-19 pandemic. Suffused with all of these intense and often collective emotions, twenty-first-century South Africa seems like a particularly fearful place to be.

Nonetheless, as I write this preface some years after my return to South Africa, it is clear that life continues amongst these powerful emotional currents. The insecurity of township existence is interspersed with the warm hospitality of community celebration. People navigate treacherous taxi ranks and reckless cross-country drivers to maintain connections with faraway family and friends. Children grow up knowing both bustling cities and grandparents' villages. Sangomas and psychotherapists alike do a busy trade, while suburban elites continue to enjoy cheap domestic labour

alongside high-end cars and handbags. Queer people escape conservative homes to emerge phoenix-like into the hybrid Afro-chic
aesthetic of the big cities. People develop friendships and love affairs
across differences of class, race, language and nationality. Daily life
is suffused with soap opera, celebrity, consumption, negotiation
and other common components of the everyday in the burgeoning
cities of Africa. For all its negative consequences, anxiety in South
Africa does not impede existence; it has rather become part of existence, unsurprising, quotidian, expected. This condition is inherently linked to South Africans' hypermodern subjectivity as citizens
of late capitalism, and has much to tell us about contemporary
popular cultural imaginings of selfhood, identity and Africa.

As its contribution to thinking through such imaginings, this book
is concerned with four stories. The chapters that follow consider the
'white genocide' conspiracy theory that has been propagated by
Afrikaner elites; the murders of three young women, attributed to
the influence of an evil satanic cult, or even literally to the devil; an
urban legend around violent and occult crime in Alexandra township, Johannesburg; and folk theories about citizenship and safety
among suburban residents in Melville, also in Johannesburg. Taking
in various locations and concerning people of different economic
classes and racialised categories, these stories reveal that themes of
fear, crime, precarity, safety and belonging criss-cross South African
society in wildly different ways. Anxiety, this book argues, is a
constant condition of South African life; but rather than meaning
only one thing, it is entirely different for different people and communities. Anxiety does not unite us. Its manifestations depend on its
proximity to whiteness and power, on the varying narratives that
underlie it, on the conditions of life of those who find themselves
at its mercy. For some of us, anxiety is a manifestation of woolly,
often repressed mythologies; for others, it is a response to the daily
risk and grind of life in this most unequal country. Cultures of fear
also add to our distance from each other by demonising difference,
fostering paranoia and closing communities. These particular tales,
while radically different in terms of the risks, concerns and conditions that foster them, have in common their imbrication in narrative; their racialised, gendered and classed components; and their
emphasis on the secret, the hidden, the uncanny or the occult.

First, each of these episodes is an instance of narrative by which incidents or experiences become subsumed in larger structures of story that are used to explain and interpret the world. In the introduction to her book on the murder of British tourist Julie Ward, Grace Musila writes that 'narrative [is] an intervention on historical reality which must not be read in terms of how faithfully it represents a given historical reality, but rather what knowledges, truths and insights it yields into these realities' (2015, p. 5). Narrative involves not just telling and retelling, not just historical or political 'fact', but also an ongoing process of sense-making and interpretation, helping to solidify diffuse individual experiences into collective understandings of 'how things work' and how different conditions impact people's shared social worlds.

Second, each of these narratives is embedded in historical formations of gender, class and/or race, whether obviously or covertly. Each instance of fear that I discuss here is in some way a consequence of the country's past and present. Apartheid and its afterlives influence all South Africans' experiences of insiderness and outsiderness, precarity and belonging, access and abandonment, safety and vulnerability. The conditions under which these cultures of fear manifest and the forms that they take are a consequence of the spatial and social racialisation that has been a feature of South Africa for centuries, and of the class and gender configurations that intersect with it. Race in particular slips in and out of view throughout this book, but as with any conversation about South Africa, it is never entirely absent from the frame.

Third, all of these racialised narratives have some thematic commonality. All are concerned with conspiracy theories, moral panics or urban legends that emphasise the threat posed by the supernatural, the secret and the hidden. Dangers may not be what they seem; crime is not necessarily 'just' crime; even seemingly helpless outsiders can present an unexpected and shocking threat. Government plots to murder and destabilise rural white communities, satanic cults that stalk and sacrifice young women, devious gangs that use indigenous magic to rob their neighbours, homeless people who are actually part of well-connected criminal drugs gangs – all of these stories revolve, to some extent, around arcane forces or hidden structures that threaten the safety of 'normal' people. Ideas about the imperceptibility of power – the impossibility of ordinary people really understanding or influencing the world around them – are a common element of contemporary cultures of fear (Bauman 2007). The four stories in this book are examples of how different communities, with different levels of agency and economy, express fears about power and powerlessness.

In our current historical moment many of the manifestations of these anxieties, and many of their swiftest transmissions, are most apparent in the media that comprise our primary mass communicative platforms. From newspapers to Twitter feeds, from radio phone-ins to memes forwarded on WhatsApp, South Africans energetically listen to, read about and share stories that shape our social theories and daily practices. Of course, access to such media forms is far from universal, especially where they require smartphones, digital data, decent bandwidth and reliable electricity. Here, as elsewhere on the continent, we cannot claim that the realm of mass media offers a clear indication of what happens in most people's everyday experiences (Mutula 2005). A media discourse project based in the global south can never be representative of an entire population, but must always acknowledge the contingent nature of its arguments, which are confined to media users.

Nonetheless, those of us who are engaged with the mass media are often deeply affected by it. Media represent and intercede in our understanding of the world in influential ways, shaping our experiences and understandings as well as impacting on our belief systems and modes of communication. Media are both a conduit for and an element of power (see, for example, Couldry 2000, Couldry and Curran 2003). They offer an invaluable approach to the kinds of anxious episodes I am concerned with here, which emerge chaotically and disappear just as suddenly, digital versions of the rumours that 'contest hegemonic truths … [and] highlight the vulnerability of modern state institutions' (Musila 2015, pp. 113–114). Mass media, and social networks in particular, also allow for an accelerated spread of affective narratives. Each of the stories that I follow in this book is notable for its mediatisation, which, far from being incidental to its form, plays a substantive part in the shapes it takes. My primary sources for the discussions that follow are these media texts. These allow me to consider each incident *as a story*, as a piece of narrative or an instance of discourse. In so doing I am able to approach it as a social artefact rather than an individual experience.

Much of this book was completed before the coronavirus pandemic that began in 2020, which, as I write this, is still very much in full swing. My students and I have moved our classes online, no small undertaking in a country where access to wifi, phone data, reliable bandwidth coverage and even electricity for charging devices can never be assumed. South Africa is reeling from the highest (known) death rate on the continent, a devastated economy and rolling revelations about corona-related corruption. Under some of the world's most stringent lockdowns, city streets have become even more ghostly. Racial and class anxieties stalk everyday conversation in some parts of the country, while in others daily survival has become almost impossible. It has been tempting to rethink this book as a pandemic project: tempting, but not entirely useful. The pandemic, notwithstanding its huge global effects, has merely laid bare existing fissures – and existing fears – in South African society. Anxiety as a structuring principle long pre-dated 2020. It is important for scholars in the humanities to remind ourselves that, despite its enormous presence, the pandemic is not the originary site of our concerns, that such issues have longer histories which remain compelling.

This book contributes to a number of intellectual projects. It is part of an ongoing reconfiguration of global cultural knowledge that refuses the view of Africa as surplus, derivative, a place of bluff, mimesis and unreal imposture that is only ever a poor copy of the wealthier world (Newell 2012, p. 15). Instead, it understands Africa and the south as places where modernity reaches its current apotheoses of inequality, fluidity, hybridity, motion and extraction (Mbembe 2012), what Zygmunt Bauman (2006, 2007) calls the 'liquid' nature of the modern. It is part too of a move to take emotion seriously as part of the culture of fear, to examine the work of emotion as a collective and political force (Ahmed 2014) rather than to dismiss it as 'soft', feminised, unimportant, individual and easily managed.

In looking at South Africa, a place that combines high violence and crime levels, desperate poverty and ostentatious wealth, we can see how the public script becomes suffused with stories of the uncanny, of fear and of threat. These stories affect the way in which we read our societies and their relics, the information that we share, how we feel about our location in the world.

Note

1 Middle-class transport taboos in South Africa's major cities have shifted since the introduction of some improved public transit networks and the meteoric rise of ride-hailing apps like Uber.

1

Risk, anxiety and moral panic

It should come as no surprise that daily life in South Africa is infused with anxieties. Considered one of the most unequal countries in the world, it has the dubious distinction, alongside Brazil, India and the Middle East, of a top 10 per cent of the population that owns over 50 per cent of national income (Assouad *et al.* 2018). Colonial and apartheid histories of expansion and extraction have left the bodies of poor, usually black people locked within what Achille Mbembe calls an 'aesthetics of superfluity' (2008), the ongoing results of which can be seen in the paucity of services, infrastructure and opportunities in townships and rural areas that were formerly legislated as 'black zones'. This disparity is placed into stark, often shocking relief when compared with the glamour and luxury of the country's high-end malls, suburbs, resorts and private safari destinations. Rates of violent, property and domestic crime remain consistently high.[1] Suburban residents of all racial and ethnic groups turn to militarised private security while poorer South Africans resort to vigilantism and sometimes aggressive protest in the face of state failures to ensure safety and services (Comaroff and Comaroff 2016). 'South African society is saturated not just with violence but with the pervasive fear of violence' (Dawson 2006, p. 132).

Despite its appeal to tourist dollars, South Africa retains a reputation as a site of chaos, drawing on old ideas about Africa's uncivilised darkness (Gikandi 2002). National and global media repeat beliefs about the risky nature of the country, sometimes blithely, sometimes hysterically, feeding people's senses of living under siege or at constant risk of danger. Regardless of experiences of actual insecurity or violence, the emotional consequences of this volatility can have a significant effect on the daily lives of all sorts of people, impacting on health, politics, economics, identity and belief systems.

South Africa is not, of course, unique in this, as journalist Niren Tolsi highlights when he warns us about the country's 'innate, misguided sense of exceptionalism' (2018a, n.p.). According to Gabeba Baderoon, 'The tendency to underplay the complexity of the country's history supports the notion that it is exceptional, and therefore has no relevance to the rest of the continent or any other context' (2015, p. 115; see also Nuttall and Michael 2000). In this respect, as in so many others, South Africa – while it offers a profoundly representative example for discussing the issues I am interested in – is far from alone. Collective anxieties may manifest differently in different locations but their existence is a feature of modern life, a consequence of a globalised world in which fears about mad cow disease in Britain, Ebola in Sierra Leone, Zika virus in Brazil, bird flu in Hong Kong and coronavirus variants in India spread pathogenically, transmitted by global media systems and digital communications as much as by human contact. Fear of crime is not restricted to South Africa, Africa or the south, or even to places with unusually high crime rates (see, for example, Hale 1996, Altheide 2002, Glassner 2010, Lee 2011). Rather, these emotional conditions affect people all around the world, from all sorts of backgrounds and with all sorts of different life experiences, in ways that are often strikingly different but nonetheless consistent in their capacity to influence and unsettle.

Although these are global phenomena, their localised instances depend on social, economic and historical context, on language, on communication, on migration, on inequality. Global media over-emphasise and even over-value fear, and the feelings, beliefs and experiences associated with it. These include the way in which we manage risk, whether present, potential, exaggerated, misrecognised or imagined; the pervasive anxiety that characterises much of our everyday life and cultural production; and the rolling moral panics through which these features of fear often manifest.

In this chapter I argue that fear, anxiety and associated experiences are important social formations and have significant effects on our macro- and micro-political lives. I show that these emotional conditions provide some of the most powerful underpinnings for late modern life. I present them as sites of narrative, as the kinds of stories that people tell each other to make sense of their worlds. I go on to suggest some of the ways in which these symptoms of late capitalist globalism materialise within the specific locality of twenty-first-century South Africa, embedded in structures of race, class, gender, poverty and inequality that persist decades after the end of formal apartheid.

Fear and feelings

Numerous scholars have written about what Barry Glassner (2010), among others, calls the 'culture of fear' that pervades modern life (for example Giddens 1991, Altheide 2002, Furedi 2006). They have employed this idea to talk about everything from state repression in response to terrorism (Mythen and Walklate 2006) to childbirth (Reiger and Dempsey 2006). Others think about fear in broader terms, treating it as an aspect of mass culture that has its origins in political economy, that is influenced and constructed rather than being 'natural', and is then internalised and popularised. One of the most insightful of these is Zygmunt Bauman, who conceptualises fear as part of his definition of 'liquid modernity'. Within a liquid modern society, 'the conditions under which its members act change faster than it takes the ways of acting to consolidate into habits and routines ... Liquid life, just like liquid modern society, cannot keep its shape or stay on course for long' (2005, p. 1). Within liquid modern life, change is permanent. Structures of society, politics and economics shift constantly. Nothing is entirely certain, and this fluidity creates new possibilities for fear to take hold. Poised on the shifting sands of an unreliable modern world, fear becomes flexible and can be cast adrift from its original sources, let loose to attach itself to new objects. Chas Critcher writes,

> Bauman's account sees fear as constructed by cultural and political agents and dependent upon a psychological mechanism of projection. Its roots, however, are to be found in the changing nature of economic and political structures which leave us more and more exposed to whatever may befall us, anxious and fearful for ourselves and of others. (2011, p. 268)

Fear is not, then, meaningless or random. It does not 'just' exist; it comes from somewhere and actively does things. It is a practice as well as an experience. It affects people and their life-worlds as much as the larger social, political and economic structures within which they find themselves. The culture of fear that infects our societies and media systems is a consequence of context rather than an ahistorical and apolitical feature of the human condition. According to Bauman,

> Fear is arguably the most sinister of the demons nesting in the open societies of our time. But it is the insecurity of the present and the uncertainty about the future that breed the most awesome and least bearable of our fears. That insecurity and that uncertainty, in their turn, are born from a sense of impotence: we seem to be no longer in control. (2007, p. 26)

In this formulation the culture of fear is a symptom of both modernity and globalisation. Bauman blames its increase on the way in which political power, and the ability to actively impact on one's society and conditions of life, have shifted away from the local and towards the global and multinational, meaning that individuals are disconnected from the centres of power. Decisions are made by vast corporations and institutions; what we once thought of as politics has become largely empty. 'The fear is one of furtive, invisible power, the power of the quasi-state, the entity that lays no claim to any physical boundaries' (Soyinka 2007, p. 9). This iteration of fear, which moves it from the personal to the collective, allows us to define it as a hypermodern state driven by hypermodern circumstances. The speed and flows of liquid modern society are the direct antecedents of the explosion of cultures of fear.

Of course, fear as a collective experience is not new. History is littered with examples of outbreaks of group anxiety, from witch trials and scares about vampires and disease to 'black peril' and 'red peril' panics about, respectively, black male sexuality and communist incursion (Goode and Ben-Yehuda 2009, White 2000, Swanson 1977, McCulloch 2000, Gibson 2002). Fear has always been a component of human social life, but one significant change comes in how we speak about it. Contemporary cultures of fear are characterised by their amplified legibility. Experiences and manifestations of collective fear are now discussed, analysed, shared and spread both locally and transnationally. They are visible and audible and form part of public life, with an expanded temporality and elastic lifespan. David Altheide writes that we are immersed in a discourse of fear, which he defines as 'the pervasive *communication*, symbolic awareness, and expectation that danger and risk are central features of the effective environment or the physical and symbolic environment as people *define* and experience it in everyday life' (2002, p. 2, emphasis added). Communication and definition are vital here. We do not just experience fear: we also talk, write, read, post, spread rumours, make art, vote, protest, burn and legislate in response to narratives of risk and threat. Media profusion is an unmistakeable element of this increase in the epidemiological quality of fear. 'Modern society is more able to communicate fear because it has pervasive and centralised means of communication whose entertainment formats utilise fear' (Critcher 2011, p. 264). Altheide, Critcher and Bauman all suggest that fear draws on the circumstances of contemporary life but also that its pervasiveness is intertwined with the excess of information we are exposed to by our mediatised mass cultures. Popular culture is complicit in building a cognitive environment that emphasises danger.

Fear is not only, or not always, a wholly negative or disagreeable experience. Fear can confirm prejudices we may already hold and can be solidified by powerful individuals, groups or institutions, adding pleasurable certainty to our impulses. Alongside this, 'a lot of commercial capital can be garnered from insecurity and fear' (Bauman 2007, p. 12). From media houses and private security firms to pharmaceutical companies, political fundraisers and the insurance industry, fear can easily be translated into currency. Fear can also be enjoyable and even thrilling. It can create social cohesion by providing convenient scapegoats, as a consequence of which 'group security is thrust to the fore because of the generation of righteous anger' (Walby and Spencer 2011, p. 110). Rather than being empty vessels who are filled up with worries constructed by powerful elites, we are active consumers and producers of discourses of fear, with agency and impact. We share these stories by choice and often exaggerate them in the telling. We use them to encode diffuse moral messaging that comes not only from elites but also from grassroots social formations. Stories of risk help us to shore up boundaries of race, space and identity, to mark insiderness, even just to enjoy the titillation of coming close to danger. The multiple nature of the culture of fear means that it is not monodirectional, transmitted from authorities to a passive populace. Like hegemony itself, fear as a cultural phenomenon often involves at least some degree of consent.

Thinking about fear in this way, as something embedded in rather than surplus to culture, allows us to understand fear as pervasive within contemporary life. Fear exists under and alongside other emotions. We cannot think about how people live today without thinking about how they feel within those lives. It thus becomes necessary to, as feminists have long argued, take emotion seriously as a political force (see, for example, Åhäll 2018). Popular conceptions tend to represent fear as the solipsistic experience of solitary individuals. But fear, and the beliefs and behaviours associated with it, are networked phenomena that flow between social, political and communication systems.

Cultures of fear are located within the wider frame of human emotion, which requires careful consideration as a social force. Sara Ahmed, in her important book *The Cultural Politics of Emotion*, shows the way in which emotions have been culturally coded as both 'feminine' and 'not white', meaning that the hard body of the nation (in her case Britain) must dismiss emotion if it wants to retain its status and power (2014, p. 2). She writes that 'evolutionary thinking' has influenced the way in which emotions 'get narrated as a sign of "our" pre-history and a sign of how the primitive persists in the present' (2014, p. 3). Understandings of emotion as feminine, foreign and primitive – indeed, as subaltern – posit a world view in which feelings are both easily dismissed and potentially destabilising. They are not experiences we should acknowledge within ourselves, nor should we take them seriously within others. Doing so distracts us from the supposedly rigorous pursuit of empirical fact, which is represented as ideologically neutral and 'true', despite the ways in which *all* kinds of knowledge slip and entangle over time.

Ahmed argues that feelings do not simply 'reside in subjects or objects': rather they are produced as 'effects of circulation' that possess a fundamental sociality (2014, p. 8). Emotions are part of the making of meaning and relation that comprises human society. They 'are not "in" either the individual or the social, but produce the very surfaces and boundaries that allow the individual and the social to be delineated as if they are objects' (Ahmed 2014, p. 10). Citing a number of sociologists and anthropologists, Ahmed writes that 'emotions should not be regarded as psychological states, but as social and cultural *practices*' (2014, p. 9, emphasis added). Emotions are performative (Ahmed 2014, p. 13), and that performance is part of the making of meaning and of the social world. They are political rather than ahistorical; they are done as well as experienced.

The notion of performativity allows us to think of emotions also as instances of narrative. These are feelings that we *share*, by talking, writing, reading, listening and posting about them, and that we make and remake in the act of sharing. Communicative practices are an essential part of the collectivity, the sociality, of emotional experiences and conditions. They do not happen to us in isolation but are rather part of a set of co-created meanings that we impose on our worlds. Like rumour and urban legend, stories of fear are 'important sites for negotiating social truths, meaning and popular knowledges' (Musila 2015, p. 99). Narratives of fear can help us to interpret confusing situations, both to ourselves and others. They can allow us to make sense of things by placing them within a register with which we are already familiar and drawing on existing belief systems, folk devils and social theories to explain events or threats that feel otherwise inexplicable.

Anita Waters, discussing conspiracy theories within African American political culture, calls these social phenomena 'ethnosociologies'. Far from being nonsense that is easily dismissed, these kinds of stories are the 'theories that ordinary people use to explain social phenomena' (1997, p. 114), appearing within social, cultural or even population groups. She argues that they are 'not necessarily less reasonable than other ways of explaining disturbing and unexpected happenings' (1997, p. 115), particularly as they may be 'more metaphoric than literal' (1997, p. 122). I want to expand this notion of ethnosociologies beyond conspiracy theories and into the other sorts of stories that people relate as part of the transmission of

cultures of fear. The term is useful firstly because, as a form of sociology, it suggests the theorisation, the drive to explain the world,
that underlies such stories; and secondly because the approach to
*ethno*sociologies in particular contains within it an acknowledgement that such stories are shaped by the specificity of who tells
and shares them. Ethnosociologies are fundamentally impacted by
race, class, gender, sexuality, religion, nationality, income, geography. While they may be common among groups, they are seldom
common *to* groups: the stories we tell, and the anxieties that they
transfer and stand in for, depend on our living conditions, our
safety, our histories, our relation to power. Again, this reveals the
way in which emotional experiences or beliefs, collective narratives
of the culture of fear, can never be neutral or empty of meaning but
are always embedded in political life.

Taken together, Bauman's understanding of the cultural-political
valence of fear, Ahmed's understanding of the cultural-political
connectivity of emotions and Waters' explanation of the cultural-
political sociologies of group narrative suggest that we need to
consider manifestations of the broader culture of fear within their
contexts and communities.

Shifting southwards

The scholars named above have done much to explain the way in
which we think about emotion and fear in particular as components
of social, political and communicative life. However, there remains
something of a lacuna in this body of knowledge. The majority of
these authors are from, or based in, institutions in Europe, the US
and Britain, and much of their writing thinks about these types of
places. Waters' work is concerned with African Americans, in particular with how conspiracy theories are used to explain the racial
inequality that continues to plague the US (1997, p. 118). Ahmed
offers the example of Britain early on (2014, p. 2), making clear that
this is the area framework for her discussion. Bauman acknowledges this gap at the very start of *Liquid Times*, where he states that
he is talking about 'the "developed" part of the planet' (2007, p. 1).
Much of his writing is concerned with manifestations of fear in

Britain and the US as a consequence of the 9/11 attacks and of other shrinkages of agency experienced by the citizens of these countries. His discussion of human migration is focused on the countries to which migrants go rather than those from which they come; he writes that the primary industry of what he calls 'developing' countries is the 'mass production of refugees' (2007, p. 33). In this analysis, 'less developed' countries are mostly interesting for the way in which they produce fear elsewhere.

Studies on fear and emotion emerging from western scholarship sometimes treat the rest of the world as merely a source of powerful anxieties that travel globally.[2] Such places are stereotyped as the origin of the migrants and refugees who threaten jobs and local cultures; the terrorists who bomb churches, synagogues and media houses; the diseases that are brought home by tourists and visitors; the pollution and emissions that add to climate disaster; the headscarves, female genital mutilation and forced marriage that have no place in 'civilised' countries; the corruption that threatens good governance; the wars and lawlessness that unsettle an otherwise apparently stable global order. These assumptions have little interest in what luxury, mobility, creativity, insecurity or violence might feel like for people who inhabit the rest of the globe.

What happens, then, when we try to apply these ideas to a place like South Africa? How do they shift and change, in what ways do they need to expand? Part of the animating drive of this book is to ask what risk, anxiety and moral panic look and feel like in South Africa, how they are communicated, what forms they take, how these are influenced by the country's histories of racial violence and segregation. I am inspired by Wole Soyinka, whose beautiful – but less cited – book *Climate of Fear* (2007) locates the nodal point of contemporary cultures of fear not in the 9/11 attacks on New York but on the 1989 terrorist attack that brought a passenger plane down in the Republic of Niger. Rather than inaugurating a new global order of collective fear, 9/11 was, he writes, 'only a culmination of the posted signs that had been boldly scrawled on the sands of the Sahara, over decades, written in blood' (2007, p. 18). Soyinka situates Africa at the heart of contemporary cultures of fear rather than dismissing it as either a source of danger to the west or a collateral damage for the west's reactionary violence.[3]

According to Critcher, 'a safer society produces paradoxically more fear' (2011, p. 259). Bauman blames this on politicians and other actors who amplify and manipulate fear out of proportion to its cause, which often poses little empirical threat (2007, p. 14). These and other theorists suggest that explosions of fear and anxiety are a consequence of more rather than less empirical security. They argue that physical risks have been replaced by broad speculative anxieties that are more difficult to articulate, and that global cultures of fear are responses to the existential threat posed by vast and invisible power structures. While they have merit, these arguments do not take into account the often empirically higher risk that is common in South Africa, where inequality, violence, poverty, disease and environmental degradation affect almost everyone, albeit in very different ways.

While there can be no doubt that terrible poverty exists in richer nations, this seldom plumbs the depths found in the worst informal settlements that dot South Africa's urban outskirts. The poor in northern cities in Britain may depend on charity, food banks and welfare grants, but it is unlikely that their homes will be destroyed or that they will be violently evicted without warning from the shacks or buildings they occupy (Ramutsindela 2002, Chilemba 2015). Poor African American children may encounter substandard education and racist policing but they need not worry about drowning in pit toilets at their criminally under-resourced schools, as happened to South Africans Michael Komape in 2014 and Viwe Jali in 2018, when both children were just five years old. These conditions are not particular to South Africa: the same or worse can be found in Indian slums and Brazilian favelas (see, for example, Fischer *et al.* 2014, Nolan 2015). Poverty is humiliating and dehumanising regardless of its location, but the extreme conditions of poverty in the global south add an extra layer of risk to the lives of people who scrape for survival along the margins.

Middle-class and wealthy South Africans, while not equally subject to risk, can also not avoid it. Those who can do so invest heavily in privacy and security (Comaroff and Comaroff 2016), but such investment has limits. Barring the super-rich, even privileged residents of South African cities cannot avoid traversing dirty or dangerous roads once they have left their gated communities, leaving them at risk from car accidents, hijackings and the everyday 'intrusions' presented by hawkers, beggars and other poor urban citizens. This is by no means a phenomenon that is restricted to South Africa. In many of the more dangerous megacities of the south, the wealth that might elsewhere act as a shield can be an attractor for aggression. The children of the rich in Mexico City and Bogotá are disproportionately at risk of kidnapping by gangs aiming to collect ransoms. Upper-class residents of Lagos must invest in generators and boreholes if they want to free themselves from unreliable state power and water systems. Long before the pandemic, salaried corporate workers in Shanghai relied just as heavily on face masks to filter air pollution as poor labourers did. Car-owning, white-collar workers in Delhi and Nairobi plan their workdays around the traffic caused by ineffectual city planning. Class and status do not necessarily protect a person from threat, as they may be expected to do elsewhere.

Within South Africa, then, the uncertainty that people face on a daily basis as a consequence of corruption, ineffectual government, unreliable infrastructure, inequality, violence, climate change and health problems must be factored into an understanding of how cultures of fear operate. Collective fear in South Africa is not the consequence of a safer society. Rather, the experience of existential fear here is bolstered by real world conditions, which impact on South Africans in vastly different ways depending on their access to privilege.

Critcher (2011), Bauman (2007) and Altheide (2002) argue that fear is constructed and disseminated by popular cultural and media systems. These systems are pervasive across regions and cultures. Information, news and entertainment are global products with local forms and qualities. People in South Africa, a county that voraciously consumes international popular culture, are often prey to the global mass media's transmission of diffuse anxieties, as evidenced by the recent rise in vaccine conspiracy theory and popularisation of snake oil coronavirus 'cures' like Ivermectin. However, it is not sufficient to assume that cultures of fear in South Africa are merely an echo of the metaphysical insecurity that characterise wealthy nations, a mimesis or bluff (Newell 2012) of what is observed elsewhere. South Africans have not simply imbibed global cultural conditions and adopted them uncritically alongside international slang, fashion and fast food. On the other hand, we must also not assume that fear in South Africa is simply related to higher levels of risk rather than to deep structures of feeling that question the individual's place in the world order. We need to acknowledge the higher risk that characterises South Africa *as well as* its imbrications in globalised flows of culture and ideology. Rather than being an atavistic throwback that has nothing to tell us about how the world works now, South Africa, like elsewhere on the continent, is overwhelmingly part of the circumstances of modernity.

Following Musila, we must be willing to consider 'a riskier, more adventurous reading of the ostensible tensions between local particularities and conventional "universal" epistemes', which can 'offer important insights into contemporary interactions between Africa and the rest of the world' (2015, p. 4). The writing of fear and emotion in South Africa emphasises the meaning-making of life, culture and politics here, unsettling geographies that draw Africa as an addendum to the 'main' part of the world, a homogenous place that can best be understood by counting and quantifying. This is not a margin but a centre of its own, communicating with other diverse and scattered centres in ways that are sometimes new and sometimes part of existing postmodern and/or postcolonial systems.

Critcher writes that fear 'distorts and misrecognises social realities' (2011, p. 259). Its major effect is that 'we are led to misrecognise real problems in order to support simplistic solutions which often worsen the problem they are supposed to tackle' (Critcher 2011, p. 262). The things that we are afraid of will not necessarily harm us or endanger our communities, and the things we do to counter or avoid them will not necessarily make us safer. In Europe the risk of death by terrorist attack is lower than the risk of death by lung cancer but far more anger is directed at people who are perceived to be Muslim than at tobacco company executives. Poorer and working-class white Americans are more likely to suffer because of tax cuts to the rich than because of Central American migrants, but Mexican Americans are more likely to be blamed for job losses than billionaire politicians. In many instances this misrecognition takes a distorted form, where the original 'threat' is substituted for hysteria around something almost entirely invented.

During the Cold War in America, gay men were stand-ins for communist spies and saboteurs who apparently threatened the safety of the nation (Morris 2002). In the 1980s the US Christian right associated role-playing games like Dungeons and Dragons with youth suicide, drugs and Satanism (Waldron 2005). In Taiwan in the 2000s a growing uptake of ketamine use among young people was seen as emblematic of an incipient youthful revolution (Hsu 2014). Not just the source but the nature of the danger it poses is misrecognised.

The tendency to misrecognise sources of fear is as prevalent in South Africa as it is elsewhere. However, the kaleidoscopic shifting of view that takes place here is sometimes a question of narrative rather than of degree. This book is centred on four episodes where communities worry about the 'right' things but attribute them to the 'wrong' causes. Rather than a minor or even non-existent issue being presented as a threat, a legitimate source of risk is misrecognised in favour of a more spectacular source for *the same risk*. A new object of fear develops within the collective imaginary, but it has the same effects – albeit with additional meanings attached – as the original threat that has mutated. This small but crucial difference may well be a consequence of the conditions of life in South Africa, where risk can be more immediate than theoretical. Social practices shift understandings of the causes of these events but the events themselves are tangible, countable and often unavoidable.

Fear and modernity in South Africa

Binyavanga Wainaina, one of the most important contemporary African writers, says in his satirical advice to those wanting to write about the continent,

> Broad brushstrokes throughout are good. Avoid having the African characters laugh, or struggle to educate their kids, or just make do in mundane circumstances. Have them illuminate something about Europe or America in Africa. African characters should be colourful, exotic, larger than life – but empty inside, with no dialogue, no conflicts or resolutions in their stories, no depth or quirks to confuse the cause. (2006, n.p.)

Similarly to global news media and literary fiction, which sometimes present the continent as a series of flat vignettes to be gazed
at, the social science approaches that dominate scholarly literature
on Africa and South Africa often treat them as a set of problems
that need to be solved, problems that are conceptualised as outside
of or other to the 'civilised' or developed part of the world. Writing
about Africa that counters these tendencies has the potential to dis-
organise the spatialised power relations that roost within the global
imagination. In this way we can learn to think differently about
the shape of the world and about what is assumed to be modern.
As Dilip Gaonkar explains, the question of the modern is subject
to all sorts of contestations about ownership, origin and meaning:
'The encounter with modernity does not take place in isolation but
is invariably mediated by colonialism and imperialism in the past
and today by the implacable forces of global media, migration, and
capital' (2002, p. 4). We must then consider the possibility of a
'multiplicity of continually evolving modernities' (Eisenstadt 2000,
p. 3), foregrounding the fact that 'modernity and Westernisation
are not identical; Western patterns of modernity are not the only
"authentic" modernities, though they enjoy historical precedence
and continue to be a basic reference point for others' (Eisenstadt
2000, pp. 3–4).

The complexity of what should and should not be considered modern is a prevailing tension within imaginings of Africa.
According to Gikandi, 'The problem of modernity and the opposition it generates remains the most powerful explanatory mode
[for the] politics of culture in Africa' (2002, p. 141). Similarly,
Musila points out the 'value-laden tensions between modernity and
tradition, Africa's alleged position outside history and therefore
modernity, and African "cannibalisation" of modernity' (2015,
pp. 17–18). Western expositions of the continent have often been
embedded in this refusal of modernity, this repetition of a prelap-
sarian 'dark continent' in which colonial settlers went forwards
in space but backwards in time into an 'atavistic' world before
history (McClintock 1995, p. 66). Of course these representations
have been resisted by African scholars, artists, philosophers and
politicians, many of whose work I cite here. In arguing for the
modernity of the culture of fear I am arguing also for the modernity

of South Africa, which is implicated in multiple ways within this culture as part of its immersion in global flows of media, money and migration.

South Africa is not the most anxious or frightened place on earth, nor is it the most dangerous, unsettling or precarious. It is not a unique exception to existing knowledge. It is, however, a powerful example that allows us to consider the sociality of emotion, particularly fear, outside the contexts that usually interest theorists. Its richness comes in its legible manifestations of commonplace structures and conditions, which can appear here in startlingly extravagant or visible ways. It offers, too, an intersection of the local and the global that highlights the multiple strands of affective life. Its imbrication in cultures of fear is part of a global phenomenon; the incarnations of these fears, however, are highly localised.

South Africa's social and economic conditions add to its value as a site of study. The country plays hosts to both extreme poverty and extreme wealth. Its membership in the BRICS grouping, while somewhat tenuous given its periodic economic instability, locates it ideologically within a south-focused twenty-first-century neoliberal geopolitics (Magubane 2004, Bond 2013). Inequality levels continue to widen despite a rapid pace of social change and the much-discussed rise of the black middle class (Alexander *et al.* 2013), while service delivery – the provision of basic state and municipal services like running water, electricity and waste collection – is glaringly uneven. Its larger cities feature both dismal, barely resourced slums and glossy high-end malls (de Vries 2008, Heer 2017). Violence is commonplace, on streets and in townships, on university campuses and in political rhetoric. Rates and threats of rape and other sexualised harm leave women locked in what Pumla Dineo Gqola calls a 'South African nightmare' (2015). Internecine prejudices are rife and outsiders, particularly from elsewhere in Africa, are often approached with fear or hatred (Nieftagodien 2008).[4] Aggression, self-enrichment and tribalism can seem disturbingly common.

These trends offer abundant examples of the ongoing consequences of the colonial project. Indeed, we cannot properly begin to think about twenty-first-century South Africa without acknowledging the continuing impact of apartheid and the colonial states that preceded it, which, in designing the racial landscape of South

Africa, impacted on its spatial and economic formations, its industries and farms, its cities (Murray 2011), its legislative frameworks, its ownership patterns, its attitudes to gender and understandings of class, its obsession with counting and codifying, currently expressed in a sinister emphasis on biometric technology (Breckenridge 2014). It is not hyperbolic to argue that just about every element of South African life and politics exhibits some or other feature that we can trace back to centuries of white minority rule, whether this is a continuation of previous patterns or a reaction to them. Of course we must not claim that apartheid, colonialism and slavery are always and only the causes of all the country's ills; over twenty years since the start of ANC rule, endemic corruption and the country's ambivalent embrace of a neoliberal global order have much to answer for. That said, it is vital that we continue to talk about the role of the past in creating the present, that we push back against those who insist that we should 'get over it'. The transition to democracy did little to upend the inequalities that mean race is still a principal marker of success or stagnation. The fear and anxiety that come alongside such extreme inequality are a direct consequence of minority rule, which may have formally ended in 1994 but still haunts the country's social, economic and institutional structures. South Africa's traumatic history, both its festering wounds and its aftermaths of violence, mistrust and greed, are part of what makes it a powerful archive for the study of cultures of fear.

All of which said, South Africa's importance for this project is not confined to doomy statistics and talk of violence. The country is socially, linguistically, culturally and racially diverse. It is home to a robust and pluralistic media landscape, to a globally influential creative industry, to a wealth of competing voices within a constantly mobile public sphere and to frequent shifts in political discourse. South Africans are avid consumers of global media but also deeply invested in local celebrity and cultural production (see, for example, Bogatsu 2002, Mhlambi 2016, Smit 2016). Music, broadcast media, fashion, celebrity and other consumerist art forms are vibrant and enthusiastically contested. The realms of culture and discourse are highly valued here, despite periodic moods of despair about formal political parties and processes. This is not a place that is just 'bad', or one that can be considered only in terms of economic goals, natural resources, unemployment rates or potential development; or, as Wainaina makes clear, the cheerful exoticism of its people. It is, rather, sophisticated and heterogeneous, with literary, artistic and media cultures that speak to each other and across transnational borders rather than constantly referring back to the north. According to the writer Sisonke Msimang, '[Courts, media and civic sectors] do not see themselves as part of a tragedy. Instead, they have recurring roles in an ongoing drama that is chaotic, complicated and sometimes comedic but always utterly resistant to a single narrative' (2018, n.p.). This is a nation that is more than the sum of its colonial and postcolonial history. It exhibits a form of modernity where precarity is unexceptional and flux is presumed.

Risk, anxiety and moral panic

There are valuable arguments that can be made around the differences between terms like fear, anxiety, dread and suspicion. Ahmed does so to great effect, drawing on sources including Freud, Fanon and Heidegger to define the gap between fear and anxiety (2014, pp. 62–68). For my purposes, however, it is more important to note that so many scholars, in so many ways, are talking and thinking about this kind of emotion as a factor in the making of African imaginaries. My concern is not to build a new theoretical architecture of affect or emotion but rather to examine the artefacts created by particular episodes of collective fear in order to show their empirical consequences for the social in South Africa. I aim to reveal how these fears were constructed, disseminated, shared and indulged in, and how they may impact on identity, selfhood and otherness for certain people at certain moments.

I have chosen to use the terms risk, anxiety and moral panic not because they offer perfect theoretical positions but rather because they have useful connotations. As I have suggested throughout this chapter, risk is central to the consideration of cultures of fear in South Africa. Risk can often be empirically higher here; alongside this, though, we see the same overdetermined misrecognitions of risk that characterise fear in the north. Risk is both a 'real' thing and an often dramatic over-reaction that is evoked in line with existing prejudices. The processing of risk in South Africa takes into account knowledge about the dangers people face on a daily basis, but also engages in mythological and ideological narratives in which risk is overblown, invented and marketised. Ideas about the kinds of risks that threaten people and communities often entrench existing beliefs about rights, race, security and power, with the support of news reports and quickly circulating rumours that 'critique postcolonial manifestations of colonial modernity's selective distribution of the privileges of modernity' (Musila 2015, p. 108). Living in a state of risk, whether actual or imagined, has emotional consequences. When experienced as looming and ever-present, as is common in the varying precarity of the liquid metropolis, risk can go hand in hand with persistent feelings of anxiety that are stoked by politicians, the press, community leaders, celebrities and other 'moral entrepreneurs' (Becker 1995).

I use the term anxiety for its descriptive rather than its psychoanalytic or biomedical connotations. Anxiety is useful because it suggests an underlying and low-level state that is not necessarily related to a specific cause. 'The detachment from a given object allows anxiety to accumulate through gathering more and more objects, until it overwhelms other possible affective relations to the world ... anxiety becomes *an approach to objects* rather than ... *being produced by an object's approach*' (Ahmed 2014, p. 66, italics in original). Anxiety in this reading can be constantly present, awaiting an object upon which it can be projected. Such an object can be easily misrecognised so as to feed anxiety's subtle but demanding hungers. Anxiety is also useful for my purposes because it can be historical and collective. These kinds of feelings are often transmitted within families, communities and larger groups and may draw from past histories of trauma. Anxiety is quick to spread, more so when passed through narrative. Thinking about contemporary South Africa in terms of anxiety allows us to understand the deep emotional qualities that inform peoples' and media sources' responses to perceived risk and threat.

Despite well-documented theoretical weaknesses in its most common uses (see, for example, Critcher 2008, Altheide 2009, David *et al.* 2011), the idea of moral panic remains valuable because of its component parts. I am interested not just in fears about safety, security and belonging but also in the particularly moral component of those fears. As well as concerns about personal vulnerability, they also suggest that society as a whole may be at risk. Like anxiety, the idea of the panic suggests the viral quality of these sorts of events and their tendency to spread, showing once again the way in which emotion is political, social and performed. We need to be able to consider moral panics as misrecognitions rather than simple over-reactions in acknowledgement of realities of insecurity and the fact that empirical conditions of higher risk often underpin these stories of collective fear.[5]

At this point I need to add a brief note about my approach. I am an interdisciplinary scholar and define this as an interdisciplinary project. The label does not, however, simply free me from disciplinary intersections. This book sweeps in and out of engagement with multiple fields of study, chief among them affect studies, urban studies, critical race and whiteness studies and South African/ African studies. Why not, then, name my project within one of these areas, for the sake of legibility, keywords, access? My resistance to this possibility is partly personal, born from somewhat unorthodox scholarly training (my PhD at the now-defunct London Consortium was explicitly framed as 'Interdisciplinary Humanities and Cultural Studies') and a distrust of the urge to file difficult things into broad categories, and partly conceptual. If we are to take seriously the Comaroffian injunction to make and read 'theory from the south' (2015), we need to do more than adopt ideas developed in the wealthy institutions of Euro-America and use them on African case studies. All the fields that I mention here receive the majority of their energy from scholarship based in the global north, and this includes African studies (Odugbemi *et al.* 2019). Of course much of this writing is enormously valuable across contexts, but to apply it wholesale to South Africa – to simply claim that I am 'doing' affect theory, or moral panic theory, or critical race theory, *to* as well as in South Africa – runs the risk of shutting down a way of thinking about this location that takes it as its own starting point. Following Gloria Wekker (2016, p. 26), I engage what Jack Halberstam calls 'scavenger' theory and methodology (1998, p. 13). I use these conceptual and disciplinary frames, these kinds of writing and arguments, when they are useful, but I do not situate this book as the latest intervention in an ongoing disciplinary list. Readers may feel differently, and may choose to locate it as part of a broader pre-existing curriculum of whiteness studies, affect theory, urban studies or other fields; in which case they too become scavengers, selecting what works for their own reading and what does not. In this way, with our practices of dissonant reading and resistant writing, we might just manage to collectively wobble the pedestals of canon and find new ways to approach the dichotomy of 'northern' versus 'southern' theory.

Four stories

The main body of this book is comprised of four chapters, arranged into two pairs that feature very different but thematically linked stories. The first pair of chapters focuses on responses to disturbing instances of extreme violence. These take place in very different communities, but in both cases they are narrativised by various actors to explain something about the worlds in which they occur. The second pair of chapters is concerned with fears of and responses to crime, both actual and imagined, and with related social theories and moral panics that emerge in different locations in Johannesburg. Each of these stories shows the power of narrative to support frameworks of identity and meaning-making. Each is implicated in the social, spatial, cultural and economic patterns that structure South Africa in multiple ways. Each is laden with emotional content, with myth, symbolism and fear of the hidden and the secret, and read through its manifestations in various forms of mass media.

South African incarnations of the culture of fear are often focused on crime and precarity, and tend to feature mythical, hidden or uncanny components. The stories I have examined here are examples of this trend, united by a shared association with violence, either actual or anticipated. They discuss thefts, attacks and even murders that have happened or are feared to be possible or inevitable in the future; but also acts of marginal survival that are classified as violence by anxious insiders. The expression of these kinds of collective fears is often an act of mediation. They are spread through the stories that we tell and hear, both in person and through the media we consume. This is why I have chosen to approach them through texts (social media posts and videos, newspaper articles and some interviews focusing on sharing narrative) and to treat them as instances of discourse, the written, verbal or visual communication that produces knowledge, meaning, power and social relations. Discourse is 'a vital component in the successful functioning of power … modern power is only effective to the degree to which it succeeds in blending its operative forms with various "languages" of truth, knowledge, utilitarianism and freedom' (Hook 2007, p. 72). Taking a discursive approach to these kinds of texts allows me to show the way in which stories of threat and risk are intertwined with questions of power, and transmit theories about race, gender, security, consumption, desire, status and identity in South Africa. Acknowledging mediation and discourse allows me to investigate these episodes as multi-modal and flexible elements of a popular cultural landscape.

Chapters 2 and 3 are concerned with murder. They discuss affective narratives that emerge among certain communities to explain certain types of killings, which involve certain kinds of perpetrators and victims. I am interested in murder because it often appears as the apotheosis of violence, the (il)logical end point of all of South Africa's instabilities and failures. Murder here feels political as well as criminal, implicated in issues of race, of poverty, of injustice, of collective trauma, of the continuation of violence despite the apparent 'miracle' of negotiated settlement. Talk of crime (Sasson 1995) reaches its peak when we are faced with the reality of murder and the human need to make sense of the loss of life. In thinking through such contrasting cases we can see the contradictory valences that exist within different cultures of fear, underpinned by very different experiences of South African life.

Chapter 2 considers the myth of 'white genocide', a conspiracy theory propagated by white Afrikaans pressure groups that present themselves as working for minority – meaning white – rights in South Africa. White genocide myths claim that rural whites are the targets of a sustained and intentional campaign of mass murder and cultural erasure. They are employed to explain so-called farm murders, the term used for the often brutal murders of white people in rural areas, which simultaneously suggests that no other deaths that happen in these places are important. Here I examine YouTube videos made by campaign groups and their supporters. These help to disseminate a paranoid fantasy of 'transnational whiteness' (Willoughby-Herard 2015) which is invoked to harness and marketise white South African fears, continuing a strategy that was extremely effective during apartheid (van der Westhuizen 2007). In these videos, the 'moral entrepreneurs' (Becker 1995) who are invested in this myth employ a variety of rhetorical tools to entrench notions of white victimhood as exceptional and unnatural. The chapter shows how these propagators of the genocide myth use scapegoating, discourses of rights and minorities, the dehumanisation of black people, the equation of property to personhood and claims over the meanings of words and symbols to entrench anxieties about white people in South Africa as a special category of victim in need of special protections. The white genocide myth, which features lurid theories about shady operatives and state-sponsored death squads and which claims that whites suffer more violence than anyone else in South Africa, replicates the racist trope that some lives, and some deaths, matter more than others.

Chapter 3 discusses newspaper coverage of two cases of violent femicide, in which young women were brutally killed by young men who they knew (assisted, in one case, by a teenage girl). In both cases, the presence of satanic or occult elements overwhelmed any other possible meaning-making and the murders were defined by press and police as 'satanic'. Invoking Hannah Arendt's formulation of the banality of evil (1963), I argue that this tactic allowed the media to disavow difficult questions about South Africa's crisis of male-on-female violence in favour of a story about monstrousness and exceptionalism. Newspapers' emphasis on Satanism obscured the realities of the country's rates of gender-based violence, not least by refusing to acknowledge any continuities between these murders and gender-based crime or, indeed, any gendered component to these killings. This allowed the press to avoid discussing the structural features that underlie such violence in favour of an overly simplistic biblical narrative of good and evil, which defined both causation and response. It also allowed for a deferral of the uncanny echoes of apartheid savagery in the forms of such murders, which are underpinned by historical as well as by structural factors. Alongside these consequences of newspapers' obsessions with Satanism, the chapter gestures to the different meanings with which people in affected communities themselves invested in the satanic narrative, and how this operated within a Christological frame of good and evil that has a long history in South Africa.

Chapters 4 and 5 are concerned with more general fears of crime and are located within different parts of Johannesburg, the country's largest and wealthiest city. Joburg is, like other urban African centres, 'itself a kind of medium, broadcasting through the circular migrations of its residents' (Newell 2012, p. 10). It has 'a particular set of mediated associations that connote specific experiences of being urban' (Falkof and van Staden 2020, p. 3). Lorenzo Rinelli and Sam Opondo argue,

> Contemporary cities connect people in ways that complicate the way we experience and imagine cities. However, the most quoted urban theorists ... rarely discuss African cities as global cities because for them, the term 'global' pairs too often with the economically 'developed' Western city ... When some of these authors turn their attention on African cities, they rarely see African cities as generators of global processes or sites where one can imagine a different kind of cosmopolitical existence. (2013, p. 248)

Following scholars like AbdouMaliq Simone (2004, 2008), Lindsay Bremner (2004, 2010) and Sarah Nuttall and Achille Mbembe (2004, 2008), I write from *inside* Johannesburg, treating it as a necessary site of investigation in and of itself rather than as a local exemplar of trends that are more importantly visible elsewhere.

As with the previous two, this second set of chapters considers cases that highlight the ways in which crime and imaginings of crime manifest under wildly varying conditions. People in townships, who are largely black, experience crime very differently to people in suburbs, who are often white. Statistics suggest that violence has 'the greatest impact on people who are black and poor' (Gould 2018, n.p.), notwithstanding the monopoly of the white and wealthy on public discourses around risk and crime. These two chapters illustrate some of the ways in which such gaps are experienced within contemporary South Africa. For the township community in Chapter 4, who live in conditions of heightened insecurity, the real threat of crime led to misrecognition of existing risk, meaning that stories of danger became overdetermined and allowed for the more existential expression of generalised feelings of precarity. For the wealthier, largely white, suburbanites in Chapter 5, fear of crime presented an opportunity to define community character and to further cement the imaginary and even physical boundaries of their neighbourhoods.

Chapter 4 is located in Alexandra, a township to the north of Johannesburg. Using a combination of personal interviews and posts on Twitter and Facebook, it discusses an urban legend about a particular form of crime that was prominent in Alex in 2013. The interviews and social media texts reveal the widespread nature of stories of so-called 'plasma gangs' that used indigenous magic to break into people's homes and steal their plasma TVs, with the aim of accessing a mysterious white powder that could only be found within such technology, and which was, according to the story, used in the production of a street drug called nyaope. This story coalesced a number of existing anxieties – xenophobia, fears of crime, of drug dealers and of police corruption – into one overdetermined folk devil that allowed for the collective expression of local senses of insecurity. Drawing on South African studies of class and consumption (Posel 2010, Alexander *et al.* 2013, Iqani 2015a), I argue that the plasma gangs story shows the complexity of living a hypermodern, aspirational and urban life within a high risk space, meaning that everyday citizens are caught between the neoliberal desire to own and display high status goods and the fear that doing so leads to risky visibility. The chapter also offers a corrective to much existing literature on fear of crime, which overwhelmingly focuses on middle classes to the exclusion of working-class and poor people, who are equally if not more subject to these anxieties (Mosselson 2020).

Chapter 5, the book's final story, considers the paranoid performances of white suburban life. Discussing a community Facebook group in the neighbourhood of Melville, in the west of Johannesburg, it examines quotidian expressions of the racialised fear of crime, showing how poorer people are demonised as drug users, criminals and members of organised, well-connected gangs that threaten the suburb's residents and reputation. Alongside this, though, it reveals another side to these community discourses: a secondary urge to undertake acts of visible humanitarianism. The collective desire for safety involves an ongoing low-level anxiety about the presence of poor and black people while the desire to do good involves collective actions of providing money or goods to poor and black people. The chapter uses the work of Richard Ballard (2003, 2005) and Mark Hunter (2016) to think about what this online community means as a racial, spatial and social designation, and Lilie Chouliaraki's ideas about 'post-humanitarianism' (2010, 2012a) to consider the contradictory nature of these urges. It discusses racialised fears and performative humanitarianism to show how white suburban South Africans attempt to construct their identities within intersecting discourses of risk, rights, safety, charity and tolerance.

South Africa is an anxious nation; but the experience of anxiety is not the same for all South Africans. The fears of the privileged cannot be equated to the fears of the powerless simply because they display related epidemiological features. These stories are not interchangeable – but they do intersect. The conditions and consequences of power, the peculiar lineaments of South Africa's history, mean that often oppositional types of fear feed on each other in multiple ways. The monopolies of the privileged further unsettle the unprivileged. Discourses of security and insecurity impact on the suburb's as well as the township's fear of crime, sometimes leading from one to the other.

Together, these essays about white genocide, Satanist murders, township urban legends and suburban community groups present an always-partial and necessarily contingent picture of some of the ways in which cultures of fear structure life and meaning for various people in various communities. They show how narratives of risk, anxiety and moral panic underpin everyday life, informing both self-making and meaning-making in contemporary South Africa.

Notes

1 According to statistics released in Parliament on 11 September 2018, in 2017/18 police recorded 20,336 murders, up from 19,016 in the previous year. The murder rate increased from 34.1 to 35.8 per 100,000

people (Africa Check 2018). Murder rates are often used as a general indicator of overall crime as they are one of the easiest statistics to access.

2 There are, of course, exceptions to this trend. Meaningful work on fear and anxiety in Africa has been produced by scholars like Grace Musila (2015), whose work on Kenya I cite throughout this book; Gabeba Baderoon (2015), who writes on the anxieties associated with Muslims in South Africa; Lorenzo Rinelli and Sam Opondo (2013), who explain the multiple meanings of Somali migrants in Nairobi; and Vincent Crapanzano (1985), who places the political worries of South African whites during the late apartheid period within the realm of the affective.

3 See also Cobus van Staden on crime in Johannesburg as a 'symptom of wider trends that are adding to anxiety everywhere' (2020, p. 38).

4 These issues are discussed in more detail later in the book. Gender-based violence forms a crucial part of Chapter 3, while Chapter 4 deals with South Africa's ongoing xenophobia crisis.

5 I have made this argument at length elsewhere – see Falkof (2018a) for a fuller discussion of how moral panic theory could be advanced and expanded to account for the global south.

2

'White genocide' and the marketing of minority victims

On 10 October 2013, about 160 white South Africans set up a protest on the seafront in the small city of Port Elizabeth. They wore red shirts and decorated their cars with red balloons to 'protest the oppression of whites in South Africa'. Amateur footage from the event, posted to YouTube by the videographer, shows well-dressed Afrikaans-accented protesters standing in the sunshine in front of rows of shiny bakkies, the open-back pick-up truck that is the vehicle of choice for many South Africans. Everyone in the footage is white, barring an ice cream seller who can be seen cycling down the promenade in one shot, three car guards wearing high visibility jackets in the background of another and two women wearing domestic workers' uniforms, filmed standing among the crowd and shaking their heads sympathetically. Protesters hold up signs that read 'South Africa: Designed by geniuses, now run by idiots. Stop White GeNOcide', 'Stop killing <u>our</u> farmers' and 'Our children have the right to live without fear'. According to one of the organisers of the march, 'Nobody reports the death of our people ... They say that this is crime. But this is not crime. The way that our people are murdered is racist ... When you see the hate in that, it's racist.' The event was part of the Red October campaign, designed to raise awareness of what protesters insist is an ongoing and ignored mass murder of white people in twenty-first-century South Africa ('Port Elizabeth').[1]

The myth of white genocide in South Africa is mostly propagated by small but vocal groups from the far right of white politics. It positions white people – specifically rural and conservative Afrikaners – as particularly at risk: extraordinary victims of an orchestrated campaign of violence, murder and land and property theft. Talk of a supposed genocide of rural and Afrikaans whites gains more global attention than what Pumla Dineo Gqola (2015, 2021) calls the 'female fear factory', the shocking prevalence of violence against women that includes the kinds of murders discussed in Chapter 3. This narrative erases black South Africans who experience violence; repeats racial and gendered myths about the moral superiority of whiteness; and erases the structural, historical and economic causes of inequality. The longstanding aggression of whiteness – what bells hooks calls 'whiteness as terrorising' (1995, p. 37) – is ignored and whites become the sole (relevant) objects of racial violence. Like cases in the US that 'evoke the spectre of "reverse discrimination"', the white genocide myth 'turns the tables on the history of race ... ascribing to whiteness the minoritised, racially traumatised position from which to reclaim forms of racial expression once sanctioned, even celebrated, by the social and legal practices of segregation' (Weigman 2012, p. 145). This fantasy not only places real and imagined white suffering at the centre of South Africa's current crises; it also attempts to overwrite apartheid, obscuring histories of white cruelty and dominance behind disinformation and weaponised anxiety. Given the excessive volume of white voices in media coverage in South Africa and internationally, such fantasies shift the discursive frame away from black experiences of trauma and violence. In undertaking a detailed analysis of their social media manifestations I speak alongside, firstly, contemporary studies of the far right that have tended thus far to focus primarily on the US, UK and Europe (see, for example, Mondon and Winter 2020); and, secondly, critical considerations of whiteness that spotlight its disavowed ethnic nature as well as the powerful mythologies that maintain its varied senses of exceptionalism and supremacy (see, for example, Wekker 2016 on white Dutch identity). I view this kind of paranoid, reactionary and often violent South African whiteness both as an anxious racial fantasy that is particular to this context and as a local instance of global racist-populist white discourse.

In South Africa the white right wing supports its claims of genocide with reference to the violent crimes known as farm murders, or 'plaasmoorde' in Afrikaans, a term that is generally understood to mean the killings of rural white people only. Conspiracy theories that swirl around farm murders implicate the ANC, the state, even shady operatives who are said to cross the Zimbabwean and Mozambican borders specifically to undertake these killings. At the more extreme edges of the genocide story, these murders are seen as 'part of a secret plot to fulfil the unachieved aims of a socialist revolution' (Pogue 2019, n.p.), in keeping with paranoid white South African theories that were common during apartheid. With its emphasis on secret plots and violent intrigue, the white genocide myth illustrates the tendency of South African cultures of fear to obsess about the hidden, the unseeable, the secret.

White people are not the only victims or, indeed, only the victims of rural murders. Black labourers, though seldom spoken about in these terms, are frequently among the victims of murders perpetrated by outsiders, and are also killed by white managers and employers; rates of femicide and domestic violence on farms are thought to be high, affecting both black and white women (Burger 2018, p. 3, Pogue 2019, Parenzee and Smythe 2003). Nonetheless the trope of the farm murder as a specific type of violent crime featuring white victims and black killers is frequently invoked to provide evidence for the alleged genocide, and the two ideas are often discussed interchangeably (Steinberg 2002).

There have been many incidents of brutal violence on South African farms. These are real deaths with real consequences and they deserve the same empathy and outrage as all victims of violence. But murders of white people on farms are not proof of genocide. A 2003 committee of inquiry into farm attacks investigated 3,544 cases that took place between 1998 and 2001. It concluded that 89.3 per cent of attacks were motivated by robbery; 7.1 per cent by intimidation; 2 per cent by political or racial causes; and 7 per cent by labour issues (Special Committee of Inquiry into Farm Attacks 2003). Despite the hyperbolic claims of the moral entrepreneurs who drive this panic, no credible evidence has emerged to show that farm attackers are military trained; come from Zimbabwe, Mozambique or other neighbouring countries; belong to organised crime syndicates; operate at the behest of the South African government; or are engaged in a systematic programme of genocide.

The fact-checking organisation Africa Check has discredited the statistics used by moral entrepreneurs to 'prove' that more murders happen on farms than elsewhere in South Africa, and therefore that whites experience higher murder rates than other people. One such group, the Freedom Front Plus political party, claimed in Parliament in 2017 that the farm murder rate was 133 per 100,000 people. Africa Check's researchers have shown that the number used to determine the overall population of farmers in this statistic was drawn from the 2007 census and only included people who were registered as farmers on properties with a minimum annual turnover. However, the number used to define the *victims* of crime does not have these restrictions and includes attacks on farms that were too small to be counted in the census as well as victims who were workers, family members, spouses, visitors and others. This leads to an inflated statistic in which a large number of crimes is applied to a small population (Wilkinson 2017). Government data from 2018 shows that 'in a country where almost 20,000 people were slain, most of them black, there were only 62 farm murders ... According to one of the country's largest agricultural associations, murders of farmers are at a 20-year low' (Pogue 2019, n.p.). According to the Institute of Security Studies, the number of farm attacks corresponds with the 'gradual increases South Africa is experiencing regarding murder and house robberies since 2011/12' (Burger 2018, p. 6), rather than rising exponentially faster than crimes elsewhere. Night shift workers and Uber drivers are statistically at greater risk of being killed than white farmers (Pogue 2019). There is evidence for murder, atrocity, even torture; there is no evidence for genocide (see, for example, Bueckert 2018, Gedye 2018, Walsh 2019). The genocide myth is an iteration of longstanding white justifications for racist domination. To put it another way, the intense and formative anxiety of whiteness – that it is always under threat – would appear among South Africans *regardless of whether farm murders happened or not*. Within this chapter I argue that white genocide is a discursive tactic to justify the normal workings of racial capital that ghettoise black people on the basis of marketised white anxiety.

This is made clear by the fact that egregious claims of white genocide are not unique to South Africa, or indeed to places with high rates of violent crime. The phrase and its associated ideas have resonance among far right groups in Europe, Australia and the US, in news sources like Breitbart and on social media networks like 4chan, Reddit, Twitter and Facebook (Jackson 2015, Daniels 2017, Johnson 2018). Its global reach contributes to the current form of what Tiffany Willoughby-Herard (2015) calls 'transnational whiteness': the broad manifestations of ideas across countries, cultures and media that characterise whiteness as multiply exceptional and in need of special protections. The transnational 'designates that which exceeds and crosses boundaries of nation-state and region without thereby erasing or negating them' (Dosekun 2017, p. 169). Within this transnationality white people are represented as the victims of a new order that reverses previous racial logics, creating uncanny mirror images of apartheid, Jim Crow, even slavery. Genocide 'as an idea set out via liberal, legal definitions becomes a term used to critique a liberal political agenda' (Jackson 2015, p. 212). It becomes associated with apparent threats to white culture, which in practice means threats to the *dominance* rather than to the existence of that culture. As Robyn Weigman writes in the context of the US,

> To be injured – by the economic transformations of Emancipation, by the perceived loss of all white social spaces, by the seeming dissolution of whiteness as the condition of citizen subjectivity – provides the basis of white supremacist collective self-fashioning, which has and continues to function by producing the threat of its own extinction as the justification and motivation for both legal and extralegal responses and retaliations. (2012, p. 146)

White genocide has been invoked to define everything from the Obama presidency and Pride marches to international migration and COVID-19 mask mandates as organised threats to whiteness. Jews, Muslims and people of colour are part of its primary narratives. These discussions 'regularly centre on the theme of white people being subjected to genocidal politics by governments acting on the wishes of a deeper Jewish conspiracy to control the world' (Jackson 2015, p. 210). After the Australian mass murderer Brenton Tarrant shot and killed 50 Muslim people praying in a mosque in Christchurch, New Zealand, in 2019, a 73-page manifesto emerged in which he claimed that the motivation for the massacre was to avert a white genocide (Moses 2019).

The South African manifestation of the genocide myth is linked to ideas about land and culture that have played a role in white nationalist imaginaries for well over a century. It also continues the hegemonic uses of white fear that provided powerful political currency during apartheid (Ballard 2002, p. 2). White genocide in South Africa is nothing new: it is part of the sense of 'rolling apocalypse' (Thornton 1994, p. 14) that characterises white imaginaries. Unsurprisingly it has little currency among the majority of white South Africans, and is mostly passed around discrete, self-sustaining digital and physical communities. Sometimes, though, the myth bursts through the undergrowth and gains mainstream attention. In this chapter I discuss two such episodes, featuring two high-profile right-wing campaign groups. I am interested in the strategies that these actors invoke to construct idealised white victimhood and to weaponise white anxiety for political gain.

The first instance I consider is the Red October campaign, which included the protest mentioned at the start of this chapter. In the latter half of 2013 a group of Afrikaner rights activists spearheaded a campaign to raise awareness about the alleged genocide, which they explicitly tied to farm murders. The campaign was led by Steve Hofmeyr, an Afrikaans pop star, and Sunette Bridges, also a singer and the daughter of legendary Afrikaans crooner Bles Bridges. 10 October 2013 was designated a global day of protest. Marches took place at the Union Buildings in Pretoria, at Parliament in Cape Town, at South African embassies in London and Sydney – both key immigration destinations for white South Africans – and in parks and other public places around South Africa and elsewhere. Supporters shouted, sang, gave interviews and released red balloons into the air. The campaign claimed that 50 marches took place in seven or eight countries ('Pretoria interview'). Red October events were the first time at which the white genocide trope emerged with such force into the general South African consciousness. While the number of marchers and events was small, the campaign attracted a fair amount of press and social media attention, almost none of it positive (Calitz 2014, p. 21). My first object of study is publicly available video material about Red October: amateur and professional footage of marches and speeches as well as news and talk show interviews with leaders and supporters, all sourced from YouTube.

The second instance features the self-styled 'Afrikaner rights' group AfriForum, which defines itself as a 'credible Afrikaner interest organisation and civil rights watchdog ... [working] on national and local level to handle the impact of the current political realities facing Afrikaners, and to influence those realities, while working simultaneously to establish sustainable structures through which Afrikaners are able to ensure their own future' (About AfriForum 2018). AfriForum's 'core constituency is the same one that sustained the apartheid regime, and their accumulated wealth means AfriForum is well resourced. It has been adept in its use of social media and at linking itself to a range of allies internationally' (Baskin 2018, n.p.). While AfriForum has been active in South African politics for some time, I am here concerned with a particular period that began on 14 March 2018. On this date the Australian Home Affairs minister Peter Dutton told Australian tabloid *Daily Telegraph* that white South African farmers were experiencing so much persecution that they should be awarded fast-track humanitarian visas to Australia. Dutton stated that white farmers deserve 'special attention' from a 'civilised country' like Australia as they were 'the sorts of migrants that we want to bring into our country' (quoted in Taylor 2018). Dutton's arguments provoked much international attention, both outraged and supportive (for example Guardian 2018, Theodosiou and Sinclair 2018). While the term 'white genocide' was never used by Dutton, and seldom appeared in mainstream reporting on the episode, his description of the threat faced by white Afrikaans farmers obviously drew on the idea. Social media reactions in Australia and elsewhere in the world were awash with memes, videos, images and comments relating to the alleged genocide.

One of the effects of the international furore around Dutton's statements was increased media attention for groups like AfriForum.[2] Capitalising on this visibility, in May 2018 the group undertook a tour of the US, including interviews on Fox News and, allegedly, meetings with white supremacist activists.[3] My second object of study is AfriForum's media-making around the time of the

Dutton remarks, both formal appearances and DIY videos posted on YouTube by leaders and supporters.

In these videos, speakers from Red October and AfriForum studiously avoid using the term 'white genocide', although it does appear when individuals become particularly emotional. Nonetheless their interventions into the discursive landscape of South Africa shore up claims of genocide, whether explicit or not, and the term is often used by supporters. These videos represent an effort to popularise arguments that crime experienced by white people in South Africa is never 'just' crime. Within this perspective whiteness, rather than shielding its bearers from danger, makes them extraordinarily susceptible to it.

Many scholars have speculated that part of the intransigent power of whiteness is its ability to remain invisible, the standard state of being from which other ethnic or racial identities deviate (see, for example, Frankenberg 1993, Chambers 1997, Dyer 1997). However, as I have argued elsewhere (Falkof 2015a), whiteness in South Africa has never been invisible.[4] It has always been the object of protective legislation and taboos against social and sexual mixing. In the case of the genocide myth, the hypervisibility of whiteness equates to hypervulnerability. The fact that whites are different – better, wiser, more moral, the 'geniuses' depicted in that protester's sign rather than the 'idiots' who have taken over – is precisely what attracts genocidal violence. Those who are the 'best' are also the most at risk.

Claims of white genocide are directed towards gaining the sympathy of white publics, both locally and internationally. Nonetheless these claims do not impact only on whites. As I have already suggested, they contribute to an erasure of black lives and deaths, not least by their aggressive expansions into the media and political discursive fields, decreasing the space that is available to consider black trauma. Their outraged exceptionalism makes other kinds of murders harder to see.

Alongside this, we need to consider the relative prominence of race in different stories of murder and violence. In the case of the 'Satanist' murders discussed in the next chapter, media discourses largely ignored the echoes of apartheid trauma and the long-term consequences of white violence that play a role in these events. In the case of white genocide, however, race is one of the most visible features of the narrative. Killers are always black, victims always white. Apartheid looms large here. AfriForum's and Red October's approaches to victimhood are located within the realms of the economic, structural, historical and military (pushing for policy change, gathering funding, publicising propagandistic narratives, organising paramilitary groups) as well as the affective. Even as they lament white vulnerability, they take full advantage of white proximity and access to power.

A history of white victimhood

The genocide myth is far from the first time that white South Africans have been represented as extraordinary victims of violence. Fears about white vulnerability and victimhood in southern Africa have resulted in a rolling series of moral panics that have manifested since the late nineteenth century. Melissa Steyn writes,

> The fear of being overrun, the fear of domination, the fear of losing the purity that was supposed to guarantee their superior position, the fear of cultural genocide through intermingling – these anxieties were always present ... Whiteness in SA has always, at least in some part, been constellated around discourses of resistance against a constant threat; it was a bulwark against what at some level was sensed to be the inevitable. (2001, p. 25)

Concerns about threats to white dominance and security have manifested in an array of strategies including segregation, demonisation and nationalism. The colonial project in South Africa, as elsewhere, has always been predicated on the notion of the exceptional white victim who is in need of special protection.

Historically, claims of white victimhood often appeared within structures of gender and power in which women were 'embodiments of the nation and its attendant anxieties' (Musila 2015, p. 66). Anne McClintock describes the 1938 Great Trek re-enactment, a countrywide pageant of Afrikaner nationalism and myth-making that has powerful resonances for groups like Red October, as featuring 'white mother and children sequestered in the wagon – the women's starched bonnets signifying the purity of the race, the decorous surrender of their sexuality to the patriarchy and the invisibility of white female labour' (1995, p. 371). Both the virtue and the vulnerability of white women were highlighted in these displays: those spotless white bonnets demanded the protection of family and community leaders.

British colonial culture too built much of its symbolic imagery upon the bodies of white women. McClintock writes,

> Controlling women's sexuality, exalting maternity and breeding a virile race of empire-builders were widely seen as the paramount means of controlling the health and wealth of the male imperial body politic, so that, by the turn of the century, sexual purity emerged as a controlling metaphor for racial, economic and political power.[5] (1995, p. 47)

Beliefs about white women's virtue were discomfited by their perceived vulnerability to and complicity with black men's sexual predation. Jock McCulloch, in his book on the 'black peril' moral panics in early twentieth-century Rhodesia, reveals that scares about the rape of white women by black men were 'as much about gender conflict ... as about racial conflict', and that 'most Black Peril legislation was designed to restrain the sexual impulses of white women' (2000, p. 3) and thus the existential threat of racial mixing. Some agree that these panics were a means of rationalising colonial masters' fears of sexual competition from black men (Cornwell 1996), and policing the sexuality of white women and lower-class men (Baderoon 2015, p. 86), while others define them as a response to a perceived weakening in racial boundaries (Keegan 2001). According to Musila, 'Fixation on the black peril ... was motivated by the need to protect and affirm hegemonic white male authority and supremacy through exclusive access to white women' (2015, p. 69).

Anxieties about racial mixing did not extend to the bodies of black and brown women who experienced assault at the hands of white settlers. Within the colonial imagination indigenous women were considered inherently 'rapeable' (Maldonado-Torres 2007, p. 255; see also Stoler 2010). During the entire period of slavery at the Cape, 'not a single free or enslaved man was convicted of the rape of an enslaved woman' (Baderoon 2015, p. 84). Violations of colonised women were dismissed as part of a natural order, while imagined sexual insults paid to white women by black men inspired press coverage, public outrage, interventions from moral entrepreneurs, changes in legislation and harsh punishments (Nightingale 2015, p. 264).[6] Despite concerns about their moral failings, the status of white women – and hence of the Afrikaner or British whiteness for which they were metonymic – as a special category of victim was firmly established.

As well as intersecting with perceptions of femininity, ideas about white victimhood drew on notions of class, particularly with regard to so-called 'poor whites' (Morrell 1992, Giliomee 2003, Hyslop 2003). The plight of a burgeoning underclass of urbanised, largely Afrikaans people attracted state, cultural and philanthropic attention in the 1930s, most notably the Carnegie Commission's 1932 study into the 'problem' of poor whites (The 'Poor-White' Problem in South Africa 1933, Bell 2000). This US study was a 'quintessential example of the intersection between segregationist philanthropy and scientific racism' (Willoughby-Herard 2015, p. 2). The very existence of the commission exceptionalised whiteness by assuming that white poverty was unnatural. Black and other South Africans could be left to sink or swim in the swamp of crime, hunger, unemployment and environmental degradation that lurked on the margins of South African cities (Bickford-Smith 2016); however, a political imperative developed around the need to 'uplift' white people (Teppo 2004). Whites could not be permitted to live in the same conditions as other rapidly urbanising South Africans. The wide-ranging moral panic about poor whites was concerned with strengthening the imaginary boundaries between whiteness and non-whiteness. In embodying what Willoughby-Herard (2015) calls a 'waste of a white skin', poor white people showed that it was possible for whiteness to be wasted. The colonial state and Afrikaner establishment defined them as problems that needed to be fixed so that they could become 'normal', meaning both less materially deprived and more closely tied to white behavioural and moral norms.

The team undertaking the research 'blamed competition from and dependence on black people for causing white poverty'

(Willoughby-Herard 2015, p. 45). Not enough jobs were available and many of those that existed were taken by people who were not white, who had quickly developed the necessary skills to compete in the urban economy. This is perhaps the most ironic feature of the moral panic about poor whites. As Giliomee (2003) and others have argued, if whites were truly a superior ethnicity then they should have easily dominated their new circumstances. Poor whites were evidence that racial mythologies were flawed. For entities like the Carnegie Commission and the nascent South African state, whites who could not properly enact whiteness were both failures *and* extraordinary victims. Because poverty was seen to be unnatural to them, it must follow that competition from other races was to blame for their circumstances. As Christi Kruger has shown with her study of a contemporary white 'squatter camp' near Johannesburg, ideas about the exceptional nature of white poverty continue in the current era (2017). International media coverage of white informal settlements, which includes claims that people in these situations are victims of the ANC government, shows the ongoing power of the idea that poverty is not natural to whiteness.[7]

Collective anxiety about white victimhood reached an apotheosis after the start of National Party rule in 1948. Apartheid's mentality was fed by global fears about the insecurity of white civilisation. These dangers to whiteness were embodied most particularly within Cold War narratives, which framed the Soviet Union and China as existential threats to not just safety but also everything that the west held dear: freedom, enterprise, progress, individuality, religion, even the family. White minority governments in southern Africa adopted Cold War politics to gain moral and material support from the west and strengthen their association with western powers, locating them within the white world despite their geographical African-ness. South Africa 'was projected as staunchly anti-communist, a geopolitical "lynchpin of white civilisation" in Africa and, by extension, the world' (Dubow 2015, p. 254). Its government amplified the threat of internal communist agitation in order to 'demonise African liberation movements and to divert domestic and international attention from the real causes of opposition to racist rule' (Onslow 2012, p. 9).

As Rob Nixon (1994) has shown, Cold War rhetoric was very useful for the apartheid state. One of the first major laws brought in after apartheid began was the 1950 Suppression of Communism Act, which was so vague in its wording that it could be used to punish almost any transgression. The red peril of communism was intimately aligned with the 'swart gevaar', or black danger, with the two becoming almost interchangeable in public discourse (Ballard 2002, p. 2, Ullmann 2005, p. 45, Klein 2006, p. 17). Young white people were fed stories about the communist menace at schools, at home and at organised veldskools (bush schools) designed to prepare them to defend their homes and nation against the red onslaught. Tales abounded of 'maids', 'garden boys' and other labourers who were secret communists. White children were exhorted to perform permanent surveillance on the workers around them, regardless of the emotional attachments they may have developed to these people who cared for them. Any black South African, even a seemingly devoted servant who was 'like family' (Jansen 2019), could be a carrier of the communist contagion.

The intersection of the swart gevaar and red peril was another instance of the extraordinary victimhood of South African whiteness. Communism was not just a political menace. It was also personal – threatening 'our' way of life – and domestic, gaining footholds within the most intimate parts of the home where supposedly separate races rubbed up against each other. White South Africans routinely misrecognised autonomous black liberation movements as conspiracies managed by shady villains from across the sea. Struggles for liberation were seen as victimisation, and a minority that ruled by force recast itself as the innocent protagonist of a moral narrative.

These historical depictions of whites as special victims have persisted in contemporary South Africa. The belief in white exceptionalism appears most obviously in what Steyn and Foster call 'white talk': the 'distinctively resistant white discourses that inform much of white sense-making about living in post-apartheid South Africa' (2008, p. 26). Joseph Wambugu shows the way in which some whites 'manage to oppose affirmative action policies, yet still inoculate themselves from accusations of racism ... [by using] the strategy of appealing to discourses of "Othering" and fairness and justice.

These discourses help nurture a construction of victimhood' (2005, p. 57). As in the case of the suburban Facebook page discussed in Chapter 5, white communities may utilise these resistant discourses to position themselves advantageously in relation to other South Africans. When it comes to claims of and about genocide, though, white talk takes on different forms. Building on the representation of crime as a symbol of the collapse of society, this form of white talk implies that violence perpetrated against whites is different from everyday violence. Taboos against outright racist speech, seen both in Chapter 5 and in Steyn's (2004) and Wambugu's (2005) research, become looser as social prohibitions are weakened.

The far right interest groups who push the agenda of white genocide are invested in traditional understandings of Afrikaner nation and culture. According to Steyn,

> Afrikaner whiteness has an affinity with what has been described as *subaltern whiteness* … There certainly always has been an element of defiance in Afrikaner whiteness against the more secure, powerful, whiteness of the English … As a resistant whiteness, the constellation of the victim has been highly salient in the discourses of Afrikaner whiteness. They saw themselves as besieged, having to fight for the 'right' to their own brand of white supremacy. (2004, p. 148, italics in original; see also van der Westhuizen 2017)

What is at stake here is thus a form of white talk that draws on historical elements to support an understanding of whites as extraordinary victims of a black majority state. Within its subaltern consciousness this form of whiteness has *always* been at risk and has *always* required extraordinary fortification.

Panics and politics

The popularisation of ideas about white genocide has significant sociopolitical implications. If previously dominant white South Africans are now the victims of 'reverse racism', manifested in, for example, affirmative action policies, then it becomes easy for the leadership of groups like AfriForum and Red October to argue that white complicity in historical injustice is irrelevant and that state moves towards restitution amount to the targeted oppression of whites. In particular, claims of reverse racism are useful for resisting steps towards land reform that might threaten the current status quo, in which white people (around 9 per cent of the population) are estimated to own 72 per cent of the country's private farmland. According to James Pogue, 'To the extent that news about land reform in South Africa has reached international audiences at all, it's been refracted through the lens of a narrative promoted by white conservatives about a supposed "white genocide" … equating land redistribution with race war' (2019, n.p.). Unsurprisingly, these myths are subject to a huge amount of contestation from all sectors of society. White groups' attempts to leverage farm murders into a narrative that positions whites as the primary victims of violence in South Africa have varied effects. In order to get a broader picture of South African responses to white genocide, I begin by briefly considering press coverage of the episodes in question.[8]

All but three of the 36 articles I found that referred to Red October were critical of the campaign. Some put terms like 'oppression' and 'slaughter' in inverted commas and used words like 'alleged' to signal their discomfort with Red October's claims (*South African*, 1 October; *eNCA*, 10 October). Some repeated widely quoted statistics from Africa Check that undermine arguments about the disproportionate suffering of whites (*Mail & Guardian*, 10 October). Others mentioned the presence of the apartheid flag at Red October marches or stated that attendees were largely white and Afrikaans (*Mail & Guardian*, 10 October; *South African*, 14 October; *Daily Dispatch*, 19 October). Some used emotive language, with those opposing Red October's claims called 'respected academics' who classified the campaign as 'racist' (*South African*, 10 October; *IOL*, 11 October). Others treated Red October as an outright joke (*Business Day*, 18 October; *BizNews*, 19 October). One article reported on the popularity of white genocide claims on social media (*South African*, 8 October) but countered this with statistics about crime across racial groups. Some reported on a Twitter campaign that aimed to shut the marches down (*Cape Times*, 11 October; *Pretoria News*, 11 October; *Star*, 11 October) while others wrote about a counter-protest at the University of Cape Town, where students spoke about crime affecting all South Africans (*Cape Times*, 16 October; *Cape Argus*, 16 October). One paper concluded that 'most reactions to Red October fell somewhere between ridicule and disgust' (*Cape Argus*, 11 October).

A similar trend can be seen in South African news coverage of the Dutton speech in March 2018. Here my search produced 28 articles, 24 of which were critical of the speech. The one positive article came from *Ditsem Vrystaat*, a small Afrikaans-language paper from the farming town of Bloemfontein. It called the speech 'surprising, but welcome', and added, 'We say many thanks for that, it is necessary, but we also say humbly that we have no plan to leave SA. This country is also ours ... We are not going anywhere. As Afrikaners we have a right to at least a part of this country.'[9] Two other articles simply reported on the existence of the speech with no mention of responses. The third focused on the enthusiastic reactions of some white South Africans (*News24*, 24 March).

Critical news sources emphasised contentious elements like Dutton's claim that white farmers need help from a 'civilised country'. Some called the comments 'offensive' (*Daily Maverick*, 29 March). Many reported on the South African government's strong response (*News24*, 14 March; *eNCA*, 2 April; *Volksblad*, 3 April; *Pretoria News*, 4 April). Others used quote marks to signal their cynicism about Dutton's 'Desire to "Save" Persecuted White Farmers' (*IOL*, 15 March). Articles referred to the immigration scandals surrounding Dutton's department (*IOL*, 15 March; *News24*, 16 March; *Mail & Guardian*, 22 March) and called him 'controversial' (*News24*, 22 March) and 'right-wing' (*Citizen*, 16 March). Some used the word 'racist' to describe the plans as well as responses from white Australians and South Africans (*Mail & Guardian*, 22 March; *EWN*, 22 March; *Sunday Times*, 1 April). A number of news outlets mentioned AfriForum by name, sometimes quoting state functionaries who accused them of 'spreading fear' (*News24*, 14 March; *EWN*, 14 March; *News24*, 16 March). Others mentioned the Suidlanders, the far right group that took credit for disseminating the white genocide myth into the US (*Mail & Guardian*, 23 March; *EWN*, 23 March).

The South African press was just part of the media picture that swirled around these episodes. They attracted thousands of tweets and Facebook comments from around the world. The Dutton speech in particular received high profile global coverage, meaning that news outlets like the *New York Times*, BBC and *Washington Post* repeated – albeit critically – the claim that white South Africans were undergoing something that could be called a genocide. The idea also surfaced on right-wing media like Fox News, where Donald Trump encountered it. Trump's subsequent tweet on the subject had 40,697 retweets and 125,507 likes on 6 June 2019.[10]

This brief analysis makes it clear that interest groups' attempts to construct a moral panic around white genocide have not necessarily been successful within South Africa. Increased international attention has not, at the time of writing, had any effect on state policy. Discussions about land expropriation continue apace. Mainstream media responses classify these panics as factually incorrect, even as explicitly racist. Comedians continue to make witty Twitter jokes at the expense of groups like Red October and AfriForum. The failures of these attempts to gain mainstream legitimacy do not, however, mean that they have had no effects. One consequence of the higher profile of Red October and AfriForum is the increased presence of ideas that underpin global white supremacy within South African social media discourse. Another is the weaponisation of white fear, part of a history of the political mobilisation of anxiety in order to entrench racial schema and the power structures they support. These groups' attempts to popularise belief in white genocide, and the tactics they use to do this, are part of a larger contestation over the place of whiteness in South Africa, seen by many to be metonymic of global trends.

My purpose in this chapter is not to trace the spread of what Gedye (2018) calls the 'big lie' of white genocide. Rather, I want to consider the way in which discourse and narrative are used to stabilise ideas about the social, intellectual and moral primacy of whiteness. In order to do this I look at the websites of AfriForum and the Red October campaign as well as at video material created by and about those groups in order to understand how they represent themselves.[11] Many of the same people appear in these texts:

the pop stars and Red October organisers Steve Hofmeyr and Sunette Bridges; the author Dan Roodt, responsible for the far right website Praag; Ernst Roets, the Deputy CEO and public face of AfriForum; and Willem Petzer, an AfriForum supporter who has styled himself as a social media influencer. All of these people are educated, urban, middle-class white Afrikaners. Footage of Red October marches shows comfortably dressed people who have cars and cellphones ('Union Buildings', 'Port Elizabeth'). Interviews with these people take place in pleasant houses with swimming pools and gardens ('Street Talk'). AfriForum supporters are sufficiently well-resourced to own the tools to make and upload videos to YouTube ('Left wing meltdown'). As Bridges admits during a panel discussion on white genocide, 'I would really be dishonest if I said I was oppressed personally ... Other [white] people are oppressed daily. It's others, not me' ('The Stream'). All of this is in contrast to footage of protests undertaken by poor black South Africans in townships and rural areas, who do not have access to these media tools and are seldom granted lengthy face-to-face interviews with national broadcasters. Similarly, these actors are markedly different from the poorer white people in informal housing and rural areas for whom they claim to speak.

Of the 11 videos I found, one panel discussion is purely in Afrikaans; one film of a march is largely in English but features some Afrikaans speeches with no translation; one film of a march features a small amount of Afrikaans and includes subtitles; and all others are in English. These linguistic choices reveal that the speakers in these texts intend to spread their messages beyond their core market of white Afrikaners. Roets admits that he is using English because he aims to respond to criticisms ('Washington feed-back'). During his speech at the main Red October march in 2013, Hofmeyr apologises for using English, saying, 'I know I'm going to have to say some of this stuff in English, but sometimes I wonder why' ('Union Buildings').

In the discussion below, I draw out the common themes that appear in these texts to show the ways in which they invoke white anxiety for political gain while naturalising notions of racialised violence and victimhood.

Rights and minorities

The notion of a minority is relative and difficult to comprehensively define (Ramaga 1992, p. 104). Nonetheless it is one of the most powerful in the arsenal of these campaign groups, who subject it to shifts in meaning and intention that are far removed from its progressive origins. Both make a point of defining themselves as defenders of minority rights without acknowledging that the minority status of white Afrikaners is not the same as the minority status of groups that are marginalised economically as well as numerically, and that do not reap the longstanding benefits of whiteness in South Africa. These groups demand the right to self-determination, which draws on ideologies that have defined Afrikaner culture since its inception (Giliomee 2003). At its most extreme, the call for self-determination involves a nostalgic longing for apartheid, mythologised as an ideal democracy in which each population group made decisions for itself, ignoring the farce of the Bantustans.[12] These groups demand state protection from perceived racism, in the form of Black Economic Empowerment and other affirmative action policies that are seen to unfairly lock whites out of education and the workplace, but also in terms of instances of supposed hate speech. They insist that they deserve special protection against crime, even though whites statistically experience less violence than other population groups (Silber and Geffen 2016). They demand that their land and property are protected – which becomes complex when one considers that whites retain a hugely unequal share of South Africa's resources – and that their language and culture are valorised, even though Afrikaans is recognised as one of the state's 11 official languages and is the language of instruction in two top universities. In substance, many of these assertions suggest a longing for white rule, when the sanctity of white people's possessions, the primacy of Afrikaans and their easy access to jobs, education and status (often regardless of merit and skill) seemed guaranteed. Every one of the videos I discuss contained the term 'minority', usually more than once, used with reference to white and particularly Afrikaans South Africans, and most mentioned the idea of 'rights' in various contexts.

Opening her speech at the main Red October march, Bridges said, 'We're not here because we're right wing racist loonies, we're here because we're a minority in this country and we're not happy' ('Union Buildings'). The landing page of the Red October website featured, in red writing on a dramatic black background, the phrase 'Minorities have rights too!' The site contained a quote from Navanethem Pillay, an Indian South African woman who was a former UN Commissioner for Human Rights: 'Minorities in all regions of the world continue to face serious threats, discrimination and racism.' The centralisation of the term positioned white Afrikaans South Africans as the appropriate recipients of humanitarian efforts to combat the oppression of minorities. In this slant the word became largely about numbers: a group that has numerically fewer members than another group is entitled to be classified as a minority and thus to access hard-earned protections from bodies like the UN and South African state.

According to the UN Sub-Commission on the Prevention of Discrimination and Protection of Minorities (SCPDPM), minorities need to be both numerically inferior and 'in a non-dominant position' (cited in Ramaga 1992, p. 104). This differentiation makes clear the racial underpinnings of Red October's claims to minority status. Within the neoliberal landscape of contemporary South Africa, whites as a group maintain a superior income level to people of other racial classifications (Statistics South Africa 2017). Bridges claimed that 'we are four million white South Africans left in this country. We do not have a vote and we very rarely have a voice' ('eNCA interview'). However, white people can, indeed, vote. We can also create cultural groups and political parties, own newspapers and other media outlets, own weapons, study and teach at elite universities, own businesses and property, employ members of the majority group at minimum wage and access the legal system, public healthcare, state pensions and other support mechanisms. These rights and privileges are not in keeping with the exclusion that the UN associates with 'non-dominant' groups. For Red October, though, non-dominant seemed to be a literal term: when whites do not dominate, as they did during apartheid, they become a threatened minority. Associations of black majority rule with white minority status can be seen when supporters carry apartheid flags and sing the apartheid anthem ('Union Buildings'), or openly state that a return to white minority rule and to the Bantustan system of so-called separate development is the only thing that will satisfy them. In a series of interviews with participants at a Red October march, one explained, 'My dream, and it will never happen I know ... is that we must return to apartheid system, where everybody in his house can dictate what he will do.' Another agreed, 'Apartheid was a true democracy' ('Street Talk').

In semiotic terms, the Red October website (since removed) was designed to connote an image of diversity. The page containing the Pillay quote also showcased a quote from Martin Luther King, placed centrally to draw the eye. This suggestion that white South Africans are the legitimate inheritors of the work of one of the most important black civil rights activists in modern history was perhaps the site's most openly cynical tactic. Above the King quote was a black and white graphic of silhouetted torsos reaching upwards into a sky filled with stark white crosses, meant to represent the dead for whom Red October claims it is fighting. At the bottom of the page was a photo of a group of people: young and old, male and female, formal and casual, adults and children, standing in a line and holding hands. Visually the image was reminiscent of the style used to connote diversity, similar to what one would find in a pamphlet publicising adoption or a community project, except that every person pictured was white. Placed directly under the King quote, this juxtaposition may have been uncomfortable for many viewers. However, the casualness with which it was presented suggests that, within the world of Red October, there was nothing strange about co-opting a hero of black liberation and applying his arguments to whites only. Red October thus took a three-pronged approach to its positioning of whites as victims: discursive (using the language of minoritisation); institutional (citing bodies and experts who are associated with social justice work); and semiotic (using visual cues related to diversity work).

AfriForum also asserts itself as fighter for minority rights. According to its website, AfriForum is a 'civil rights watchdog', a 'non-governmental organisation ... with the aim of protecting the rights of minorities. While the organisation functions on the internationally recognised principle of the protection of minorities,

AfriForum has a specific focus on the rights of Afrikaners as a community living on the southern tip of the continent' (About AfriForum 2018). As well as drawing on the idea of minorities, claims to work for 'civil rights' and to defer to 'internationally recognised' principles make discursive links with historical campaigns for social justice, particularly with African American struggles in the USA and, again, with respected bodies like the UN. Its original claim to focus on the rights of minorities is quickly superseded by its emphasis on Afrikaners (as opposed, even, to whites in general). The page goes on to say that one of AfriForum's goals is for Afrikaners 'to ensure their own future'. Behind the careful phrasing is a restatement of the traditional Afrikaner desire for self-determination (Giliomee 2003).

AfriForum's self-description is more sophisticated than Red October's. It emphasises reports and statistics over dramatic graphics and imagery, with the material written in dispassionate rather than emotive style. Its logo is a graphic of two stylised and intersecting human figures with no particular defining characteristics, located within a visual paradigm of pan-humanist activism. A viewer familiar with the history of white South Africa may associate the logo's distinctive green and orange colouring with the apartheid flag, in which the same shades appeared.

All elements of the AfriForum site are available in both Afrikaans and English while Red October's site was entirely in English. Given that both groups make it clear that Afrikaners are their primary concern, these uses of English again reveal that both are designed to reach a wider audience. These sites are exercises in marketing as well as information. They provide perhaps the clearest example of how each group wishes to be perceived.

Red October and AfriForum are not the first South African organisations to adopt the language of progress and social justice in order to further the agenda of white dominance. Towards the end of apartheid, the ruling National Party engaged in a project of what Rob Nixon calls 'ideological cross-dressing' (1994, p. 223), in which it attempted to portray itself as the party of reform and progress. Discussing the adoption of feminist discourse within Blairite politics in the UK in the early 2000s, Angela McRobbie writes,

Elements of feminism have been taken into account, and have been absolutely incorporated into political and institutional life. Drawing on a vocabulary that includes words like 'empowerment' and 'choice', these elements are then converted into a much more individualistic discourse, and they are deployed in this new guise, particularly in media and popular culture, but also by agencies of the state, as a kind of substitute for feminism. (2009, p. 1)

Right-wing South African manipulation of progressive language operates in a similar way, shifting words onto different objects and blurring their original meanings. These terms, images, ways of speaking and rhetorical modes are invoked to associate whites – and *only* whites – with the progressive drive for justice that was such an important part of South Africa's self-description after apartheid. George L. Mosse defines Nazism and fascism as 'scavenger [ideologies]' (1999, p. 48), picking up any loose ends that can be used to justify their purposes; this characterisation can also be applied to the white right wing in South Africa, which adopts whatever tools and terms will further its aims.

In one such instance, Red October's Hofmeyr made the common argument that whites voluntarily, and altruistically, gave up power in the 1992 referendum.[13] He read from a dramatic self-penned poem,

> I am the Afrikaner ... the one without whose vote there would be no new South Africa ... The one without whose magnanimity you would still be facing the mightiest defence force on this continent, but the one who made a choice against blood and power only to inherit the bloodiest land in the universe. ('Union Buildings')

Within this version of history, white South Africans are 'not only victims of violence but also victims of ingratitude' (Calitz 2014, p. 56). Bridges, when asked whether apartheid was a system of racist oppression, said, 'Absolutely, which is why it was voted out in 1992 by white people' ('eNCA interview'). These claims suggest that majority rule in South Africa is entirely the legacy of white people, negating the freedom struggle, international anti-apartheid movements, National Party attempts to derail the transition process in the 1990s and the blunt, and often hypocritical, pragmatism of whites who voted for an election rather than a ravaged economy.

The struggle becomes invisible and white voters become the heroes who saved South Africa, only to see it destroyed.

If whites are the oppressed then it must follow that blacks are now the oppressors. The media material released by Red October and AfriForum makes this suggestion in various ways. Speakers appealed to the constitution and to white people's constitutional rights. They alluded to government complicity in the murders of white farmers, either by omission – not caring enough about these deaths to make them a priority crime – or directly – by inspiring and even sponsoring murderers. Protesters used racialised language that emphasises the divisions between 'them' and 'us' to define their perceived lack of opportunities as a direct consequence of other groups being awarded preferential treatment. Taken together, these kinds of speech add to an impression that apartheid has been reinstated, but this time black people are dominant and whites are excluded. Sometimes this was made explicit, for example when a US television show host claimed that 'government has announced a policy of taking land away from people on the basis of their skin colour' ('Fox News'), when an AfriForum supporter accused the ANC of 'racist theft of land' ('Left wing meltdown') or when a Red October organiser cried, 'I don't understand why we have laws that talk about black and white. I thought that was supposed to change 20 years ago. Now it's worse than ever' ('Union Buildings'). This 'new apartheid' is the apotheosis of claims of reverse racism that have long characterised far right white arguments.

These groups design their appeals to provoke maximum emotional engagement with the plight of whites. Both draw on the rhino, one of the most powerful contemporary symbols of white fear about the decay of South Africa at the hands of black people and foreigners. Roets mentioned the state's classification of rhino poaching as a 'priority crime' and bewailed the fact that it won't do the same for farm murders ('Washington feedback'). Hofmeyr, affecting a fake 'black' accent that drew sniggers from the crowd, told them, 'They tell you that the whole country is dying ... Everybody is a victim. Ja but this we know because we are also South Africans, we are also counting the bodies. That's like telling me listen you must help all the dying animals, not just the rhinos' ('Union Buildings').

Anti-rhino poaching efforts gain an extraordinary amount of attention in South Africa. Rhinos, to the exclusion of other threatened species, have become a cause célèbre for white people, with game rangers represented as heroes and poachers' deaths publicly fêted. According to Bram Burscher, the 'politics of hysteria' surrounding rhino poaching 'should be understood within historical and current (South African) political-economic contexts that emphasise the connections between race, nature, affect and control. The central element of this context relates to the interconnectedness between histories of (white) belonging through the environment and (black) dispossession through conservation' (2016, p. 982). Much of the talk around rhino poaching laments the fact that 'they' – meaning, variously, the ANC, the state and black people in general – cannot properly look after South Africa's natural resources. In line with widespread discursive constructions of African bush and wildlife, this suggests that the land is only safe when whites are in charge (Musila 2015, pp. 145–166).

In comparing 'endangered' white South Africans to the animal that is most often associated with threats to the natural world, speakers from Red October and AfriForum both emphasised the danger that whites are in and highlighted their specialness, the fact that they deserve the same sort of attention, funding, campaigns and emotional investment as rhinos. Minority status thus becomes not just about numbers or risk but also about a subtler type of value judgement.

White selves, black others

The sense that white people, like rhinos, are unusually special was emphasised by the way in which these videos centralise white selfhood. One of these groups' primary rhetorical tactics was to tell individual stories. The leaders of both groups made a point of providing gruesome details of the horrors that victims had undergone. Many of these stories featured women and children who had experienced horrific violence, from rape to torture to murder. When men were mentioned it was usually in the context of their families: fathers killed in front of children or husbands in front of wives. Speakers also mentioned victims' ages. The young and old were particularly present. In all of these instances real names were used. Within the videos in my sample there is no mention of farmers fighting back, protecting their neighbours or arming themselves in anticipation. Afrikaners were presented as helpless and denuded of agency, with no capacity to defend themselves in the face of the almost supernatural wave of violence that encompasses them.

Attacking a critic who queried AfriForum's statistics, Roets said,

> I'm curious if [she] would say this to Corey Nel, who's now raising his two grandchildren, who were very small toddlers when they saw their mother, Venessa Stafleu, being murdered in front of them on a farm ... I'm curious if she would mention to Mariandra Heunis who's now raising her four little children alone after the husband Johannes was murdered in front of her. I'm curious if she would say that to the family of Willemien Potgieter, who had to stand by and watch as her father was stabbed 151 times with a garden fork. ('Washington feedback')

Deborah Posel, writing about SABC television news during the most violent periods of the 1980s, discusses the different ways in which people were depicted onscreen. Black protesters were shown from a distance as faceless crowds with no leaders, names or signs of individuality. Whites, on the other hand, were almost always represented as individuals, even when they were members of anti-government platforms (1989). Contemporary white right-wing groups use the same tactic: white victims of farm attacks are mentioned by name, in contrast to the de-individualisation, and concurrent dehumanisation, of other victims of violence. This tendency was repeated in the representation of historical violence. In some instances speakers acknowledged that apartheid did lead to deaths and was an unfair system ('Union Buildings', 'Pretoria interview', 'eNCA interview'). However, no mention was made of particular crimes perpetrated against black South Africans and no names were given for people who suffered under apartheid. In general these campaigns 'effectively developed a narrative of victimhood while simultaneously displaying amnesia about the role of ... Afrikaner identity in the oppressive practices of apartheid' (Baskin 2018, n.p.). Petzer, in his video supporting Roets, alluded to one instance of white-on-black violence that gained much press coverage and sparked angry protests ('Left wing meltdown'). However, this was only introduced so that he could make the argument that this case gained *more* media attention than the murders of white farmers. He did not mention the names of the victims or of the accused.[14] The discursive positions presented here separated people into selves – named individuals with stories and histories, who inspire empathy, horror and ideally action – and others – those whose suffering is invisible, or who are themselves the causes of suffering.

A further consequence of this differentiation is the naturalisation of violence related to black people, both as victims and as perpetrators. The failure to ascribe personhood to black people who experience crime, and the failure to assign meaning to those forms of violence, suggest that they do not need to be interrogated, like the idea of 'black-on-black violence' that allowed apartheid-era politicians and journalists to dismiss violence as a normal feature of township life.[15] In his video Petzer stated, '100 percent of the attackers have been black males. I cannot emphasise that enough. 100 percent' ('Left wing meltdown'). Blackness' association with violence places it in direct opposition to whiteness, to which violence is seen to be alien. This is despite the often violent structure of the traditional Afrikaner family (McClintock 1995), the apartheid state's aggressive masculinist militarisation (Conway 2012) and the way in which whiteness, for black people, has often been seen as threatening rather than reassuring (Malan 1991).

The tendency to naturalise violence for black people and to exceptionalise it for whites reached a ludicrous peak in one of Hofmeyr's interviews, in which he told journalists, 'We are not used to being raped by other races and ethnicities' ('Pretoria interview'). His statement, which was gleefully reported across mainstream media, makes clear the conceptual underpinnings of such naturalisation: it is not normal for 'us' to experience violence at 'their' hands. This may suggest that what we could call white-on-white violence is not really classified as a problem. Despite their emphasis on female and child victims of farm attacks, the activists in my sample never mentioned high rates of femicide, domestic violence and child abuse in South Africa, common among all racial classifications

(Sibanda-Moyo *et al.* 2017). This naturalisation also regularises a situation in which blacks experience violence at the hands of whites. Petzer, arguing that whites do not perpetrate rural violence, claimed that many such cases involve not 'murder or torture' but rather a 'guy that got a slap from the farmer or someone that was kicked or something like that' ('Left wing meltdown'). Within this version of events, violence performed by black people is illegitimate whereas violence performed by whites is benign: part of a colonial legacy that disciplines, and thus improves, 'uncivilised' natives (McClintock 1995).

Personhood and property

One of the most common features of the narrative of white genocide is the elision of physical safety with the sanctity of rights to property, particularly land, and lifestyle. This suggests that 'white people are not merely treated unfairly, but they face a sustained threat to their ongoing existence' (Jackson 2015, p. 210), embodied by diversity work, land restitution, affirmative action and similar policies. Speakers in these videos repeatedly shifted between the two, making claims about the threat to white people's lives that segued into fears about threats to their land, homes and jobs. In associating personhood and property so clearly, these speakers insinuated that losing white land, homes and other possessions is equivalent to losing white lives. Threats to property became existential issues of the continued physical survival of Afrikaners.

At the start of one of his videos, Roets explained AfriForum's US tour as being about gaining support 'against the murdering and torturing of people … and not to have people's private property taken from them without compensation' ('Washington feedback'). He began a press conference by telling the cameras that he would first talk about farm murders and then about land expropriation, making it clear that, within AfriForum's version of the world, these are two sides of the same coin ('Land expropriation'). This tactic also appeared in his interview with right-wing US talk show host Tucker Carlson ('Fox News'). Carlson began the segment by stating that South Africa is 'under attack' and, in a clear instance of the adoption of progressive discourse, that the ANC government is trying to make the country 'less diverse'. He and Roets went on to discuss the 'barbaric' killings of white farmers. Roets quickly shifted from murders to land expropriation. He mentioned Zimbabwe as a site of farm attacks and theft of private property in a move that reiterated late apartheid anxieties about South Africa becoming too 'African' (Manzo and McGowan 1992).[16] Roets also claimed that international investment would be 'expropriated' if the state had its way. At the end of the interview Carlson asked what concerned Americans could do to halt the process and Roets entreated them to 'put pressure on the government to abandon this policy' of land expropriation. A segment that started with sensationalist claims about targeted mass killings of white South Africans ended with a plea for Americans to push against an African state's policy in which whites could lose property. This interview makes it clear that AfriForum's project is about entrenching white property rights and securing white economic power rather than about countering a genocide.

Red October also centralised the connection between materiality and personhood, but sometimes went further than this, equating personhood to quality of life. Explaining why she decided to start the campaign, Bridges said that she constantly received messages 'from people whose family members have been murdered or tortured'. She continued, 'My eldest is just finishing school this year ... as an 18-year-old, who was born in 1994, he will most likely not find a job in South Africa and will have to leave this country' ('The Stream'). She moved seamlessly from the horror of murder and torture to the more quotidian threat of joblessness and (comparatively privileged) emigration. A supporter on the Cape Town march told a camera crew that she had joined in because 'enough is enough', insisting, 'We're marching for the genocide that is happening in South Africa. We have 44 murders a day ... We have had enough of corruption, of fraud, of governance that's not accountable' ('Street Talk'). Here mass murder of solely white victims (with unsubstantiated statistics) blended seamlessly with the problems of a wounded state.

The most prominent text on Red October's website emphasised farm attacks and physical threats to whites. Smaller text, however, made it clear that the campaign's aims were more diffuse. Red October wanted to counter 'the destruction of our infrastructure, our filthy government hospitals, our pathetic educational system, dirty dams and rivers, uninhabitable parks and public areas, dangerous neighbourhoods and filthy streets' (Red October 2014). Although the site's main page exhorted all visitors to 'join us', the visuals used and the emphasis on the murder of whites made it clear who the projected 'us' is. A campaign that was ostensibly about a genocide was actually concerned with what it viewed as the sinking quality of life of white South Africans. Of course, South Africans of all racial groups are concerned about failures to provide acceptable healthcare, education, infrastructure, environment and public space. But like Hofmeyr's claim that 'we' are not used to being raped by 'other races', this association of social decay with whites alone, as the 'we' who will no longer countenance such destruction, suggested that the problem is not that South African public services are failing but that they are failing white people. Hofmeyr made this clear when he stated that Red October is actually about 'some people' – meaning whites – marching to prove that they 'refuse to acclimatise to the substandard' – meaning standards of living that are not acceptable for them but are, by extension, fine for other groups – because they 'know they deserve better' ('Union Buildings'). This position is a contemporary iteration of 1930s narratives of poor whiteness, in which dirty parks and failing infrastructure, like poverty, are not 'normal' for whites.

The slippage in these videos between dramatic scaremongering about targeted racist violence and anxiety about property ownership and lifestyle reveals their ideological foundations. They activate white anxiety about physical safety that has been whipped up by South African press and politicians for decades (van der Westhuizen 2007), and then apply this to threats to white ownership of land and related economic privilege. These groups invoke the names and bodies of murdered Afrikaners in order to further a political agenda that is less about security and justice than about retaining the advantages of apartheid.

Fights for meaning

Contestation over the meanings of numbers, symbols and words was a prominent feature in the rhetorical toolbox of AfriForum and Red October during these periods. Speakers who represented or supported them were relentless in their use of statistics and insisted on the veracity of their numerical information. According to Roets, 'Everything we say is fact-based, based on research' ('Fox News'). They frequently referred to 'research' undertaken by Afrikaans organisations, drawing on the rigour that the term connotes without giving specifics for what was researched or how (for example 'Left wing meltdown', 'Washington feedback', 'KykNet panel').

Statistics were either employed to support their arguments or dismissed as unreliable when produced by other bodies. Roets claimed that AfriForum's data is more reliable than the police's ('Land expropriation'). A Red October supporter stated that 'police do not keep accurate statistics' and went on to relate how hospitals record causes of death as heart attacks or illnesses rather than writing on death certificates that Afrikaners died in 'race-based hate crimes' ('Street Talk'). Research and information-gathering were represented as useful and reliable when performed by 'us' but as troublesome and disputed when provided by 'them'. The use of questionable statistics was combined with the individualisation of victims, discussed above, to create a two-pronged argument about the murders of white people as more frequent and more significant than other South African deaths.

This contestation extended beyond numbers and into discussion of how we talk about these killings and what they mean. While organisers of these groups generally avoid explicitly claiming that a genocide is underway, they are quick to dive on the term when it is raised by others. In one interview Bridges stated,

> The definition of a genocide is not a mass murder – one night they rush into the streets and they hack people to death with pangas [machetes]. You'll get away with it if you do it systematically, in other words. For twenty years now white people have been murdered. Our population has dropped with [sic] seven percent in 20 years, while theirs has grown with 36 percent. ('KykNet panel')

When the interviewer asked how much of that population drop is down to white emigration out of South Africa she answered that 'there are reasons for emigration'.

Roets was more careful in his approach to the term (indeed, AfriForum in general avoids mentioning white genocide, while simultaneously gesturing in its direction). Responding to an Afrikaans academic on Twitter who questioned his statistics, he distanced himself from the myth entirely, saying, 'Who's talking about white genocide? It's you and your friends in the media screaming white genocide.' However, he then went on to ask, 'Why is she referencing Rwanda? What's the point? Something is only called genocide once it's been denied' ('Washington feedback'). He ostensibly rejected the term as a fabrication of the 'liberal' media but then proceeded to associate South African and Rwandan violence, with the implication that the true plight of white Afrikaners will only be acknowledged once it is too late.

Like the Red October organiser quoted at the start of this chapter, many of the speakers in these videos made the argument that farm attacks 'are not crime'. Protesters held signs bearing the battered faces of white victims under the words 'IS THIS NORMAL CRIME' ('Union Buildings'). A Red October supporter said, 'They're killing our people because of our race and they call it burglary. They're slaughtering us' ('Street Talk'). These claims have the effect of again exceptionalising white victims of violence. Crime is a universalising term in South Africa, used to describe a vast array of circumstances and consequences (Comaroff and Comaroff 2016). In characterising farm attacks as something other than crime, these activists rejected universalisation, insisting that the whiteness of the victims gives different meanings to violence. Interestingly the same case is not made for violence against urban white people: the home invasions, rapes, robberies, even murders that suburban residents fear are classified as crimes despite the fact that urban whites, like farmers, often agree that they are disproportionately at risk. Similarly, murders of or attacks on black farm labourers are simply called crime. Despite their concurrent location, there is no sense that these kinds of killings are linked by ideology.

The white activists in these videos argued that speech, language and symbols can themselves be equated to violence and thus blamed for genocide. One powerful narrative strand insisted that the erasure of familiar symbols is in itself an act of violence. Speaking of the ANC government's policy of changing place names, Bridges told a panel discussion that genocide 'is about changing names of towns and not teaching in our languages' ('The Stream'). She said, 'I don't want to drive through towns where I don't recognise anything' ('Union Buildings').[17] Similarly, Hofmeyr told reporters, 'It doesn't matter that we're not dying en masse. It's genocide if we're losing our language' ('Pretoria interview'). He called Afrikaners 'the only minority on the continent that is fighting for own language education. Everyone else wants to speak English' ('Union Buildings'). He too made a point of mentioning the changes to street and town names as a component of the crisis ('Union Buildings'). Another supporter said, 'For me it's not about the colour. They're taking away our language' ('Street Talk'). In redefining genocide as related to changes in South Africa's symbolic landscape, Red October placed itself within a historical trajectory of Afrikaner resistance that includes the codification of Afrikaans as a formal language and the creation of a political mythology featuring dates, monuments and commemorations (Thompson 1985, Witz 2003). It also displayed a kind of 'white self-representation' that, according to Wekker, 'experiences a sense of deep loss, that things aren't the way they used to be anymore', although unlike in her Dutch case the loss here was defined as physical as well as cultural violence (2016, p. 146).

According to supporters, words themselves have the power to enact genocide. Speakers in these videos are particularly enraged by a struggle-era song called 'Kill the Boer'.[18] Both then-president Jacob Zuma and Julius Malema – leader of the self-proclaimed radical Economic Freedom Fighters party, a skilled purveyor of political theatre and white South Africans' current favourite bogeyman – have sung this song in public, leading to fierce outcry. Roets defined 'Kill the Boer' as a 'very popular song'. He called it hate speech ('Land expropriation', 'Fox News') and argued that it is 'particularly troubling' that the ANC is willing to overlook this when other forms of such speech are censured ('Fox News'). According to Bridges, the song was directly responsible for murders: 'Our president says "Kill the boer, kill the farmer, shoot them, rape them, rape the dogs!" And every single day we bury more of our people' ('KykNet panel'). Red October supporters used Zuma singing the song as an example of state-sponsored racism. One said, 'My people, my heritage is being eradicated by the slogans that ... people in the top positions in government are in fact propagating' ('Street Talk'). In these claims, harmful speech can be directly blamed for physical violence and threats to property.

Ironically, though, the same actors ignore or angrily repudiate the potential for their own verbal and visual symbols to cause harm. Despite Hofmeyr's insistence that 'everyone is welcome here', video recordings of the main Red October march in Pretoria in 2013 show participants enthusiastically waving the apartheid flag and singing the full Afrikaans apartheid anthem ('Union Buildings').[19] Despite its powerful visual and symbolic associations with the previous regime, Bridges insisted that Red October has 'never used racist discourse' ('The Stream'). During the period in question Roets launched a spirited defence of the 'old' South African flag after suggestions were made to ban its public display.[20] Both Roets and AfriForum's CEO Kallie Kriel are on record arguing against the UN classification of apartheid as a crime against humanity. AfriForum has vocally supported a number of white South Africans who have been legally censured for racist speech.[21] Indeed, the group has an entire section on its website devoted to 'hate speech' (Hate Speech Archives n.d.). At the time of writing, just one post on these six pages related to racist speech aimed at blacks by whites, a general comment asking South Africans to refrain from using a particular offensive word. Every other post referred to black South Africans as the purveyors and white South Africans as the victims of hate speech, and many of these situated AfriForum as the expert body on this kind of speech, taking cases to court and commenting on existing prosecutions and episodes.

As with the paranoid exceptionalism that elevates white victims of crime, so AfriForum and Red October activists' understandings of the harmful power of language and symbols applied only to themselves. Changing a street name that celebrated an apartheid general is classified as actively harmful, but exhibiting the symbols of a racist minority regime is a simple display of culture, and criticising it is tantamount to an attack on and attempted erasure of that culture.

Fear and folk devils

The folk devil, if present, is usually one of the most potent elements of the moral panic, an 'unambiguously unfavourable symbol' (Cohen 1972, p. 41) around which a panic can coalesce and which can be easily scapegoated for all the social ills that the panic allows us to misrecognise. Moral entrepreneurs can activate existing folk devils or present new ones so as to increase public support for hegemonic positions. South Africa has had its fair share of folk devils, from African migrants to Satanists to gay white men (Banda and Mawadza 2014, Falkof 2018b). The far right groups who popularise white genocide invest much of their narrative energy in isolating and demonising folk devils.

Perhaps the most significant of these is also the most surprising. Speakers from Red October and AfriForum frequently raised the spectre of communism to explain the alleged threat that is posed to white people. In the twenty-first century, apartheid-era fear of communism – which allowed whites and their government to dismiss calls for black liberation as a foreign plot – has retained some of its power. Some references to the communist menace take contemporary forms, drawing on language used by conservatives around the world to delegitimise feminist and anti-racist thought and action. This is clear when Roodt referred to a critical Afrikaans scholar as a 'cultural Marxist' ('The Stream'), one of the most popular dismissals that right-wing discourse aims at so-called 'social justice warriors' (Lux and Jordan 2019).

More frequently, though, South African communist phobia takes older forms. Roodt, again, stated that 'the ANC are communists' and called them an 'extreme left wing terrorist group' ('The Stream'). A Red October supporter dreamed of a time when 'every South African can do what he wants to do in South Africa, under a set of ... god-abiding laws, not socialist, communist' ('Street Talk'). Petzer insisted that a university must take action against another Afrikaans scholar because she is a communist, and then defined the *Huffington Post*, which published a critical article on AfriForum's US venture, as a 'socialist communist narrative' ('Left wing meltdown'). Roets argued that policies of land redistribution are 'in fact about nationalisation of land, it's about having the state own the land' ('Land expropriation'). These classifications of the ANC as communist are unrecognisable when one considers the neoliberal economic policies of the South African state (Magubane 2004). Nonetheless, in raising the historical spectre of communist takeover, which has terrified white South Africans for generations (Nixon 1994), Red October, AfriForum and those who support them energised a longstanding folk devil in order to amplify and exaggerate the threat that is apparently being posed to white safety and property.

Leaders and supporters of Red October and AfriForum also made a point of demonising intellectuals and the media, who were often conceptually linked. I mentioned above two instances in which Afrikaans academics who publicly questioned AfriForum and Red October were the targets of vicious attacks and accusations of being communists. Roets blamed genocide denial on 'so-called progressive professors' ('Washington feedback'). Petzer gleefully reported that AfriForum's US visit had led to a 'meltdown from public intellectuals, other public figures as well as the mainstream media', adding, 'Now I do have to point out that these people are a fringe hateful minority of the population here in South Africa and they do not at all represent South Africans.' This video contains multiple uses of emotive words like 'lies', 'fringe', 'horrible' and 'hateful'. The association between these groups suggests a conspiracy in which academics and journalists work together to undermine the cause of ordinary people, who do not have a voice in South Africa and reject the 'vile' opinions of those who are 'allowed to say these things just as long as they are anti-white' ('Left wing meltdown').

Many of the speakers in these videos argued that the South African media is biased and fails to report on violence against white people, particularly farm murders. Research suggests that white victims of violence appear more frequently in the South African press than victims from other groups (Brodie 2020), in line with global media trends (see, for example, Meyers 1997, 2004a, Gilchrist 2010). Nonetheless Roodt castigated 'radical left wing journalists' who blame white men for the country's problems and Bridges accused the media of ignoring farm attacks entirely ('The Stream'), while Petzer said, 'Unluckily in South Africa our media is extremely left-wing' ('Left wing meltdown'). Red October marchers in Cape Town insisted that the press simply do not report 'black-on-white-violence' while 'any white-on-black violence is blown up out of proportion' ('Street Talk'). Roets accused both the English-language and the 'very balanced' Afrikaans media ('Washington feedback') of ignoring farm murders.[22] Sometimes speakers who denigrated the media also, contradictorily, invoked its importance to support their claims. Despite his frequent criticism of press bias ('Fox News'), Roets argued that 'white-on-black violence' cannot be an issue since so few incidents appear in the press ('Washington feedback'). The media was thus framed as both an ideological problem and as a viable source of information, depending on which argument is being made.

While speakers were quick to emphasise their own reliance on supposedly scientifically legitimate research and statistics, the people who are generally associated with those practices were scapegoated. Afrikaans academics who are critical of these groups came in for special censure. In one particularly disturbing episode, Roets posted a late night video from his trip to Washington in which he attacked the legal scholar Elmien du Plessis after she used Twitter to query AfriForum's statistics on farm murders. He began by accusing her of making threats and spreading propaganda and spent some time dismissing her arguments as 'blatantly false'. He called her position 'postmodernist', echoing the accusations of cul-tural Marxism mentioned above. Towards the end of the video, in another act of 'ideological cross-dressing', he quoted the journal of Holocaust survivor Victor Klemperer, who he refers to as both as a 'Jew' and 'an intellectual himself':

> If one day the situation were reversed and the fate of the vanquished lay in my hands then I would let all the ordinary folks go, and perhaps some of the leaders ... but I would have all the intellectuals strung up, and the professors three feet higher than the rest. I would have them left there for as long as was compatible with hygiene.

After this threat, Roets added, 'Of course, we have no inten-tion to harm anyone.' He contrasted du Plessis to 'rational truth seeking people' and condemned her 'hatred and bigotry', once again attempting to turn racist speech back in on itself so that the purveyors of the white genocide myth become its victims rather than its progenitors ('Washington feedback'). Following Roets' lead, Petzer accused du Plessis of '[instigating] hatred' so that 'low IQ people' will be 'more hateful to AfriForum'. He claimed to be shocked that a university professor would push 'extreme propaganda' ('Left wing meltdown').

Fear as social capital

The leaders of groups like AfriForum and Red October invoke old ideas about race, selfhood and institutions in order to gain support for their political aims. They adopt progressive discourse to emphasise the claimed uniqueness and moral superiority of white people, skewering global understandings of injustice to claim the status of an oppressed minority under a racist regime. They discursively position white people as exceptional victims for whom violence is shocking and unnatural, in the process dismissing black South Africans as a faceless horde for whom the experience of violence is nothing out of the ordinary. Their claimed anxieties about bodily safety slip quickly into panic about rights to property, particularly land. They interrogate and reconceive the meaning of symbols, terms and languages to suit their purposes and invoke historical folk devils to suggest that their core support base is threatened by powerful forces beyond their control. Taken together, these strategies construct a world view that is suffused with paranoia, self-righteousness, horror of the other and anxious imperatives towards group cohesion and boundary-making.

While the term itself is not always mentioned and is sometimes repudiated, white genocide refracts much of this ideological posturing. Leaders and supporters insist both explicitly and obliquely that the violence white people experience is not like other violence and that they should be awarded extraordinary protection. These campaigns imply that only white people deserve to feel safe and comfortable and ignore the painful truth that safety and comfort are elusive for most South Africans. In exceptionalising the brutal violence that some white farmers experience as different from and more important than other forms of brutal violence, such as the horrific femicides discussed in the next chapter, they contribute to a narrative that turns victims of crime who are *not* white farmers into numbers rather humans. These people experience a double erasure: first of their bodies by other people's acts of violence, and then of their meanings by these attempts to delete them from the public space. The genocide myth undermines, ignores and further brutalises many South Africans who have suffered the country's structural and physical violence.

These campaigns' targeted appeal to the darker corners of global whiteness has led to international attention and a greater potential market for the genocide myth, which certain right-wing white South African activists utilise in order to further undermine the state. Deep anxieties about safety, belonging, status and power become tools in an arsenal that the far right employs to further its ideological aims. Regardless of how many people in South Africa actually believe that a genocide is occurring, this weaponisation and marketisation of the anxiety that is a constant component of South African whiteness help to keep racist ideas in the forefront of national debate, contributing to the polarisation of a social world that is already dangerously underpinned by risk and fear.

Notes

1 See Appendix 1 for details of the videos discussed in this chapter.
2 Investigative journalist Lloyd Gedye (2018) links the 'spike in advocacy' around white genocide to a 'a co-ordinated campaign by right-wing group the Suidlanders to bolster international support for white South Africans'. While the Suidlanders are extremely interesting, I have chosen to focus on AfriForum as they have a greater public presence. See also Pogue (2019) for an enlightening interview with Simon Roche, the head of the Suidlanders.
3 AfriForum has denied these claims, but has also refused to release a full list of who representatives meet on their US visits 'for reasons of confidentiality' (Essa 2018; see also Bueckert 2018).
4 See also Sara Ahmed (2004) and Robyn Weigman (2012, p. 160), who make the salient point that whiteness has never been 'invisible' for the people whom it negatively racialises; that is, everyone else who has to live with its consequences on a daily basis.

5 As in the US, white women often supported rather than resisted patriarchal racism (see, for example, Apel 2004). Women were complicit in
   perpetuating myths of violent, animalistic black men, embellishing or
   inventing tales of attacks and insults that could lead to horrific punishments and even death for the accused.

6 While 'violations' of white women by black and brown men were
   heavily penalised, white women were also subject to rapeability under
   specific conditions: wives and prostitutes were always sexually available to white men. McCulloch (2000, p. 5) notes that no white man
   in the history of Southern Rhodesia was executed for the rape of *any*
   woman of any racial or ethnic group.

7 Over 14 million South Africans currently live in extreme poverty in
   informal settlements and squatter camps. According to government
   estimates, 13,310 of them are white. Nonetheless white poverty has
   been extensively covered by international news outlets, many of whom
   repeat 'a wildly inflated estimate by "Afrikaner-rights" activists that up
   to 400,000 whites were living in camps, which is a number that it later
   became clear the activists had made up' (Pogue 2019).

8 For this analysis I undertook searches using the terms 'white genocide',
   'Red October' and 'Dutton' respectively. I used Google news searches
   and the SA Media database, a press cuttings service that offers full-text
   searching of over 120 South African publications, to look for a month's
   worth of coverage of each episode in physical and online South African
   news sources. For the Red October protest, my search took in the
   whole of October 2013 on the assumption that there may have been
   some coverage before the main march happened on 10 October. For the
   Dutton incident I began my search on 14 March 2018 and ended it on
   13 April.

9 'Verrassend, maar welkom'; 'Ons sê baie dankie daarvoor, dit is nodig,
   maar van ons beskeie kant sê ons, ons het geen plan om SA te verlaat
   nie. Hierdie land is ook ons s'n … Ons gaan nêrens heen nie. Ons het
   as Afrikanervolk 'n reg op minstens 'n deel van hierdie land.'

10 'I have asked Secretary of State @SecPompeo to closely study the South
   Africa land and farm seizures and expropriations and the large scale
   killing of farmers. "South African Government is now seizing land
   from white farmers." @TuckerCarlson @FoxNews' (23 August 2018).

11 In order to find this material I undertook Google Video and YouTube
   searches for the terms 'AfriForum' and 'Red October' for two months
   after the date of each event. I collected a total of 11 videos that related to
   farm murders and/or white genocide, seven featuring the Red October
   campaign and four featuring AfriForum. All videos were accessed and

downloaded in August 2018 (see Appendix 1 for details of these). As the Red October website is no longer online, the discussion here is based on screengrabs taken in 2013 and draws on an article I wrote for the *Daily Maverick* news outlet the week before the main marches took place (Falkof 2013).

12 Bantustans, or 'homelands', were areas that the white minority government designated for black residency. One of apartheid's primary means of segregation, they were designed to legislatively remove black people from South Africa, classifying them by often spurious tribal categories and forcing them to live in these nominally independent areas which were nonetheless economically crippled and entirely dependent on the South African state. In effect, Bantustans were cheap labour reserves that kept white South African farms and mines productive while entrenching the transparent fiction that black South Africans had their own countries, rights, citizenship and governments.

13 This referendum, in which only whites could vote, measured white enthusiasm for the already-initiated process of 'negotiated reforms' to the apartheid system. It simultaneously undercut support for the Conservative Party and other burgeoning far right groups that threatened the National Party's dominance among whites. The referendum was a significant victory and formalised the NP's mandate to move towards ending legal apartheid. It is often narrativised as an act of self-sacrificing altruism on the part of whites, who 'voluntarily' gave up power. This perspective fails to acknowledge the unrest, economic consequences and enormous internal and international pressure that had already made the system untenable.

14 It is likely that this statement refers to a murder that occurred on 20 April 2017, when two white Afrikaans farm workers near the town of Coligny came across 15-year-old Matlhomola Moshoeu allegedly stealing sunflowers worth R60 (about $4). The men loaded him into their bakkie but then, according to the prosecutor in the case, intentionally threw him in the road and drove off. The boy died of his injuries soon after. Both men were found guilty of murder.

15 I have more extensively discussed the trope of black-on-black violence during the late apartheid period elsewhere (Falkof 2015a).

16 White moral entrepreneurs often repeat this fear of so-called Zimbabwefication. Within my sample, Dan Roodt mentioned both Robert Mugabe and Tanzania during an Al Jazeera panel discussion ('The Stream').

17 Wekker (2016, p. 149) points to a similar anxiety about naming among white Dutch people who were challenged on the inherent racism of the

blackface stereotype Zwarte Piet/Black Pete. In that instance the fearful reaction was about changes to food names rather than place names: 'First it was negerzoenen [Negro kisses]. What is going to happen to Jodenkoeken [Jew cakes] and blanke vla [white flan]?'

18 The exact translation of boer is 'farmer'; however, the word is often used to refer to Afrikaners in general, sometimes in a positive iteration of traditional identities and sometimes with derogatory connotations.

19 Segments of *Die Stem* were incorporated, in both English and Afrikaans, into the anthem of the 'new' South Africa. However, the original version remains tied to Afrikaner identity and associated with white dominance of the country.

20 In August 2019, South Africa's Equality Court partially banned the display of the so-called apartheid flag, ruling that gratuitous display amounted to hate speech.

21 In 2018, in one of a series of similar incidents, an estate agent named Vicki Momberg was convicted of *crimen injuria* after being filmed hurling racist slurs at a police officer. AfriForum condemned the conviction as an instance of 'double standards on race' (Sentence imposed on Vicki Momberg confirms double standards in South Africa regarding race 2018).

22 A search on the SA Media database reveals a total of 119 English-language newspaper articles that refer to 'farm attacks' and/or 'farm murders' in the six months between 1 January and 30 June 2018.

3

Christian nightmares

One warm Saturday evening in October 2011, a group of eight friends, a mixture of male and female, white, black and coloured, aged between 15 and 23, walked up a small hill behind a swimming pool in the racially mixed, working-class suburb of Linmeyer in the south of Johannesburg. They went equipped to spend the night drinking, smoking marijuana and chatting around a campfire, as they usually did on weekends. But this was not a normal weekend.

Hours later the majority of the group had fled, while two of them stumbled and crawled back to town: Kirsty Theologo, 18, most of her body covered in third and fourth degree burns, somehow assisting Bronwyn Grammar, then 16, her arms and body burned from trying to roll her friend in the sand and douse the flames that were covering her. Soon after, her brother found Kirsty in the kitchen of their home, so heavily burned that she was barely recognisable. She was rushed to hospital where she lapsed into a coma. The fire had severely damaged her lungs and upper body and she died days later.

A story began emerging almost immediately of a planned attack in which the other members of the group soaked Kirsty with gasoline, set her on fire and left her to burn to death. Lurid details, including a bloody ritual, five-pointed stars drawn on the ground and the desecration of a bible, led to a swift diagnosis by press and police that this was a 'Satanist murder', a phrase that has a long resonance in South Africa. Six people were arrested: five male, the oldest of them 21, and one 15-year-old female. None tried to flee or deny their presence on the hill, although all tried to shift the blame for the attack to others.

The Theologo murder shocked South Africa, garnering a comparatively large amount of press coverage for a country with a high rate of violence against women. Journalists, editors, religious leaders and politicians flocked to report and comment on Kirsty's brutal fate.

Hers was far from the only story of 'satanic' killing to appear in the South African press in recent years. In the summer of February 2014, just days after some of the accused had been jailed for Kirsty's murder, a man working in the veld near Dobsonville in Soweto, Johannesburg, stumbled across the mutilated bodies of two local teenage girls. Best friends Thandeka Moganetsi, 15, and Chwayita Rathazayo, 16, had been missing since the previous day.

The girls, both pupils at nearby George Khosa Secondary School, were found metres apart, still wearing their school uniforms, with open wounds on their backs and cuts on their hands and necks. Three razor blades and a black candle were found near the bodies, once again leading to a quick diagnosis of Satanism from press, police and parents. Distraught friends told tales about satanic cults operating within the school that may have 'sacrificed' the girls. Two teenage boys, pupils at the same school, were quickly arrested. Religious and political leaders descended on Dobsonville to decry the scourge of Satanism in schools. Once again, these killings received an unusual amount of media and public attention in a nation that often glosses over public violence.

The deaths of Kirsty Theologo, Thandeka Moganetsi and Chwayita Rathazayo are part of a gruesome chronicle of so-called Satanist murders of women in contemporary South Africa. Other victims include Nofoundation Gomba, 73, and her granddaughter Siya, eight, 'hacked to death' in R1 Village near Butterworth in 2010 (*Daily Dispatch*, 27 April 2010); Yonela Sikweyiya, nine, killed by a pastor, his wife and a traditional healer in Ekuhurleni in 2010 (*Sowetan*, 7 August 2012); Sinethemba Dlamini, killed by a group of relatives in uMlazi in 2012 (*Daily News*, 20 March 2012); Michaela Valentine, 25, Natacha Burger, 31, and Joyce Boozaier, 68, members of the Gauteng-based Overcomers Through Christ ministry, all stabbed to death by a 'Satanist group' in 2012 (*The Times*, 12 October 2012); Refilwe Ramohlabi, two, drowned by a 13-year-old girl in Jan Kempdorp in 2013 (*Star*, 2 December 2013);

Nokubonga Mhlongo, six, killed by a relative in Eshowe in 2013 (*Times*, 11 February 2013); Keamogetswe Sefularo, 17, killed by a group of 10 classmates in Mohlakeng, Randfontein, in 2013 (*Star*, 6 March 2013); and Nadine Esterhuizen, 'almost beheaded' by her girlfriend in Mitchell's Plain in 2017 (*IOL*, 22 June 2018).

In this chapter I discuss newspaper representations of the murders of Theologo, Moganetsi and Rathazayo, from initial reporting until the eventual sentencing of the accused.[1] I argue that, while there were undoubtedly features of the events of both nights that could be described as 'satanic', the media's overdetermined focus on these elements of the murders meant that they were defined as bizarre and unusual occult crimes rather than as part of South Africa's ongoing epidemic of gender-based violence. My analysis in this chapter has two overarching aims: firstly, to highlight the consequences and ethical-conceptual weaknesses of media over-investment in this satanic panic, and secondly, to suggest a reconfiguration of narratives of 'exceptional' Satanist murders alongside critical writing on femicide and violence against women (for example du Toit 2014, Gqola 2015, 2021, Brodie 2020, Falkof *et al.* 2022).

As I suggested in Chapter 1, everyday violence is rampant in South Africa. The country's rate of sexual assault is one of the highest in the world. During the 2013 to 2014 period, 46,253 rapes were reported to the South African Police. The Medical Research Council estimates that only one in nine rapes are reported, making the overall number much higher than this (Institute for Security Studies 2015).[2] Research conducted on statistics from 1999 showed that four women a day, or one woman every six hours, were killed by an intimate partner in South Africa. Only 37.3 per cent of these female homicides resulted in conviction (Matthews *et al.* 2004). Further studies estimate that between 43 and 56 per cent of South African women have experienced intimate partner violence and 42 per cent of men report perpetrating it (quoted in Mathews *et al.* 2011, p. 960). Recent research suggests that around eight women a day are killed in South Africa, more than half of them by current or former partners (Brodie 2020, p. 16). Women in South Africa are disproportionately likely to be harmed by men, particularly by men they know.

The press narratives that surrounded the deaths of Kirsty Theologo, Thandeka Moganetsi and Chwayita Rathazayo were not just examples of news sensationalism. In repeating moral panic tropes around Satanism to the exclusion of all other potential contributing factors, newspaper reporting on these cases disregarded the disturbing truth that violence in South Africa is usually structural and often gendered. The focus on Satanism also allowed newspapers to avoid considering the *forms* of these murders, which, in their echo of late apartheid violence, recall historical trauma. Within the reporting, anxieties about the alleged threat of Satanism displaced knowledge of how male violence and the residue of apartheid atrocities shape contemporary life, especially for the poor. At the same time, however, newspaper interviews with affected families and communities offered some sense of the Christological frames that have resonance particularly for working-class and black South Africans, which resurfaced here as part of an affective investment in the spiritual as a way of living in and through unimaginable violence.

In focusing on newspaper coverage, this chapter discusses the mediated appearances of reactions to the murders rather than the reactions themselves. Such media narratives are generally simplified for mass consumption. They may emphasise the shocking and the outrageous and may employ tone in a way that fosters empathy or disdain in the reader. The stories of these murders that were told by newspapers are not the full or the only stories, notwithstanding their use of direct quotations from grieving communities. They can give us some sense of what the satanic diagnosis meant for those affected, but such an analysis can only ever be partial as it is filtered through the gate-keeping and agenda-setting functions of the news (McCombs 2002). Rather than claiming to explain why and how South Africans believe in satanic murders, this chapter reveals how the discursive field around these murders was shaped and considers what it might mean when brutal killings that are part of a trajectory of femicide are defined instead as occult crimes with no relation to gendered violence.

Evil, violence and spectacle

In *Eichmann in Jerusalem*, Hannah Arendt writes,

> Despite all the efforts of the prosecution, everybody could see that [Eichmann] was not a 'monster,' but it was difficult indeed to suspect that he was not a clown. And since this suspicion would have been fatal to the whole enterprise [of the trial], and was also rather hard to sustain in view of the sufferings he and his like had caused to millions of people, his worst clowneries were hardly noticed and almost never reported. (1963, p. 54)

Arendt's description of the 'banality of evil' has been enormously influential. She shows the significance of Adolf Eichmann's ordinariness and his failure to appropriately embody an idea of evil, but also of the Israeli judicial establishment and international media's compulsion to disavow that ordinariness and insist that Eichmann must have been a monster. According to Zygmunt Bauman, 'It is not only monsters who commit monstrous crimes … if it were only monsters who did, the most monstrous and terrifying of crimes we know of would not have happened' (2005, p. 66). Nonetheless a monstrous act leads almost inevitably to a popular diagnosis of the monstrosity – the literal inhumanity – of the perpetrator.

Arendt's formulation inaugurated a theoretical turn that draws out the ways in which mass media respond to events that are described as evil: beyond 'normal, everyday' violence, perpetrated by people who are separate from 'normal, everyday' humanity. What is at stake here is not a philosophical debate about the nature of evil but rather the roles that the idea of evil plays within popular cultural discourses.

Bauman writes that the category of evil exists to help us explain the inexplicable: '"Evil" is precisely the kind of wrong which we can neither understand nor even clearly articulate … We call that kind of wrong "evil" for the very reason that it is unintelligible, ineffable and inexplicable' (2005, p. 54). But the category of evil can also allow us to *make things inexplicable*, thus avoiding the need for closer examination. Discursively constructing certain types of acts simply as 'evil' (specifically, in these cases, as satanic) can free us from the need to consider them more carefully as a part and consequence of social, political, historical and economic structures. Evil can signify only itself, can be a justification in itself, can disguise more meaningful understandings of violence. In over-investing in evil as the sole explanation for these spectacular murders, media representations avoided the need to interrogate them, even while drawing on ethnosociologies like Satanism that parse complex understandings of the meanings of violence.

In his influential (if now somewhat dated) book *Society of the Spectacle* Guy Debord refers to spectacle as an 'instrument of unification' operating in the service of the ruling hegemony (1994, p. 3). It is 'the existing order's uninterrupted discourse about itself ... the self-portrait of power' (1994, p. 24). This description defines the spectacle as a direct consequence of power, a collection of metaphorical (and sometimes literal) fireworks that distracts the confused population from power's workings. However, spectacularity does not only come into play in the division between oppressive hegemony and oppressed subjects. Where violence is experienced as spectacle – perhaps because of its unusually extreme nature, or because it is related to a particular political modality, or because of its heavily mediatised appearance – it can be a means of deferring realities of risk or trauma, or even the painful meaninglessness of such acts. Spectacle can be diffuse, particularly in the way in which it intersects with collective social anxieties. Groups or societies sometimes turn to spectacle in order to deny or disavow the more unsettling risk of commonplace violence. Cultures of fear are not simply monodirectional; societies, communities and individuals invest in them affectively for a variety of reasons and with a variety of outcomes. In the case of supposedly satanic murders, exceptionalising such killings into the work of a devilish cult might be one way for media producers, police and other moral entrepreneurs to evade the anxiety and 'moral blindness' (Bauman and Donskis 2013) of being overwhelmed with stories of violence against women. These narratives reveal the need for an explanatory framework for violence that offers the possibility of resistance: it is easier to pray for redemption from the devil than to acknowledge the social causes of South African men's seemingly infinite capacity for violence.

Feminist media scholars have shown how, in both news and fictional representation, emphasis on the spectacular details of a crime, the monstrousness of its perpetrator, the ideal innocence or implied complicity of its victim or the exceptional nature of its circumstances distracts us from the social and structural qualities of gendered violence (see, for example, Meyers 1997, Carter 1998, Gilchrist *et al.* 1998, Cuklanz and Moorti 2009, Rentschler 2015). Similarly, feminist sociology reveals that, in certain contexts, 'a privileging of the extreme nature of political terror has amounted … to a neglect of the more "ordinary" forms of violence' (Roy 2008, p. 317). This is congruent to what Nancy Scheper-Hughes, writing on Brazil, calls 'the violence of everyday life' (1992). Violence perpetrated against subaltern women and men on an everyday basis can be easily forgotten, unlike violence aimed at other types of bodies and people, like the 'exceptional' victims of the alleged white genocide discussed in the previous chapter. Ordinary women disappear along with ordinary violence. In defining the murders of Theologo, Rathazayo and Moganetsi as the acts of depraved Satanists rather as part of a continuum of violence against women, the South African press effectively ignored any other explanations for them and avoided having to mention the multiple other female victims who were killed or harmed in these same weeks or months. Murders performed by satanic monsters have different proximities to murders performed by husbands, friends, sons.

Meyers asks 'whether news studies grounded in cultural studies can adequately examine the ideological implications of the reporting without acknowledging gender, race, and class as interconnected signifiers of domination and exclusion' (2004b, p. 213). Issues of class, race and gender were deferred in the coverage of these murders in favour of over-emphasis on the satanic narrative; nonetheless, a careful reading shows the way in which these intersecting positions impacted on the stories. News reporting on both cases avoided discussing gender almost entirely, although traces of gender-based violence can be found in the coverage, particularly of Kirsty Theologo's murder. Theologo was white and the men and young woman accused of her murder were black and coloured, but, uncommonly for South Africa, these race markers were also barely mentioned by the press. Similarly, signs of her class position (she was one of seven children of an unemployed single mother) were generally glossed over. It is likely that Theologo's whiteness contributed to her representation as an exceptional, and therefore an ideal, victim, outweighing considerations of class that often impact on reporting of violence against women.[3]

In the case of Chwayita Rathazayo and Thandeka Moganetsi, class – and concurrently race – was a little more visible. Both girls and their two male killers were black, living in a poor area of Soweto. Unlike in the Theologo case, press coverage sometimes dwelled on Moganetsi's situation as an orphaned child being raised by a financially struggling grandmother and Rathazayo's history as one of many children of a poor mother, although these backgrounds were never explicitly cited as causes for their deaths, in contrast to the common news tendency of blaming a victim's circumstances for the violence inflicted upon her (Howard 1984, Grosholz and Kubrin 2007, Suarez and Gadalla 2010). Much of the coverage was concerned with community reactions to the apparent outbreak of Satanism. In some of these instances the tone taken by newspapers was patronising and dismissive, presenting residents' fears of Satanism as nothing but superstitions. These depictions are in keeping with South African newspapers' usual representations of witchcraft, magic and indigenous belief systems, which dismiss them as sensational and hysterical, notwithstanding their internal meaning and coherence (Boshoff 2013).

It is impossible, in contemporary South Africa, to divorce approaches to class from race. Race cannot be said to have 'trumped' class, regardless of the much-written about rise of the black middle class, when the majority of black South Africans remain in poverty.[4] Being poor and being black are largely intertwined in the public imagination, in contrast to the continued denaturalisation of white poverty discussed in Chapter 2. While race may not have played an obvious role in news coverage of these deaths, the whiteness or blackness of victims, perpetrators and affected communities impacted on the presentation of their class positions, albeit in subtle ways that were overshadowed by the persuasive satanic narrative.

To summarise, then, certain extreme acts of violence, like the murders of Chwayita Rathazayo, Thandeka Moganetsi and Kirsty Theologo, are spectacularised in news coverage in a way that distances them from other, more everyday acts of violence, disavowing the relation between violence and structural conditions of power, poverty and inequality in favour of individual monstrousness. This debases everyday violence as unworthy of attention, something that can pass almost unremarked as yet another sign of a violent society in which 'girl bodies', in Sarah Nuttall's phrase, are routinely sacrificed (2004).

This claim is not confined to South Africa or to violence specifically against women. Globally, acts of extreme violence undertaken by white male perpetrators are often exceptionalised in a similar way, with media coverage 'preoccupied with psychologizing' these 'monstrous' white killers (Sebro 2013). Anders Breivik, the far right Norwegian terrorist who shot dead 69 people on a summer camp in 2011, is often referred as a 'lone wolf' killer (Pantucci 2011, Ranstorp 2013, Berntzen and Sandberg 2014), a term that crops up repeatedly in discussions of domestic terrorism perpetrated by white men in the US (McCauley *et al.* 2013). This suggests that the killer acted alone not only in a practical sense, but also in that he was not part of any larger social problem. Defining 'lone wolf' actors as both individual and monstrous distances them from other acts of racist and right-wing violence that emerge from similar ideologies, even as these increase in the west. The spectacularity of white male violence, like the spectacularity of Satanist murders, is presented as unnatural and uncommon rather than structural and social.

Satanism in South Africa

Moral panics around Satanism have appeared in a variety of locations (DeYoung 1998, La Fontaine 1999, Hjelm *et al.* 2009). Such panics can be a site for the displacement of other, less manageable, concerns: risks that cannot be easily legislated against, which are resisted by anxious communities and the pronouncements of moral entrepreneurs who incite popular crusades against social ills (Richardson *et al.* 1991). They draw on the uncanny, the bizarre and the supernatural.

During the last years of apartheid, one such moral panic around Satanism sprang up in the South African media, which over a period of years repeated claims that deviant white youth were being pulled into evil cults that indulged in murder, drug dealing, pornography, paedophilia and even cannibalism.[5] These imaginary Satanists were scapegoated by anxious whites, performing the role of what Stanley Cohen calls folk devils (1972). Fearful rhetoric around violent African nationalist revolution as well as dangerous communists, corrupting foreigners and unruly youth were all pulled into its narrative axis, creating fears of a supernatural enemy that threatened the social fabric of the white Christian nation. Despite decades of press coverage, legislation, political intervention and even the establishment of a dedicated police unit, still in existence today, no credible evidence has ever been uncovered to support claims that a large-scale Satanist conspiracy exists in South Africa or elsewhere.[6] While some people have been prosecuted for minor crimes like vandalism and drug possession, they tend to be individuals who self-define as Satanists or invoke iconography that could be said to be related to Satanism, rather than belonging to an organised group.

By the mid-1990s the word 'Satanist' no longer connoted white deviance. It had become part of an existing South African occult framework, a hybrid supernatural cosmology that also featured witches and zombies. But despite these shifts, Satanism has retained its emotive power. Jean Comaroff and John L. Comaroff speculate that the apparent increase in the late 1990s of occult panics may have been related to 'processes of globalisation and the forms of capitalism associated with it ... with postcoloniality ... with the sociology of postrevolutionary social worlds' (1999, p. 282).[7] Jeffrey Victor, writing on the US Satanism scare in the late 1980s, says that satanic tales 'arise as a response to widespread socioeconomic stresses ... The Satanic cult legend says, in symbolic form, that our moral values are threatened by evil forces beyond our control' (1991, p. 221). These scholars suggest that occult narratives are a consequence of social and political stresses that require explanation in a vocabulary that makes sense to those it speaks to. Claims of supernatural activity can mask other anxieties, such as the rumours about vampires in colonial East Africa that encoded concerns about extractive white settlers within dramatic narratives of blood theft (White 2000). In many cases these claims manifest as moral panics: overarching narratives of sudden threat, propagated by journalists, editors, religious figures, politicians, teachers and parents and usually embodied by folk devils, which, we are told, must be countered if society is not to be undermined.

Cohen wrote in his later work about the psychic formation of denial as a social concept, in which authorities responded in three ways to threats that could launch potential moral panics: '*literal denial* (nothing happened); *interpretive denial* (something happened but it's not what you think) and *implicatory denial* (what happened was not really bad and can be justified)' (2013, p. xxxiii, italics in original). In the case of these murders, Cohen's second category applies: drawing on the power of existing beliefs about Satanism, press discourse insisted that *something* had happened to these young women but that it was not what it seemed. This narrative centred on real tragedies involving real people; however, their causes were collectively misrecognised by the media.

The first of these causes is masculine violence. Classifying these murders as the acts of monstrous Satanists allowed the press to defer awareness of the crisis of femicide and the responsibility that we as a society have for it. As with coverage of domestic violence, 'by perpetuating the idea that violence against women is a problem of individual pathology, the news disguises [its] social roots' (Meyers 1994, p. 60). Poverty, inequality, joblessness, political frustration, the normalisation of violence, institutionalised misogyny, media prejudices and the social and spatial legacies of apartheid all contribute to the rise of the kinds of toxic masculinities (Haider 2016) that are prevalent in South Africa, masculinities that scholars like Kopano Ratele (2016) consider urgently vulnerable and in need of social support. Rather than thinking about what that support might look like, or how we might raise, educate and nurture male children differently, media investment in the overpowering narrative of Satanism allowed the press to ignore masculinity in favour of a horrifying, even supernatural, danger that could be blamed for these young women's deaths.

The second threat that was deferred by the satanic narrative was in the form these murders took, and can be considered a looming return of an apartheid repressed. A young woman covered in fuel and set on fire to burn alive; mutilated girls with their throats slit;

broken bodies abandoned in fields and warehouses outside townships; people cooked like meat and slaughtered like goats; people
drowned, stabbed, ripped apart. These kinds of murders painfully
recall apartheid-era urban and political violence. They echo the late
night work of state execution squads, the necklacings (Gobodo-
Madikizela 1999), the mob justice, the accused collaborators found
murdered on urban outskirts, the resistance fighters' bodies burned
on open fires (Feldman 2003). These types of violence were the by-
blows of the apartheid state, trade-offs for the serenity of the tree-
lined suburbs discussed in Chapter 5. Few of those killed by security
police, the apartheid army, urban crowds or internecine political
violence during the 1970s, 1980s and 1990s have seen justice. Their
ghosts haunt the project of democracy, despite the efforts of the
Truth and Reconciliation Commission to lay at least some of them
to rest (Gobodo-Madikizela 2003).

Outside of their horror at the obvious brutality of these killings, the media discourses discussed below made little attempt to
locate them as part of a continuum of urban violence. In treating
them as the incomprehensibly evil acts of Satanists (who are presented as outsiders rather than members of 'normal' society), they
painted these modes of murder as ahistorical and apolitical. The
uncanny remnants of apartheid violence stalk these narratives, but
referring to them as 'satanic' killings meant that traumatic memo-
ries could be repositioned onto a narrative that is disturbing in a less
immediate way. Anxieties about the threat posed by the incursion
of Satanism into schools and social lives present a different problem
to the deep-set awareness that, when it comes to the intersection of
poverty, precarity and violence in South Africa, formal apartheid
may have ended but its structures remain. In this sense, we must
think about both the murders and the reactions to them as part of
a system of racial injustice that includes myths of white victimhood
and heightened suburban perceptions of risk, in which certain kinds
of deaths are still seen as more important than others.

While it is largely outside the purview of this chapter and its
methods, it is nonetheless important to consider why Satanism
'worked' as an explanatory framework for these murders. Of
course, one reason for this was the appearance of supposedly
occult paraphernalia at the murder scenes. But there is no evidence

that these killers were Satanists in any real sense. As the trials revealed, the so-called Satanists undertaking these killings learned about Satanism from the same media that later defined them as Satanists, illustrating the circular nature of youth-related moral panics (Cohen 1972). Nonetheless, the satanic explanation must have had some resonance for the community members who were interviewed about the occult threat. Here it is important to remain cognisant of what M. Jacqui Alexander calls 'the Sacred', without which 'the majority of women in the world ... cannot make sense of themselves' (2006, p. 30). Alexander's formulations illustrate the way in which a sense of the spiritual, the mystical, pervades the lives of those who have been most bitterly abused by colonialism and slavery – and, we can add, by apartheid. Of the descendants of people who were forced into the Middle Passage, she writes, 'Cosmological systems housed memory, and ... such memory was necessary to distil the psychic traumas produced under the grotesque conditions of slavery' (Alexander 2006, p. 341). Amongst South Africans who suffered under apartheid, it may be the case that cosmological systems – in this instance a Christian frame that foregrounds the workings of the devil in everyday life – help to maintain stores of memory that are part of the collective work of resistance and survival. Explanations that rely on a Christian frame are not just about providing answers but also about providing comfort. Religion, in whatever form it may appear, can provide what Linda Elaine Thomas calls 'spiritual resilience', deferring collective anxieties and engaging beliefs and rituals that 'blend worldviews to form a cosmology that helps people live with everyday challenges' (1999, p. xv). Spiritual communities served this purpose during the darkest days of apartheid (Graybill 1995) and they continue to do so today. Like other forms of narration, South African stories of Satanism are part of a 'search for and an expression of meanings and truths' (Musila 2015, p. 5). They are sense-making processes for people who need to explain and understand the violence of their societies. While we critique the media's obsessive over-valuation of satanic causes, we must also remind ourselves that there are other currents behind these belief systems.

The Theologo murder[8]

In this section I trace the process that the story of Kirsty Theologo's death followed, considering the way in which the developing master narrative – that of a ritual murder performed by a group of Satanists – consistently outweighed any other possible meaning-making. The trial was heavily reported on, with coverage focusing on the murderers' testimony rather than on public responses. As is to be expected with news media about a murder trial, the reporting largely took a horrified and censorious tone. It never interrogated the veracity of the satanic motivation or whether the perpetrators believed in it.

The Star newspaper in Gauteng, the region where the killing happened, carried a disproportionate amount of coverage in comparison to newspapers elsewhere in the country. A brief quantitative survey makes it clear that the articles in question took a similar perspective throughout the case, from initial reporting on the death through two years of arrest and trial. Of the 55 articles I found, 44 used variations on the term 'satanic ritual' or the Afrikaans 'sataniese rituual'. Seven called the killing a 'satanic murder' while the terms 'ritual murder', 'satanic ceremony', 'ritual killing', 'satanic slaying', 'satanic killing', 'satanic rite' and their Afrikaans equivalents appeared a total of 14 times. Only three articles took different perspectives on the diagnosis of Satanism. One was an opinion piece that critiqued the use of Satanism as an excuse for the murder; one, discussed in more detail below, suggested that the killers' adoption of the term 'Satanism' followed rather than preceded its appearance in the media; and only one of those surveyed did not mention Satanism in any form. Twenty-five of the articles used words like 'apparent' and 'alleged' to describe the murder as satanic or placed the satanic descriptions in quote marks. But although some articles used these markers to signal the dubiousness of the satanic claim, no other narrative was offered to explain what had happened to Theologo or even to speculate on how it related to the larger picture of violence in South Africa. The remaining 30 articles referred to Satanism or ritual murder uncritically in their headlines or standfirsts. Eighteen referred to the killers' plans to 'sacrifice' (rather than to murder) Theologo, while evocative words like 'cult', 'devil', 'ritual' and 'soul-selling' cropped up repeatedly. Theologo's death appeared seven times in articles that listed cases of satanic or ritual violence in South Africa but only once in a general article about violence in the country.

One of the first articles on the attack, in the *Daily News* on 24 October 2011, is a paradigmatic example of the power of satanic stories to claim a spectacular crime. Running under the headline 'Girl set alight in "satanic ritual"', it referred to an 'apparent satanic ritual', 'some sort of satanic ritual' and police 'speculation that the attack was a satanic ritual'. The article ends with a reference to another case of alleged Satanism in which a teenage girl was kidnapped and brought to a 'type of church' where another teenager was murdered. The framing of the story here is clear. Readers were invited to place the attack in dialogue with other satanic acts and thus with an ongoing panic around Satanism. There was no sense in this article that anything connected the young female victims other than their torturers' occult intentions.

With Theologo badly burned and still in hospital, reporters clamoured to interview her mother, Sylvia, who further classified the attack as satanic by emphasising her daughter's Christianity. The killers had 'joined Kirsty's and Bronwyn's church in a bid to befriend them' (*Star*, 25 October 2011) and the girls had been lured to the hill by text messages sent during 'their church's youth service' (*Star*, 26 October 2011). Sylvia told journalists that 'Kirsty [was] not a devil worshipper. She [had] been going to church since the age of 8 ... They befriended her under false pretences. They used to go to church with her. They convinced my Kirsty they were Christians' (*Citizen*, 27 October 2011). Theologo, her mother insisted, 'loved God. She would never leave the house without her cross' (*Citizen*, 27 October 2011). She repeated this at the end of the trial: '[Kirsty] trusted them. These boys, they came to us as good Christians. They were always praying, preaching and carrying on about God' (*Saturday Star*, 9 November 2013).

In emphasising these claims about Christianity, Sylvia Theologo implied that her daughter was both respectable and innocent. Despite framing the murder as satanic rather than gender-based, she nonetheless drew on the moral discourses around which narratives of femicide and sexual assault often hinge. Studies of news coverage have shown that women are often blamed for their own victimisation (Berns 2001, Meyers 2004a, p. 97, Halim and Meyers 2010, pp. 90, 101). The emphasis on Theologo's virtuous Christianity made her subject to the same 'good girl/bad girl or virgin/whore dichotomy' (Meyers 2004a, p. 97) that is common to reports of violence against women. This depiction only began to falter towards the end of the trial, when a more complex image of the victim emerged. In a much later article, containing interviews with her mother, brother and best friend/fellow victim, Theologo is described as a 'freaky wild chick', a 'party animal', a rebel who was constantly 'preening' (*Star*, 8 November 2013). This portrait of a complicated young woman is in total contrast to the idealisation of the innocent Christian daughter that characterised the majority of the reporting. These interviews, as well as the mention of her nickname 'Thirsty Kirsty' – given because she 'liked a party' – had the potential to undermine the image of Theologo as an innocent victim of evil forces, and it is notable that no newspaper chose to publish any of this information until after the trial was concluded.

Theologo's mother's original statements insisted that she did not deserve this death *because she was not a Satanist*. As well as attempting to create an acceptable public face for her daughter-as-victim, this perspective also positioned Satanism as a legitimate force in opposition to Christianity. The murder thus became framed as a religious rather than a social problem. Unlike community responses to the deaths of Rathazayo and Moganetsi, discussed below, Theologo's mother invoked Christianity as part of a narrative about her daughter's victimisation rather than as a strategy for countering the Satanist threat. Her Christian framing seemed designed to connote respectability rather than to offer spiritual succour.

On 28 October Kirsty Theologo died in hospital from the wounds she sustained during the attack. Press reporting remained dramatic, with headlines emphasising the cultic aspects of the murder: '"Satan" ritual teen dies' (*Witness*, 29 October 2011), '"Satanic" case may go to high court' (*Citizen*, 2 November 2011). Many articles did use quote marks around words related to Satanism. But at the same time as loosely signalling that the satanic claims had yet to be proven, they also repeated one of the most lurid aspects of the story, in which Courtney Daniels, the youngest and only female accused, had her hand cut and smeared onto a bible as part of the group's ritual. The continued reference to blood and bibles alongside journalistic markers like quote marks suggest that, despite attempting to appear critical, press outlets were already wedded to a pre-existing discourse that provided a convenient and legible – albeit horrifying – explanation.

As the case progressed more information began to emerge about the night of the murder. According to Daniels, the killers' plan was to 'burn [Theologo] alive and then eat her body ... in honour of "Satanism practice"', based on details apparently drawn from a 'bible verse about a prostitute' (*Citizen*, 17 November 2011). Newspapers focused on the group's consumption of alcohol and marijuana as well on as their occult paraphernalia. Alongside this, however, the prosecutor Colleen Ryan is reported as saying, 'They brought those items there for a purpose. It is clear that the offense was planned and premeditated,' and that 'the nature of the crime is so horrendous that there has been a public outcry' (*Star*, 18 November 2011). While her statements classified the murder as exceptional, they also described it as a *crime* rather than as a ritual, locating it within a national criminal problem rather than within a religious framework. This alternate discourse was undermined by the article's headline, 'Two accused in "Satanic ritual" killing denied bail', which made it clear that this was no 'ordinary' crime.

It was soon revealed that some of the accused had criminal or otherwise compromised histories. Lindon Wagner, then 21, had suspended sentences for housebreaking and possession of marijuana. Lester Moody, then 18, had been sent to a rehabilitation facility after pleading guilty to assaulting a man while drunk (*Star*, 24 November 2011). Harvey Isha, then 23, was a refugee from the DRC, had a three-month-old baby and an 'undisclosed medical problem'. Robin Harwood, then 18, had been suspended from school for smoking marijuana (*Star*, 22 November 2011). Wagner had 'become a chronic drug user as a result of his troubled upbringing in a single-parent family struggling financially. Wagner had often skipped school and exhibited antisocial behaviour ... [he experienced] satanic delusions and had an extensive history of mental illness including schizophrenia and bipolar disorder' (*Star*, 23 April 2013).

Again the potential for an alternate narrative emerged here, one which took into account the killers' backgrounds and placed their actions within histories of poverty, mental illness, migration, trauma, substance abuse and family dysfunction, many of which are implicated in South Africa's femicide crisis (Vetten 2005, Lamb and Snodgrass 2013, Gouws 2015, Gqola 2015, Ratele 2016). However, the headlines of these articles, 'Two accused in Satanic ritual killing denied bail', 'More satanic murder accused fail to secure bail' and 'Cult murder accused can be held accountable', made it clear that, whatever their circumstances or structural imbrications in violence and inequality, these young men were being tried in the public imagination for a specifically *satanic* killing. Early the following year *The Star* stated that 'the six alleged Satanists' would appear in court again in February, implicitly suggesting that they were on trial for Satanism as well as for murder (18 January 2012). Their involvement in Satanism became a key determinant of their guilt.

In March 2012 Moody and Jeremy King pleaded guilty to the murder and were sentenced to 17 years each after agreeing to testify against Wagner, Harwood and Isha. According to their lawyer, Rod Montano, the pair admitted that a plan had been made to 'sacrifice' Theologo three weeks earlier, on the basis of a dream of Wagner's. The magistrate 'asked if the two were admitting the incident related to the occult and Montano replied: "They were never involved in a satanic ritual before"' (*Citizen*, 30 March 2012). The Afrikaans newspaper *Beeld* wrote that 'Kirsty Theologo's friends were curious about Satanism, but did not know entirely what it involved ... Nobody truly understood Satanism and they discussed how it had to be done' (20 April 2013).[9] The fact that the accused did not know how to 'do' Satanism suggests that such skills are attainable and therefore that Satanism poses a genuine threat when performed by people with the appropriate knowledge.

The statements of the five defendants made it clear that, rather than belonging to an organised cult, they had little idea of what they were doing. The ritual elements had only a tangential relation to common descriptions of Satanism in South Africa and sometimes veered into confusion. Moody explained that the group had referred to Theologo as 'braaivleis' (barbecue meat) when planning the murder and that a 'divine force, like God', had led her to joke about being sacrificed, which the accused decided to take seriously (*Saturday Argus*, 27 April 2013). This description of a human victim of violence as meat on a barbecue bears an uncanny relation to some of the most chilling acts undertaken during the last years of apartheid, when the bodies of murdered black liberation fighters were burned by white state operatives, who stood around the fires drinking beer as though at a family barbecue (Feldman 2003, pp. 243–245). It also suggests something about which kinds of bodies, in contemporary South Africa, are considered suitable for sacrifice. While men and boys are frequently victims of brutal violence, the performative spectacularity of 'ritualised' killing – the burnings, dismemberments, gang rapes, physical humiliations – that characterises the murders of Theologo, Moganetsi and Rathazayo seems largely reserved for women and girls (Gqola 2015).

Daniels, meanwhile, stated that the group 'drew a five-pointed star on the ground the evening of the murder. [Moody] was of the opinion that a "spirit" would "rise" out of the middle of the star and then each one's wishes of wealth, power and wisdom would be fulfilled' (*Beeld*, 30 April 2013).[10] Moody is reported as saying, 'It felt like something had control over me … I do not know if they were spirits … Jeremy also wasn't himself. He ran around strangely' (*Beeld*, 1 May 2013).[11] Wagner later told the court that he was 'zoned out' during the murder (*New Age*, 11 October 2013). The confused and confusing testimony suggests that the accused's experiences of the event were not set: they were open to co-optation and alteration by the dominant narrative and its single-minded focus on Satanism. These claims of possession were not reported with high modality but neither were they interrogated. Press discourse may have had no real interest in whether these young people were possessed by devils, but neither did it cast doubt on whether *they* believed in this possession. Indeed, the occult reasons for the murder had by now become common knowledge: Theologo was 'set alight at the climax of a satanic ceremony where [the defendants] offered their souls to the devil in return for material benefits' (*Star*, 22 May 2013). Regardless of whether individual journalists or editors believed in satanic or supernatural activity, they rarely questioned its validity as a motivation for murder.

The reporting took an increasingly surreal turn during the testimony given by Wagner, who was fast becoming seen as the mastermind behind the murder. Crucially, Wagner told the court that 'it was the media that labelled the killing as "satanism" and that he started to refer to the ritual that way only because "it made sense to use the word". Before that, he said, they never spoke about satanism' (*Star*, 18 October 2013). This reveals in the clearest possible way that the discursive construction of the murder was assembled by a homogenising press that drew on familiar tropes to explain an otherwise unthinkable event. Wagner embedded himself in that emergent narrative, telling the court that the defendants were 'willing to sell their souls that day'. He repeated the claims of possession, saying that he cut his hand and put it into the fire but could not feel the flames (*Star*, 11 October 2013) and that his lawyer had advised him not to plead guilty as the 'court wouldn't accept that something took over me' during the murder (*Saturday Star*, 12 October 2013).

Wagner comes across as a fantasist, lifting elements from popular culture to construct the shaky mythology that was built in the run-up to and the wake of Theologo's death. He told the court that the idea for the killing came from a six hour long movie called *The Anti-Christ*, parts of which he had watched on his phone.[12] He is quoted as saying, 'I wanted power to be able to lift you up with my eyes and then throw you on the other side of the room ... When I heard of American artists selling their souls, it was something I wanted to be part of, like Tupac, Bone Thugs and Snoop Dogg' (*Citizen*, 18 October 2013). While the strange intersection of satanic stories and hip-hop celebrity culture deserves closer analysis, more relevant here is the repeated desire for power, also mentioned by other defendants. Indeed, one article on Wagner's testimony used the headline 'Deadly "power" talk' (*Star*, 18 October 2013). However, none of the reporting asked *why* young people would be so desperate for power that they would perform a brutal murder to get it. Feelings of powerlessness – due to poverty, lack of opportunity, even the perception that women, foreigners or different racial groups are taking one's allotted place – are a feature of life in South Africa for many, but these conditions were barely mentioned as part of the circumstances that led to Kirsty Theologo's death.

During the trial another important and disavowed counter-narrative began to emerge: that of sexual violence. Questioning Isha, a prosecutor asked, 'Did you think that she needed help? ... You thought at that time that you were witnessing two girls getting raped, didn't you?' (*Star*, 23 May 2013). This was the first time that the possibility of gendered violence was explicitly stated in these articles, despite the fact that the extreme brutality of Theologo's death sits on a continuum with incidents of 'corrective rape' and with the 2013 killing of Anene Booysen, one of South Africa's paradigmatic female victims of violence.[13] Questioned about the brake fluid that had allegedly been added to Theologo's vodka, Wagner said that it 'had the same effects as a date rape drug', again gesturing to a less spectacular, if equally horrific, motivation for the murder (*Star*, 5 November 2013).

An undercurrent of sexualised violence emerges from Wagner's testimony in particular. He told the court that 'one of the group suggested they have sex with Kirsty and her younger friend before sacrificing them' (*Star*, 11 October 2013). He also stated that he 'loved' Theologo, and that they had kissed but 'we never had sexual relations' (*Saturday Star*, 12 October 2013). These signs become particularly important when considered in the light of the longer interview that was carried out after the trial with Bronwyn Grammar, the second girl who was set alight in Linmeyer. Grammar related how she and Theologo would 'hang out with the accused rather than go to school', drink, watch movies and play video games. Theologo 'had a soft spot for coloured boys' and 'had a thing for Lindon [Wagner]' although she dated his brother instead. The article continued, 'It's because of the relationship drama that Bronwyn believes Kirsty's murder was motivated by lover's jealousy rather than Satanism' (*Star*, 8 November 2013). This version suggests a gendered story in which a young man violently punished a young woman for what he perceived as unruly sexual behaviour: again, an iteration of tropes of corrective rape and strongly related to performances of aggressive patriarchal masculinity. The claim that Theologo had a 'soft spot for coloured boys' suggested a dangerous or disordered female sexuality that included multiple partners and crossed racial boundaries, in contrast to the majority of the representation, which was careful to present her as an ideal victim (Christie 1986, Brodie 2020). This was, however, one of the few times during the reporting that the close relationship between victim and accused was mentioned.

On 8 November 2013, Wagner and Harwood were found guilty of murdering Kirsty Theologo and assaulting Bronwyn Grammar. Harvey Isha and Courtney Daniels were acquitted. Reportage on the convinctions continued to emphasise the importance of Satanism in the case. Headlines included 'Justice for all; Relief as two "satanic" killing accused go free' (*Star*, 8 November 2013), '"Devil's disciples" guilty of murder' (*Times*, 8 November 2013) and '"The devil destroyed us"' (*Saturday Star*, 9 November 2013). The quote marks used in the latter two headlines suggest that they refer to interview material that will be discussed in the articles below; however, this does not happen in either case. Both mention the devil in their headlines and nowhere else. Once again this reveals the extent of press commitment to the narrative of Satanism as the only possible explanation for Theologo's death, as well as suggesting the way in which South African cosmologies of Satanism emphasise not just mysterious cults but also the empirical existence of the devil.

Throughout the reporting on this murder, alternate tropes and counter-claims emerged. Traces of sexual violence and of racial, class and other inequalities appeared in the texts but were consistently disavowed or ignored in favour of the dominant account that posited Satanism as the only possible way of understanding the murder. Similar patterns appeared in press coverage of the next set of murders, although alongside this insularity the coverage also suggested some of the powerful spiritual framings that weave throughout township life.

The Dobsonville killings

Newspaper coverage of the deaths of Thandeka Moganetsi and Chwayita Rathazayo was far less extensive than coverage of Theologo's murder. Reporting within the court was not permitted due to the youth of the accused so media material does not show how the killers defined their actions. Denied access to their stories, coverage focused on the responses of the community, emphasising the panic that occurred in the wake of the murders. This emphasis fostered a different tone to reporting on the Theologo murder. Articles seemed sometimes to suggest that community reactions to the threat of Satanism were excessive. Some of the reporting implied a difference between knowledgeable, critical journalists and uneducated, superstitious residents. The lack of detail in reporting about the killings also meant that the press narrative exhibited even more clearly the features of a moral panic. Moral entrepreneurs and folk devils appeared prominently alongside a sense that the murders represented a threat to the Dobsonville community and to society as a whole.

Twenty-seven of the thirty articles I found on these murders used the words 'satanist', 'satanic' or 'satanism'. These words were placed in inverted commas or accompanied by other markers of doubt like 'suspected' and 'alleged' in just twelve instances. Twenty-two articles used the words 'occult', 'cult' or 'ritual'. Twenty-six articles mentioned that candles and razor blades, recognisable as satanic paraphernalia, had been found near the bodies. Twenty articles made reference to priests, healers, prayers or exorcism, either as events already taking place at the school in the wake of the murders or as necessary correctives to the apparent epidemic of Satanism sweeping the country. Six articles mentioned the literal presence of the devil or of evil spirits as the reason for the rise in satanic murders. A further 20 referred to apparently deviant behaviour – drug and alcohol use, adolescent rebellion, tattoos, body piercing – as signs of satanic involvement on the part of the victims or as warning signs for parents and teachers. Nine of the articles stated that the crimes were being investigated by the South African Police Service's controversial Occult-Related Crimes Unit, a division that was set up during the late apartheid satanic panic, which continues to restrict membership to Christians and which has publicly supported exorcism as an appropriate response to 'satanic' crimes.[14] Only a single article of the 30 I encountered – an editorial demanding that the Premier of Gauteng Province take action to deal with violence against children – related these murders to the general problem of crime in South Africa. None of the reporting linked these young women's deaths to rates of femicide.

Under the headline 'Girls' "Satanic" End' (20 February 2014), the first article that appeared in *The Star* emphasised elements of the case that would become common throughout the reporting. Much was made of the ritual elements of the 'Satanism-related killings', with reporting discussing the candles and razor blades, stating that the girls had been 'mutilated' and relating stories from anonymous friends about how they had agreed to join a 'satanic group' but had been 'sacrificed' after one had changed her mind. Unlike the Theologo case, initial news coverage suggested that these girls were to different extents complicit in their own deaths, which were related to their supposed flirtation with Satanism.

Also visible in this early reporting was a differing conception of the two victims, emphasised in the interview material that journalists chose to include. According to a lengthy article in *The Star* (20 February 2014), the orphaned Moganetsi's 77-year-old grandmother and primary carer, Elizabeth Potsanyane, was 'shocked' by her death, but also told reporters, 'There were days when she never came back home from school … She was very naughty. She was a stubborn and disrespectful child at times. We fought a lot because she didn't like it when she was reprimanded.' Rathazayo's mother, Philiswa, on the other hand, was described as 'emotional', and the girl's athletic success was emphasised: she was a member of the provincial swimming team and her 'swimming medals were propped against the wall in the sitting room'. A distinction was drawn here between the orphaned victim who was badly behaved and rebellious and the talented victim from a more stable and loving home. At this stage the reporting slotted the two young women into the usual good girl/bad girl iterations of female victimhood in the media (Benedict 1992).

Once again, this crime was described purely in satanic terms. The *Star* article contains two box-outs, one listing five other recent 'Satanist murders' (including Kirsty Theologo's) and another citing Kobus Jonker, the notorious former head of the Occult Unit, stating that Satanism 'involves the worship of Satan … Satanists usually make a "blood pact" with the Devil and reject Jesus Christ'. Press coverage was committed to the diagnosis of Satanism right from the start, including the possibility that these murders were part of a larger picture of satanic crime and that satanic practices led to actual supernatural events.

An article in *The Citizen* that day (20 February 2014) took the same approach, beginning, 'Something in Pheliswa Rathazwayo's [sic] heart told her to go to church yesterday to pray for her 15-year-old daughter, Cwayita [sic]'. She was soon contacted by police and taken to the crime scene: 'It was there that she heard Cwayita's name in the whispers. Then she learned that both girls had been found dead in the field. Rathazwayo fell to her knees on the ground where the two girls lay.' The article goes on to quote Moganetsi's grandmother on how the girl had left the house the previous night despite her objections: 'She said I can't control her because she knows her rights … As I prepared myself for her arrival, the call came from the police to say she is dead.' Once again reporting drew a difference between the victims, expressed in the reactions of the women who cared for them: one emotionally traumatised by the death of an innocent, the other suggesting that the victim's own behaviour had been part of the cause. The article also quotes police spokesperson Brigadier Neville Mailila explaining that police would not rule out 'the possibility of suicide or cult suicide' but that this was unlikely as 'both girls had nine lacerations on their bodies and it was improbable that they had done this to themselves'. No other explanation was offered. The mutilation the girls suffered was never connected to other attacks on female victims.

The following day two 16-year-old boys, also pupils at George Khosa high school, were 'nabbed for "Satanic" murders' (*New Age*, 21 February 2014). Minimal information about the killers was released, so media speculation focused almost entirely on the victims' behaviour and on community responses. Indeed, little was said about the boys at all other than the fact that they were still wearing their school uniforms when they were arrested and that they had been taken to a 'place of safety' rather than to prison owing to their youth (*New Age*, 21 February 2014; *Star*, 21 February 2014; *Sunday Times*, 23 February 2014; *New Age*, 24 February 2014).

The premier of Gauteng Province, Nomvula Mokonyane, classified the murders as part of a national crime problem, stating that the government 'was deeply concerned about levels of violence against women and children'. This was tempered, however, by police assurances that the controversial Occult Unit would continue to investigate (*New Age*, 21 February 2014). Despite the arrests, the characterisation of Moganetsi as a complicit victim continued, with her grandmother claiming that she had stolen money and a cellphone, threatened to murder family members, 'smoked, drank alcohol and partied a lot' and had a tattoo on her arm that she 'believed was linked to Satanism' (*Star*, 21 February 2014).

This article allowed some space for the debunking of myths in a second page box-out that quoted Dr Chaundre Gold from the Institute of Security Studies. She did not go so far as to use the term moral panic but did warn against using Satanism as a 'scapegoat' (*Star*, 21 February 2014). Despite this brief foregrounding of social science expertise, *The Star* did not take up the suggestion that different explanations should be considered.

The Citizen, meanwhile, headlined its 21 February coverage 'Satanic panic' and stated that the boys had been arrested for murdering their friends. Brigadier Mailila insisted that it was 'early days to label it an occult killing', but this did not calm the community: 'nervous parents and guardians' waited all day by the school to collect their children, alongside heavy security that meant no students could leave unnoticed. Only members of the local education department and a Lutheran priest, there to counsel students, were permitted access. A few blocks away a crowd gathered while police dug up bones buried in the yard of a private home after an accusation that these were human remains connected to Satanism, a claim quickly refuted by police. According to local resident Refilwe Camngca, the community was shocked by the murders: 'We have the usual crimes here, like housebreaking, but nothing like this. We are a close-knit community; we support each other in times of need; we talk to each other.' These responses illustrate again the way in which the murders were exceptionalised. As with the plasma gangs urban legend discussed in Chapter 4, they were represented as a novel and unexpected danger rather than as part of an ongoing problem of violence against women.

With no new information emerging, reporting on the murders continued to focus on anxiety among local residents and interventions from moral entrepreneurs. Parents continued to wait at the

George Khosa school gates and pupils continued to tell reporters that they were terrified. Reverend Gift Morane, secretary of the provincial branch of the South African Council of Churches, attempted to hold a prayer meeting at the site where the girls' bodies were recovered. Cementing the idea that Dobsonville was under threat from supernatural forces, he told reporters that he had encountered a snake that was 'a sign of the bad spirits hovering in the area'. The reverend also 'slammed individuals and groups who killed in the name of Satan ... "We don't have a religion in this country called Satanism. It's the behaviour of people who support the wrong spirits and think that this country is a banana republic"' (*Saturday Star*, 22 February 2014). Morane's statement indicates the linking of Christianity with citizenship, a marriage of politics and religion that is common across Africa (Ellis and ter Haar 2004), in which troublesome people believe the wrong things about religion as well as about the nation. The murders thus became a symptom of the apparent scourge of Satanism – described by this church official as an illegitimate belief system within a Christian and democratic country – with no relation to structural conditions of power, economics, race, class or gender.

The *Sunday Times* (23 February 2014) continued to discuss the story in terms of the girls' culpability in their own deaths. This time, however, Rathazayo, the swimming star who was being groomed as an Olympic hope, was the object of the reporting. Her mother was quoted as saying, 'I saw the signs, but I thought it was just a passing phase and peer pressure ... I did not imagine it would result in her death ... She just changed and would not listen to me.' Rathazayo had begun cutting herself, drinking alcohol and smoking marijuana, and had told her mother the night before her death that she had almost joined a satanic cult. Here the murders were decoupled from their setting, with its historical conditions of poverty, injustice and other consequences of white supremacy, and rewritten as crimes that could have happened to any teenager who had made the mistake of becoming involved in Satanism.

As with the social scientist quoted above, alternative narratives for the murders did emerge but often from sources that were unlikely to be meaningful to readers worrying about Satanism. Martin leBatte, an 'occult arch-priest', told *The Citizen* that the two boys may have had 'mental health problems' and been 'influenced by what was written about Satanism online', and suggested that police should also investigate their home lives. Offered as part of a defence of alternative religions, this perspective was not convincing to most readers. Fifty-six per cent of respondents to a poll conducted on the paper's website that same day agreed that Satanism was a 'real threat' (*Citizen*, 25 February 2014).

On 25 February Moganetsi and Rathazayo were given a joint funeral service at the Dobsonville stadium, packed with hundreds of local residents and 'inconsolable' school pupils, some of whom fainted and had to be given medical assistance. The event was characterised by the appearance of 'pastors and priests from various churches [who] took to the podium, calling on God to help in the fight against satanic spirits that they said were attacking pupils' (*Star*, 26 February 2014). These 'prayers for healing' were accompanied by condemnations of the murder from attending local ANC politicians, ANC Youth League members, rivals from the Economic Freedom Fighters party and local leaders of the Congress of South African Students, some of whom sang songs associated with South Africa's liberation struggle (*Citizen*, 26 February 2016). The funeral itself, as well as the reporting on it, recalled the emotional, politically charged and often violently suppressed township funerals of opponents of the apartheid regime. This connection was not made explicit in the coverage, but it is difficult to avoid the echoes of historical trauma that haunted these events.

Speaking after the service, Moganetsi's grandfather Reuben Williams said, 'Some children in the school are aware of this [Satanism]. Children should play far from them. Schools should hold daily assemblies because Satan is playing with our children.' Rather than the threat emerging solely from the now-arrested murderers, who were barely mentioned as individuals, in this formulation it was Satan himself who was the source of danger. Such an approach allowed these murders to take on meaning within a religious frame rather than just being random acts of violence. It also suggested that at least some agency was available to those affected, who had Christian strategies of belief and ritual they could draw on to push back against the satanic influence that was responsible for the death of their youth. Invoking the literal presence of Satan (and concurrently of Christ) could allow those affected to make sense of the senseless, to locate themselves within it and to develop affective strategies of resistance. Similarly, Khohliwe Habile, a local primary school principal, blamed peer pressure, deviant behaviour and bad religion for the threat posed by Satanism: 'Children should stay away from the wrong friends. Parents must monitor their children's friends; the clothes they wear; tattoos and body piercing because some of [these] are signs of the devil … We must monitor churches they attend because some churches worship the devil' (*Sowetan*, 26 February 2014).[15] Again there was a sense here that something could be done to mitigate the threat to children, that good Christians could save them from bad churches. In this response, the supernatural threat posed by Satanism could be read in young people's social semiotics and countered by embedding these potential deviants in 'good' religion.

While neither of these perspectives placed the murders within patterns of gender-based violence in South Africa, it is nonetheless significant that community members often located the deaths as part of a generalised satanic threat that was not restricted to Dobsonville. Where media discourses exceptionalised the murders, residents' religious narratives sometimes acknowledged that these shocking crimes were not, in fact, out of the ordinary, notwithstanding the inherent otherness of occult and moral danger.

Media discussion of the murders as solely satanic crimes was further strengthened by police revelations that the Occult Unit was at that moment investigating a total of 48 cases, including the Dobsonville case. Police Colonel Attie Lamprecht told a press conference that satanic crimes were on the rise and that an increasing number of young people were joining 'cults', lured in by recruiters who promised money and power (*Star*, 27 February 2014; *New Age*, 27 February 2014). According to Lieutenant-Colonel Hettie de Jager, provincial commander of the Occult Unit, 'satanic-related crimes, including rape and murder, [were] on the rise in black townships' (*Sowetan*, 27 February 2014). Police descriptions of murders and rapes as examples of Satanism, rather than as instances of the crimes that pervade South African society and particularly the lives of women, spectacularised sensational crimes and divorced them from socioeconomic realities.

Both of the policemen quoted here stated that young people's attraction to Satanism had to do with their desire for 'power', but as in the coverage of the Theologo murder there was no discussion in the press about the conditions of powerlessness that may be related to such an urge. Police revealed the profile of a 'dabbler' in Satanism – a young person with social problems, who experiments with drugs, is rebellious and withdrawn (*Sowetan*, 27 February 2014) – without alluding to factors like race, class, gender or poverty that could impact on the execution of violent crimes. The murders were explained as the consequence of cult recruitment and individual pathology, and adolescent behaviour was demonised as not just deviant but potentially homicidal.

The South African Council of Churches released a statement in response to the killings that equated murder, rape and sexual abuse with 'rising cultic and satanic practices' and called on religious leaders to help government resolve the crisis (*New Age*, 28 February 2014). *The Star*, in an editorial on 28 February, referred to both this case and Kirsty Theologo's death as instances in which the constitutional injunction towards religious tolerance became a problem, as Satanists were engaging in 'murder most foul' under the guise of religious practices. Police, head teachers, newspaper writers and religious leaders insisted that what was needed to curb the satanic menace was vigilance from parents and an increase in Christian activities in schools. Unlike community responses that drew on a transcendent understanding of the threat of the devil, these moral entrepreneurs were concerned with satanic *practice* alone, rather than with supernatural danger. The problem of violence in South Africa, and particularly of male violence, was disavowed in favour of a moral narrative of good versus evil, in which communities were responsibilised to watch over their children but were not granted any further agency in countering the threat.

Press coverage tailed off after the funeral, re-emerging in mid-March with a continued focus on community reactions. The girls' school was at the heart of many of the rumours of supernatural danger, with priests attending at least three times a week, holding all-night vigils 'in the hope of expelling Satanism' and '[casting] out demons' from some of the 'hundreds' of pupils who were affected. Teachers told reporters they were afraid of going to class, students refused to walk through the school alone and self-confessed Satanists reported 'horrific things' going on in the buildings (*Sowetan*, 19 March 2014). *The Citizen* wrote that 'children are dying because of Satanism' and reported that, in the wake of the killings, Basic Education minister Angie Motshekga had partnered with a teachers' union and the ANC Women's League to combat Satanism in schools. Motshekga 'said a parent of one of the murdered girls had said she could see her daughter was acting differently prior to her death ... "[We need] to educate parents on picking up signs when something is not right with their children"' (24 March 2014). This suggests that parents of victims were as responsible as parents of perpetrators for keeping adolescent deviance, and consequently the possibility of murder, at bay. It also recalls common injunctions about parental responsibility for teenage drug use, showing again the way in which narrative structures repeat across moral panics.

In April the accused boys appeared in court. Denied access to the trial, media reports continued to repeat anxious local narratives around the murders, suggesting that 'similar incidents related to Satanism were reported at George Khosa Secondary School prior to the incident' (*New Age*, 9 April 2014). Once again a possibility for alternative understandings of the murders emerged. Newspapers mentioned that social workers' reports had been prepared on the boys, alluding to a possibility of social or mental health factors that could come into play (*Citizen*, 11 April 2014). The director of a clinic for child victims of abuse warned that 'time wasted in places of safety where child offenders were kept while awaiting trials, tended to disrupt the lives of the children ... "The waiting adds to their trauma and victimisation. It can be more harmful to children in the long term"' (*Citizen*, 16 June 2014). This was the first time within these articles that consequences for the killers were mentioned, and the first time that they were referred to as children.

Despite these traces of perpetrator trauma, reporting on the various stages of the trial – including all the articles cited in the previous paragraph – continued to mention the now-canonical evidence that black candles were found near the site and that the girls' bodies had cuts on their necks and wrists (*New Age*, 14 April 2014). This appeared even in an article devoted to the fact that both killers were undergoing observation at Sterkfontein mental hospital (*Citizen*, 18 June 2014).

After this fairly minimal reporting at the start of the trial, my searches did not uncover any more press mentions of Moganetsi and Rathazayo – barring a single editorial in which their names were mentioned as part of a catalogue of recent violent crimes (*Citizen*, 28 July 2014) – until the sentencing the following year, when both accused boys, now aged 17, were given 14 years in prison under the Child Justice Act. The sentencing was covered by just a single article in *The Star* on 27 May 2015 titled 'Teens sentenced for satanic murders', which again mentioned the candles and razor blades found near the bodies. Echoing coverage of Kirsty Theologo as an idealised victim, a change from earlier allusions to particularly Moganetsi's but also Rathazayo's allegedly deviant behaviour, the sentencing judge Tshifuiwa Maumela told the court that 'two young innocent lives were lost. They are gone forever. They were completely defenceless and helpless'. Importantly, given how little reporting was possible on the details of the case, this article stated that both boys had 'confessed to being involved in Satanism and having killed the two girls'. Here involvement in Satanism was given equal importance to the enactment of a brutal murder. Satanic practice and extreme violence become equated, one explaining the other.[16]

This article also returned to Rathazayo's mother, who had appeared frequently at the start of the coverage. Repeating the trope that there could be only one way to understand the murders, it stated that Philiswa Rathazayo was still 'struggling to come to terms with the fact that her daughter died as part of a satanic ritual'. She told the paper, 'It took a while to understand. I am always crying but prayer has made life easier.' Again here we see the immense power of the religious narrative, of Alexander's 'Sacred' (2006). Understanding her daughter's murder as a Satanist crime, thereby locating it within a recognisable structure of moral warfare, allowed a bereaved mother to make 'life easier'; to retain her spiritual resilience (Thomas 1999); to manage, somehow, the unbearable burden of knowledge and the awareness of incipient violence that sit on the shoulders of women in South Africa.

As with the Theologo case, press coverage of these murders was overwhelmingly concerned with defining them as satanic crimes. Where possibilities of other explanations emerged, such as suggestions about mental health problems, these were quickly glossed over. The lack of detail available ensured that the media story of the murders of Chwayita Rathazayo and Thandeka Moganetsi remained a simplistic tale of evil powers and adolescent deviance.

Women and violence

It is undeniable that there were elements of these murders that can be defined as occult, ritualistic or satanic. During the Theologo trial it emerged that the idea to kill Kirsty had come to Wagner 'in a dream' (*Citizen*, 30 March 2012) and that the group related their plan to a bible verse about sacrificing a prostitute (*Citizen*, 17 November 2011). Wagner and the others told stories about wanting to gain supernatural powers and performed invented rituals involving blood and the cutting of hands to mark their violent acts. The killers of Rathazayo and Moganetsi confessed to being involved with Satanism and placed supposedly occult objects – black candles and razor blades – near the bodies.

These are, however, *descriptive* elements. They tell us as much as other explanations offered for violence against women in contemporary South Africa: punishment for sexual or gender 'misconduct', as in cases of corrective rape; jealousy, as in domestic violence; the influence of drugs and alcohol, as in many random acts of extreme violence that happen to women (see du Toit 2014). Any one of these causes could have been brought to bear without changing the fundamental facts of the murders. Media claims that these killers were working under the influence of supernatural evil are just one of many ways to understand violence. I have suggested above some of the reasons why the spiritual framing of satanic murder may be particularly meaningful for those affected. Nonetheless, the emotional and spiritual significance of this narrative to affected communities does not negate the fact that formal media outlets failed to consider any meaning to the murders other than Satanism, a diagnosis that they, hand in hand with police, had imposed.

In valorising Satanism as the only possible motivation for what was done to these girls, the South African press in effect legitimised its own claims.

The failure to think about these murders as femicides is important. Nuttall writes that 'gender relations are central to the success and failure of post-apartheid South Africa', and that acts of violence perpetrated against the bodies of young women of are 'non-negotiable significance to South Africa's capacity to reconcile with itself' (2004, p. 20). Despite this centrality to the national imaginary, however, the gendered nature of contemporary violence was largely denied or avoided by media reactions to the tragedies. In these cases, the spectacular violence of a Satanist act almost entirely erased the possibility of more 'normal' (equally brutal but less sensational) violence against women. The deaths of Moganetsi, Theologo and Rathazayo were made exceptional, categorised alongside other Satanist murders but never discussed in the context of the rates of death of South African women or of other acts of violence perpetrated against them. Unlike in the case of Anene Booysen, whose killing was clearly sexualised, responses to these murders almost entirely avoided talking about them as instances of the rage and aggression meted out so frequently on the bodies of South African women by South African men, resulting in Gqola's 'female fear factory' (2021). The spectacularisation of Satanist murders allowed the media to sidestep the disturbing awareness that, in fact, the greatest monsters are not monstrous at all: they are human, familiar, part of our communities and our worlds.

Like those of the other women named at the start of this chapter, the deaths of Chwayita Rathazayo, Kirsty Theologo and Thandeka Moganetsi were individual tragedies, appalling crimes and symptoms of a larger condition. They reveal the continuation of the embedded structural violence that has wounded South Africa since the start of the colonial project. The press's incapacity to see past the screening fiction of Satanism recalls the way in which apartheid-era realities were deferred by privileged white people who claimed not to know about the violence and injustice surrounding them (van der Westhuizen 2007). Like the many South African women whose murders go unreported and unnoticed, Theologo, Rathazayo and Moganetsi are victims of this willed blindness, this refusal to know and concurrently to act against both the structural causes of violence and those pathological modes of gender that work out their rage, despair and fear on the always-available bodies of women.

Notes

1 A list of the newspaper articles cited in this chapter can be found in Appendix 2.
2 The One in Nine Campaign, an important feminist activist group supporting victims of sexual violence, takes its name from this statistic. The group was established in 2006, spurred by the vitriol and violence aimed at a young woman named Fezekile Kuzwayo – known by the pseudonym 'Khwezi' – who had the astonishing courage to bring a case of rape against Jacob Zuma, then deputy president of the ANC (see Gqola 2009).
3 Sociologist Nils Christie defines the ideal victim as 'a person or category of individuals, who, when hit by crime, most readily are given the complete and legitimate status of being a victim' (1986, p. 18). These sorts of people – innocent children, older women, those who are considered weak, vulnerable, respectable – are automatically deserving of victim status, unlike other types of people, for example sex workers and women who drink or are sexually active.
4 At the time of writing, official statistics revealed that 'in addition to having worse employment outcomes, black Africans also earn the lowest wages when they are employed. Whites, in contrast, earned substantially higher wages than all other population groups. Their monthly average real earnings were more than three times higher than those of black Africans' (Statistics South Africa 2019).
5 In my previous book I offer an extensive discussion of the moral panic around Satanism during the late apartheid period (Falkof 2015a). This scare was, like most moral panics, localised among certain people and groups rather than widespread throughout the population. Nonetheless it offers a valuable site for understanding white anxiety during a moment of intense social and political change.
6 See, for example, Elaine Showalter (1997) and Lawrence Wright (1994) on court cases around high profile satanic panics in the UK and US, none of which resulted in legitimate prosecutions.
7 Published in 1999, Comaroff and Comaroff's canonical article made a case for the sudden and dramatic increase in occult narratives in South Africa. At the time of writing, twenty years later, these events show

no sign of diminishing, suggesting that they are not tied to particular political circumstances but are rather responses to social anxiety that are embedded within southern African imaginaries.

8 In order to conduct the analyses in this chapter I used the SA Media database to undertake a search from 22 October 2011, the date of Kirsty Theologo's murder, to 31 June 2014, a month after the sentencing of Thandeka Moganetsi's and Chwayita Rathazayo's killers. I performed searches bounded by these dates for the terms 'Satanist', 'satanic', 'Satanism' and their Afrikaans equivalents, as well as for the names 'Theologo', 'Rathazayo', 'Moganetsi' and 'Dobsonville'. Supplementary searches for the same terms and dates were conducted using Google. I amassed a total of 115 articles, of which 55 were on the Theologo case and 30 on the Moganetsi and Rathazayo murders. It is possible that Theologo's murder garnered more coverage because she was white; crimes with white victims are, in South Africa as elsewhere, often given more detailed reporting (Grosholz and Kubrin 2007, p. 63). Some of the coverage of her death appeared in Afrikaans-language newspapers but I did not find single article on Rathazayo and Moganetsi in the Afrikaans press. Although South Africans of various races speak Afrikaans as a first language, these newspapers are aimed at an economically elite audience (Wasserman 2009), which in practice translates to a largely white readership. The fact that no coverage of these township murders appears in Afrikaans newspapers in the region illustrates once again that black and white victims of crime are still treated differently by the South African press.

9 'Kirsty Theologo se vriende was nuuskierig oor satanisme, het nie mooi geweet wat dit behels nie ... Niemand het satanisme werklik verstaan nie en het bespreek hoe dit gedoen moet word.'

10 'die aand van die moord 'n vyfpuntige ster op die grond geteken het. [Moody] was van mening dat 'n 'gees' uit die middle van die ster sou 'verrys' end dan sou elkeen se wens van rykdom, mag en wysheid waar word.'

11 'Dit het gevoel asof iets beheer oor my het ... Ek weet nie of dit geeste was nie ... Jeremy was ook nie himself nit. Hy het snaaks rondgehard-loop.'

12 It is likely that this refers to a 2005 US television special that interviews 'clergy, scholars, historians and psychologists' to discuss the 'evil enigma' of the antichrist through the ages (Antichrist n.d.).

13 Corrective rape is the term used to describe the sexual assault of black lesbian women, particularly in townships and rural areas, a violently homophobic disciplining of what are seen to be illegitimate modes of

sexuality. Anene Booysen was a 17-year-old girl from Bredasdorp in the Western Cape who was gang-raped and disembowelled, allegedly by a group of men she knew. The murder led to outraged condemnation both nationally and internationally but overall this did not affect the discourse around sexual violence in South Africa (Mpalirwa 2015).

14 According to the journalist Jacques Rousseau, the unit 'continues to waste public resources, misdirect police attention, and stigmatise young people who are by and large more misunderstood than malignant' (2013).

15 Christianity in South Africa is heterogeneous and constantly shifting. The school principal's claim that some churches worship the devil reflects an ongoing contestation between traditional, evangelical, syncretic and other churches over what constitutes legitimate Christianity.

16 Valérie Hirsch, a Belgian journalist who interviewed the accused in prison a few months after the murders, points out important similarities between this case and Kirsty Theologo's. Both killers had traumatic personal histories that are not uncommon in South Africa. One lost his father to AIDS, after which his mother fell ill and the family descended into dire poverty. He began drinking and was a fully-fledged alcoholic by his early teens. The other was the son of a policeman whose alcoholism manifested in violence and who had been beating his wife and children severely for years. Both boys told Hirsch that they became involved in Satanism as they 'wanted power' and that their reputations as Satanists had improved their standing at school, where they were 'big men'. However, neither suggested there was any cult or organised activity behind their actions. They had learned about Satanism online rather than being recruited and no other students had been involved (Hirsch 2016).

4

Drugs, crime and consumption
in Alexandra

Around the middle of 2013 a series of stories appeared in the South African press about a new phenomenon called 'plasma gangs', presented as the latest iteration of the country's crisis of crime. Journalists, broadcasters, police and government spokespeople, social media users and local residents shared tales online and in mainstream media of the frightening exploits of these gangs, which were said to be located in Alexandra township in the north of Johannesburg. Unlike 'normal' robbers, who stole anything of value, plasma gangs had a very specific modus operandi. They were said to break into homes in the township with the express purpose of stealing plasma televisions. According to the stories, the gangs used various technologies to achieve this aim, both hypermodern electronic devices that could tell from outside which homes contained the TVs and muti (indigenous magic) techniques that sent residents to sleep while their homes were plundered. They also took advantage of township sociality and visibility to locate their victims. They were extremely violent and often caused death or harm in their pursuit of plasmas. But rather than selling these desirable consumer goods, as one might expect from criminal syndicates, the gangs were said to dismantle them and break them open in order extract a mysterious white powder that was used to make nyaope, a street drug otherwise known as wonga or whoonga. Depending on which story one heard, the gangs were either nyaope addicts themselves or professional dealers of the drug.

Nyaope is notorious in South African cities. It is extremely destructive and the subject of a large body of urban mythology.[1] Experts generally agree that it is comprised of a mix of substances, usually a base of cheap heroin with additions like asbestos, rat poison, milk powder, bicarbonate of soda and even swimming pool cleaner (Department of Community Safety 2014, Vahed 2015, p. 265). It is 'sold in powder form, smoked by rolling it with cannabis, heating it up & inhaling the fumes & of late it is also injected' (Fernandes and Mokwena n.d., p. 3). As is common with drug-related panics (see, for example, Linnemann 2010), stories about nyaope pull into their axis a range of other social anxieties. One persistent rumour suggests that dealers make the drug with antiretroviral medication that they have stolen or bought from HIV-positive patients (Davis and Steslow 2014, p. 216, Department of Community Safety 2014). Drawing on existing stigmas about HIV, this rumour adds to fears about both the vulnerability and the moral weakness of people living with the disease. As in all such epidemics, poverty and unemployment are major contributing factors to the drug's spread (Mokwena and Morojele 2014). Addiction rates are high, recovery rates are low and many poorer communities have been decimated by nyaope use (see Vahed 2015).[2]

While concerns about drug users and dealers are not my focus in this chapter, they play powerfully into the plasma gangs narrative. The nyaope connection is part of what set this story aside from 'normal, everyday' crime and helped it morph into an urban legend that continues to be disseminated as one of the risks of living in South Africa. There is no mysterious powder in plasma televisions that can be used to get high. Plasma is a descriptor for a technology rather than a substance. The powder contained in these devices is magnesium oxide, a small amount of which coats the display electrodes in a thin layer. Magnesium oxide is easily purchased at health food stores and has never been shown to have any psychotropic effects. Despite various expert attempts to disprove it, though, the story remained current throughout 2013 and continued to appear intermittently on social media for the following five or so years, set in various places around the country. The plasma gangs story shows the way in which township residents' narrativisations of their own precarity are both hypermodern and related to globalised and transnational anxieties about status, consumption, belonging and identity. It combines the local and the global, the historical and the contemporary, in ways that reveal the social utility of urban legends. The story condenses fears about security and crime, drug dealers and drug users, police failures and corruption, dangerous foreigners, unruly youth, the intersection between crime, witchcraft and technology and the insecurity and visibility of township life. It shows how myth, uncertainty, rumour and strangeness can inform South African cultures of fear, where crime is not just frightening in and of itself but also because it connotes the presence of hidden forces that undermine the predictability of everyday life. I am concerned here with a kind of 'crime talk' (Sasson 1995) that is endemic in South Africa but oddly quiet in the literature, which often associates fear of crime with whiteness and wealth. This chapter emphasises, too, the centrality of the African urban to contemporary city forms (Falkof and van Staden 2020), a perspective often overlooked in traditional urban studies, which engage 'ways of seeing and reading contemporary African cities [that] are still dominated by the metanarrative of urbanisation, modernisation, and crisis' (Mbembe and Nuttall 2008, p. 5).

Also important is the materiality of plasma TVs themselves. These are consumer objects that signify aspiration and success and have been 'incorporated into the hierarchical schematisation of modernity' (Newell 2012, p. 173). In the context of township crime, they are also lightning rods for the sometimes violent jealousy that can make one a target of criminals. Looking at plasma gangs in this way can offer us a new perspective on the intersection between consumption and anxiety in South Africa. As well as creating anxiety about whether we can keep up with social norms, consumption can lead to anxiety about our safety. The compulsion to consume and display that characterises so much of life under late capitalism can, in conditions of heightened insecurity, add risk in practical rather than existential ways. Studies of consumption in Africa and the global south often take a developmental perspective and adopt a moralising tone whereby consumption becomes 'conspicuous' – meaning excessive, tasteless and bad – when undertaken by Africans. In this chapter I move beyond that reductive position, viewing consumption, like anxiety, as a fundamental component of modernity and urban self-making. Important arguments have been made in this direction by scholars of African luxury (Iqani 2015b, Dosekun 2017, Dosekun and Iqani 2020); at the same time, however, we need to acknowledge the power of *risky* consumption and the way in which it intersects with urban affects.

I first encountered the plasma gang story in around 2012 in conversation with friends from Alex, who told me that 'everybody knew' that the gangs were a threat in the township. My interest was further piqued when the story began to appear in mainstream media, but without the occult element that had come up in the versions I had heard. Notwithstanding this absence, tales of the plasma gangs were heavy with possible meanings. The fear of having one's possessions stolen or one's private space violently invaded is nothing new in South Africa, nor is it unfounded. Nyaope is a serious social problem that is the cause of sometimes violent crime. The question, then, is about the additional elements – the mysterious substance inside the TVs, the indigenous and modern technologies used to perpetrate crime, the special skills of the criminals, the gangs' manipulations of township visibility – that make this a story of exceptional crime, crime that is somehow out of the ordinary, like Satanist murders of young women.

Throughout this chapter I refer to the plasma gangs as an urban legend. Urban legends are reactions to 'unconstructed social problems' (Best and Horiuchi 1985, p. 489), which 'often depict a clash between modern conditions and some aspect of a traditional lifestyle' (Brunvand 1981, p. 189). While urban legends may be covered by the press, their primary mode of dissemination seems to be word of mouth (Best and Horiuchi 1985, p. 492) or, in more recent times, the networked communication of social media. Urban legends are also notable for their folkloric qualities. They 'seem most likely to persist when they have a general, underlying message ... which can be tailored to fit new situations' (Best and Horiuchi 1985, p. 492). Once again, we can think of urban legends, and the rumour and hearsay through which they spread, as ethnosociologies, 'the theories that ordinary people use to explain social phenomena' (Waters 1997, p. 115) and that are 'not necessarily less reasonable than other ways of explaining disturbing and unexpected happenings' (Waters 1997, p. 115).

Luise White writes of colonial rumours of the occult,

> These stories, even when told with the conventions and constraints of hearsay, were not all received and heard the same way ... Nevertheless each repetition, each repudiation, each amendment and refinement did not make a story more true or more false, but made it a more immediate way to *talk about other things*. (2000, p. 41, emphasis added)

Hearsay, rumour and urban legend allow tellers to position themselves as particular kinds of subjects, to discuss and contest issues and to cement ways of thinking and relating. It is almost irrelevant to talk about whether people 'believe' these stories; rather, we need to consider what such stories *do*, what they achieve in terms of what people know about their social worlds. These 'marginalised discourses' are 'important sites for negotiating social truths, meaning and popular knowledges' (Musila 2015, p. 99). Musila argues that rumours 'encode anxieties' (2015, p. 97); that is to say, they provide an oblique way for people to communicate the substance of deep collective fears.

In this chapter I map how the plasma gangs scare was disseminated across traditional and social media and then discuss five thematic elements of the story, employing a combination of media material and interviews with former or current residents of Alexandra. I use the plasma gangs tale to highlight a contradiction of life in the globalised South African city: on the one hand, neoliberal injunctions towards visible aspiration and consumption, which are a feature of urban life in so many places; and on the other, the awareness that in South Africa these performances can be dangerous, that visibility can lead to vulnerability. While this kind of consumption anxiety may affect all South Africans, I am here concerned with those who cannot afford to hide their desirable goods behind high walls and electric fences, and who are also seldom acknowledged in the academic literature on fear of crime (Mosselson 2020).

Alexandra, or Alex, is one of the densest urban areas in South Africa. It is also just ten minutes' drive from Sandton, an elite neighbourhood full of high-end malls, gated housing developments and a glossy banking district. Democratic South Africa's failure to live up to its inclusive promises is 'nowhere more evident than in the contrast between Alexandra and its neighbour, Sandton' (Nieftagodien and Bonner 2008, p. 386).[3] Alex was originally designed for a population of about 70,000. The 2011 census put residency at about 180,000 (Alexandra 2016).[4] It is home to ever-increasing numbers of migrants from elsewhere on the continent, some of whom who live in extremely precarious conditions (Nieftagodien and Bonner 2008, pp. 397–401), as well as to Pakistani and Bangladeshi traders. Many residents live in traditional family homes, but many others eke out a more precarious existence in shacks that line the Jukskei River and the mishmash of formal and informal housing between 6th and 18th Avenues. The city's delivery of services like trash collection is poor and an astonishing R1.6 billion (about $112 million) has gone missing from the much-vaunted Alexandra Renewal Project (Sibembe and Simelane 2019). The area sometimes suffers from infestations of rats, while on certain roads goats and other small livestock wander unencumbered. Despite these challenges, and its reputation as a 'hotspot' for crime, Alex is brimming with social life, informal trade, small business, family networks and fashion – all the elements that make up Joburg's reputation for 'hustle'. On weekends the Pan-African Mall, with its global and national fast food chains and clothing outlets, is a bustling hub. In the evenings locals crowd around venues like Joe's Butchery and Alex The Hub to enjoy live music and skilled DJs. Unlike its image in the mass media, which tends to emphasise poverty and disaster, Alex is home to class stratification and mobility, to aspiration, to wealth as well as poverty (Alexander *et al.* 2013).

Crime and consumption

The plasma gangs story is more than just another crime narrative, and one of the elements that makes this clear is its fixation on its central object. Plasma TVs are expensive, technologically advanced and aesthetically pleasing. As well as offering the viewer a way to access information and entertainment, the television has powerful symbolic meaning. Plasma TVs are the sort of high status consumer goods that '[promise] the realisation of personal and collective ideals' (McCracken 1990, p. xv). In order to understand the plasma gang story we must think about it as a narrative of consumption, which Deborah Posel defines as 'the acquisition and use (including the display) of durable and nondurable goods, along with the cultural, political and psychological antecedents and effects thereof' (2010, p. 161). Consumption 'refers to a regulatory regime and the agency that this enables and constrains' (Posel 2010, p. 161). It is a 'social and semiotic process through which goods make concrete the abstract categories of social life' (Newell 2012, p. 209). Scholars who think about consumption are concerned with the ways in which shopping, selling, displaying, buying, importing, exporting, advertising, marketing and related activities shape and reshape not just political and economic but also social life (Miller 2005). They help us to understand that 'how money is spent on material items, from the mundane to the spectacular, is one way in which human beings say something about who they are' (Iqani 2015a, p. 48).

One of the most influential interventions into this field comes from Pierre Bourdieu (1984), who emphasised consumption as 'the institutionalisation of differentially valued tastes that function to reproduce social status and class', rather than as an instance of individual choice (Fitzmaurice 2015, p. 694). Üstüner and Holt (2010), however, argue that Bourdieu's model, based on wealthy western democracies, does not adequately explain consumption modes in what they call 'less industrialised countries'. In her path-breaking book on media and consumer culture in the global south, Mehita Iqani writes that

> although consumption has been much studied from the perspective of the west, its study in 'the rest' appears to have been limited to anthropology and economics ... It seems crucial to turn the map of research about consumption upside down, to pay attention also to the narratives about consumption which are at the margins. (2015a, p. 7)

Talk of consumption in South Africa is often disapproving. Media that engage with the consumption practices of black South Africans draw on elitist notions of taste to classify emerging middle classes as vulgar, to dismiss the practices of poorer people as irresponsible or to demonise African consumption overall as foolish, excessive and environmentally dangerous (see, for example, Iqani

2015c, van Staden 2015). Popular perspectives often view South Africans simply as hapless victims of northern production and consumption processes, ignoring the taste and agency of those who work and hustle to buy cars, iPhones, Levi's, Rich Mnisi dresses and, indeed, plasma TVs. However, if, as Daniel Miller argues, the structures, processes and acts involved in consumption underpin the whole of human history (2005), then we must acknowledge its social and economic complexities in South Africa and reject the moral and aesthetic judgements that dismiss African displays as conspicuous. We must also, however, be willing to think about the insecurities that consumption can inaugurate, which are not specific to Africa or South Africa but find visible expression here.

Histories of consumption in South Africa have always been as much about race as about class. According to Posel, there has long been 'an historically constitutive relationship between the workings of race and the regulation of consumption … the making of the racial order was, in part, a way of regulating people's aspirations, interests and powers as consumers' (2010, p. 160). During apartheid, white-made laws regulated which shops could exist and what they could sell in townships, constricting black South Africans' agency to buy, eat and wear what they chose. Africans, however, are 'longstanding consumers and participants in transnational media and commodity cultures' (Dosekun 2017, p. 167). Despite these constraints, black people during the apartheid and colonial eras engaged skilfully with western forms of consumption and self-display and hybridised them into local configurations (Odhiambo 2006, Mokoena 2017). Since the end of apartheid many have enjoyed the opportunity to consume and to display without restriction, as whites have always done. From the Maponya, Dobsonville, Protea Glen and Jabulani malls in Soweto to the Pan-African in Alexandra and the Khayelitsha Mall in Khayelitsha, Cape Town, township malls have become big business, to the detriment of the spaza shops and other smaller and informal traders who were once the backbone of township commerce (Ligthelm 2008). Malls and advertising billboards 'add to a barrage of factors that encourage people to place themselves in the new South Africa as consumers' (Ceruti 2013, p. 74). Research suggests that ownership and enjoyment of consumer goods, from cars and appliances to clothing and alcohol brands, has a significant impact on how South Africans define their own class positions (Ceruti and Phadi 2013, pp. 143–144).

A large part of the pleasure of ownership involves exhibition. However, within the sometimes dangerous space of the township, this is complicated by what Sasha Newell calls 'the ambivalence surrounding display' (2012, p. 131). Showing off your possessions can make you visible in both a desirable sense – friends and neighbours can see what you have and respect how you're doing – and in an undesirable sense, where expensive goods attract criminal attention. The plasma TV story thus allows us to ask an important question about consumption and aspiration in South Africa. What does it mean to own an aspirational object in an insecure place?

There is no question that being a victim of crime can have a detrimental effect on one's daily life. But equally, reactions to the *possibility* of crime can be deeply damaging, whether that crime actually happens or not. In the UK, US and Europe, fear of crime has long been seen as a social problem almost as pressing as crime itself, which 'continues to impinge upon the wellbeing of a proportion of the population' (Gilchrist *et al.* 1998, p. 283). According to Murray Lee (2011), a micro-industry of state, academic, NGO and corporate actors has developed around ideas of fear of crime, sometimes to the detriment of useful policy-making. Fear of crime has been 'normalised as a socio-cultural term used to describe an element of life experience in late modernity' (Lee 2011, p. 1). Fear of crime is often overtly racialised and centred on white people being, or claiming to be, afraid of black and brown people (see, for example, Skogan 1995).

In South Africa, it is clear that anxiety about crime has pernicious consequences. Numerous scholars have written about what Charlotte Lemanski (2004) calls the 'architecture of fear': the high walls, boom gates, barbed wire fencing, armed response and community policing that characterise suburban and upwardly mobile neighbourhoods across the country (for example Spinks 2001, Ballard 2005, Durington 2009, Comaroff and Comaroff 2016). Both the white genocide myth discussed in Chapter 2 and the Melville Facebook page discussed in Chapter 5 reveal how the anxieties of the privileged have an impact on the wider social and spatial landscapes of South Africa. Valji, Harris and Simpson discuss some of these:

An accelerating retreat of middle-class communities behind high walls and private security, prompting a withdrawal from public space and pre-empting the possibility of relationship-building ... Viewing the new South Africa through a prism of fear creates an identity of victimhood that is linked to race; reinforcing the divided and racialised identities of the past ... This can fuel resentment and a sense of injustice on one side of the wall, and a sustained sense of entitlement and privilege on the other. (2004)

There is far less research, however, on fear of crime among marginal and poorer communities. According to Aidan Mosselson, 'The majority of urban studies and planning scholarship has treated fear of crime as a bourgeois concern. This body of work discusses how upper class fears and discourses about crime are usually placeholders for other forms of prejudice and discomfort caused by proximity to "others"' (2020, p. 225).

It is unquestionable that 'most whites and many blacks, especially among the middle classes of the faded rainbow nation, feel themselves uniquely vulnerable to rage, attack and immanent disorder' (Comaroff and Comaroff 2016, p. 221). However, data from the 2010 South African Social Attitudes Survey (SASAS) suggests that, while white and wealthy South Africans report a consistent level of fear about crime, black people – particularly those living in insecure conditions – reported far higher daily levels of fear and perceptions of risk (Roberts 2010). Mosselson reveals that 'despite their general silence in the prevailing literature, poor black people are actually more likely to fall victim to crime and violence and frequently articulate acute fears and anxieties about this vulnerability' (2020, p. 226). Fear of crime is not restricted to the middle classes; but middle-class people, with their increased access and agency, are more effectively able to broadcast their fears and thus to make them into social and policy issues and subjects for academic research. In South Africa, as elsewhere, the audibility and visibility of white people's fears can silence or obscure the more pressing concerns of those with less economic security.

One of the consequences of the securitisation of South African cities, which has its roots in colonial segregation (Swanson 1977, Nightingale 2015), is the lack of visibility of citizens to each other. Those who live behind high walls, opening their electric gates to drive their cars to enclosed private parking lots, are invisible; they can be seen only by what they have and what they choose to display. In contrast, those who walk on the streets, do not own cars and do not live behind walls are easily visible to those who do. The tension between who can see and who is only seen is a common symptom of racialised power in South African cities. Townships like Alexandra and Soweto, however, upend this way of understanding the city. They are spatially flatter: houses and walls are lower, yards are smaller, gates are often open, families live closely and neighbours are intimately acquainted with each other. Strangers are usually welcomed. One of the consequences of township sociality and geography is that residents can both see and be seen. This contributes to the creation of strong community bonds but can also make one overly visible to unwanted eyes.

Plasma gangs in the media

The shift from the localised urban legend that I first heard about to something with broader impact seems to have been a consequence of the plasma gang story's entry into the mainstream media. In this section I offer a brief genealogy of how the story was transmitted once it made that leap.[5]

Its first significant media appearance came on 29 August 2013 on a programme on the talk radio station 702, hosted by a white South African man named John Robbie, who told listeners that Alex was in the grip of a dangerous crime wave instigated by so-called plasma gangs. According to Robbie and his unnamed informants, the gang broke into homes in the township and stole televisions that they would smash open and use for nyaope production. They were responsible for numerous murders and for a general outbreak of criminality in the area. Later that morning his official account (@702JohnRobbie) sent out two tweets on the subject, and at around midday he posted a video to his YouTube channel. Across these three platforms, listeners, readers and viewers were told that eight people had been killed in Alex by the gangs, a number that recurred without substantiating detail as the story spread further.

Tweets soon followed from the well-known spokesman of an anti-crime NGO (@Abramjee), a high profile author and radio personality (@RediTlhabi) and the official Twitter feed of the South African Police Service (@SAPoliceService), as well as from various listeners and social media followers, many of them residents of Alex. The radio and Twitter discussions quickly spread to other media, some of which reported on plasma gangs as a genuine threat, while others tried to discredit the story and classify it as an urban legend. These news sources drew on quotes from political, police, drug and community experts to make their contradictory claims (for example *New Age*, 29 August 2013; *IoL*, 29 August 2013).

Of the tweets posted on that first day, 27 were retweets of claims made by media outlets or figures, without added commentary or opinion. Forty-three discussed the gang with exclamations of fear, distress or surprise. Ten asked fairly neutral questions along the lines of what the term 'plasma gang' meant, while only seven were critical of the veracity of the story or signalled by the use of acronyms like 'LOL' that they had not taken it seriously.

By the following day the plasma gang story had firmly found its way into mainstream news (*Star*, 30 August 2013; *Sowetan*, 30 August 2013). Experts and witnesses who had been mentioned the previous day recurred, with more detail given, including names of people who had allegedly been murdered by plasma gangs. Responses to the story revealed a disjuncture between different institutions and citizens. A number of tweeters agreed that the plasma gang was either invented or was not a genuine problem. Community organisations and government spokespeople worried about the threat posed by the gangs, while police and other government figures insisted they were an urban legend. The first group drew on notions of law and order and police failure to express their concern about the danger, while the second invoked terms like 'myth' and 'rumour' to discredit the destabilising potential of the first. Moral entrepreneurs' contestations about the story were concerned not just with its details but with its credibility.

The plasma gang tale was widely repeated during that first month of its public appearance and often conflated anxieties related to crime, consumption and security. Journalists writing or broadcasting about plasma gangs linked them to drugs, xenophobic attacks, inter-community crime, police failure, taxi violence and fears of township unrest (*Saturday Star*, 31 August 2013; *Alex News*, 12 September 2013). Other outlets focused on debunking the myth, bringing in experts to argue that plasma TVs could not possibly be used to make nyaope (*Saturday Star*, 7 September 2013; *Eyewitness News*, 25 September 2013). Stories soon emerged about the gangs terrorising townships in other parts of the country (*Mpumalanga News*, 5 September 2013). Twitter engagement continued throughout the rest of 2013, with most tweets suggesting that plasma gangs were a genuine threat. Discussions there and on Facebook went on into early 2014. As time went by, the plasma gang legend began to appear as one of many elements in stories about nyaope rather than as a primary expression of township residents' fears about drugs, crime and safety.

The concentration of material on Twitter reveals how mainstream media impacted on the spread of these rumours online. Eighty-seven of the tweets (56 per cent) appeared on 29 August 2013, the day the plasma gangs story broke on Radio 702. A further 32 (20 per cent) appeared immediately after, between 30 August and 2 September. Twenty-one more tweets (13 per cent) appeared between 4 September and the end of that month. Thus, a total of 89 per cent of the Twitter activity about plasma gangs appeared immediately after mainstream media discussions on the subject. While the story had been current in Alex for some time, it was, ironically, the intervention of a white male media celebrity that had the most impact on its dissemination outside the township.

Plasma gangs in daily life

Alongside the media material discussed above, in 2017 I undertook a series of interviews with Alex residents, hoping to find out what, if anything, they knew about the plasma gang story.[6] All 21 people I interviewed had heard that plasma TVs owned by residents of Alexandra had been targeted by gangs of drug dealers or users who stole them in order to get a powder (or, in one case, a gas) that was used to make nyaope or other street drugs. Only one of them had not heard the phrase 'plasma gang' but, once I explained what I meant by it, she confirmed that this type of crime was known to have been common in Alexandra. Others agreed that everyone in Alex was aware of the gangs. Even those who had only encountered the story tangentially had some experience of its impact. Ntokozo told me, 'All I've heard is that there is a powder inside the plasma that they target. The thing is, I bought my own plasma that's in my room and I was kind of afraid. That's all I've heard.'

A series of themes recurred throughout the interviews and media material, which I discuss sequentially in this section. First, plasma gangs were classified as either normal or abnormal township crime; second, the reality of plasma gang stories was contested; third, plasma gang stories drew on the familiar scapegoats of drug users, corrupt police and foreigners; fourth, plasma TVs were discussed as material objects that connoted wealth and status; and fifth, plasma gang crimes were seen to be a consequence of township visibility.

The first theme, of defining plasma gangs as either 'normal' or 'exceptional' crime, reveals the different ways in which fears of crime and violence were expressed. When treated as an extravagant type of criminal activity, the plasma gangs story allowed my respondents to express a range of other anxieties, from the pressures facing community structures and the threat posed by witchcraft practices to the need to protect themselves from crime. For others, treating the plasma gangs as just another iteration of the everyday criminality of the township allowed them to represent their own identities and street savviness in particular ways.

Many of those I spoke to reiterated that there was a special category of often violent crime in which homes were broken into in order to steal plasma TVs because of the powder they contained. These responses often centred on the desperation of drug users. When the focus group considered the connection between drug users and plasma theft, Adele stated, 'I wouldn't put it past them because they will do anything to get hold of this drug. I even heard rumours of them taking ARVs and smoking them ... Even that thing you use to wash your swimming pools, they smoke that as well.' According to Thembani, 'Once the experimenting starts ... you use and then you need more supply ... so you start breaking into houses to steal.' Lucky agreed, 'We heard that they break into the houses at night and they find people and usually they shoot them.'

Plasma criminals were sometimes defined as exceptional or unusual for reasons other than drug-induced desperation. Thulani explained that plasma gangs were 'not just criminals ... these guys are smart'. A number of respondents described the gangs as organised and intelligent. Some online responses also classified the plasma thieves as ingenious and unusually competent. On 29 August @Tshipi4 wrote, '@plasma gang how did they know! these guys can be used to find AIDS cure ... they know things.' On the same day @Wizba wrote, 'But this Plasma Gang HOW THE FUCK did they find out about whats inside Plasma TVs!' On 31 August @Sebs_Daddy_Cool referred to the plasma gang as 'Kasi [township] chemists with expensive taste & habit'. In these instances the mythology around drug dealers defined them not only as dangerous but also as especially clever, able to use complex technologies and substances in their quest to make more money and/or to get high.

Other respondents, however, suggested that plasma theft was 'just' crime and that plasma TVs were only one of a set of desirable objects that were stolen from people's homes. According to Twitter user @MadameVG, 'We also have gangs that focus on only high end luxury goods in [Pretoria]' (29 August 2013). During the focus group Lucky said, 'I think people were stealing those TVs to sell them ... Logically you will steal a TV and sell it and get drugs for R2,000, which would be more than the thing they find in the TV.' Sandile agreed that plasma theft was part of everyday drug crime: 'I think [the white powder story] is just a gimmick. Most of these people steal these plasmas because they need money in order to buy drugs.'

Sometimes these positions overlapped. Lungile told me, 'Plasma gangs are a group of guys who steal plasmas in order to get that powder ... and they use it to mix it with nyaope,' but then continued, 'They will do anything. They steal clothes from the washing line; they mug people of their cell phones. They break in and steal TVs, they even steal car tyres.' Far from being exceptional, this second description is in keeping with general understandings of the desperation of street addicts. The meaning of the plasma gangs was not fixed; they could be both ordinary and extraordinary crime.

Some online discussions invoked exceptionality to suggest how communities should 'deal with' crime. Posters reacted with calls to a gun-toting machismo that has had long currency in South Africa (Cock 2001), echoing the valorisation of vigilante justice in which 'Lone Ranger' violence and personal firearms are seen as legitimate responses to social threat (Baderoon 2015, pp. 107–132, Comaroff and Comaroff 2016, p. 193). One wrote, 'The plasma gang r terrorising the neighbourhood. Ama buy me a gun' (@toperoM, 9 November 2013). User @MojelaTumelo wrote, 'Yes mob justice does not help, but sometimes it seems like the only solution in such cases,' while @AlPatronMaile wrote, 'The plasma gang that has re-ignited terror in Alex will be met with anarchy! Ayeza amaguerilla' ['The guerrillas are coming'] (29 August 2013). User @thogore agreed, 'Kill them that's only solution. SA government gave this rubbish some rights' (29 August 2013). This comment blames South Africa's crime problem on the imposition of western notions of human rights, a legal and ideological regime that, as Jason Hickel has shown (2015), many South Africans deeply resent. Another user claimed, 'They must come to my house. We have rifles & I've even taught my housekeeper to shoot' (@toshpolela, 29 August 2013). This tweet showcases some of the awkward social contortions caused by beliefs about crime and risk in South Africa, when 'even' a housekeeper – presumably a black female domestic worker, often a low status and poorly paid job – must become familiar with firearms.[7]

One important differential between plasma gangs and 'normal' crime appeared in stories of the technologies they used. First, criminals were said to have a mysterious high tech device that could tell which homes contained plasma TVs. Second, they were said to have access to traditional muti techniques that they used to subdue residents.

According to Twitter user @moyawamaubane, 'They also operate in Protea Glen. They have a device that can detect if a house has a plasma/not' (29 August 2013). My interviewee Lungile described the device as 'kind of like a laser'. Thembani agreed that the gangs must have some sort of technology that allowed them to find out which house had a plasma and which did not. Others, however, thought these claims must be overblown. Delia said, 'I did hear about that, but how would those junkies get a hold of such an expensive device? ... Whenever they get a plasma they don't save, they're always buying that drug that they get to get high.' Ntokozo agreed, 'Honestly, come on, where are they going to afford that technology? If you have to steal the plasma screen then how can you afford the technology to track them down?'

During my focus group an enthusiastic discussion developed around the muti techniques that plasma gang criminals were said to employ. Sandile stated, 'Especially where we come from, with muti you can do anything.' All the group participants had heard of a substance called umsila wemphisi, directly translated as 'hyena's tail', which was allegedly used by plasma gangs. When I asked David about this he answered casually,

> Oh yeah, it's called a hyena's tail ... If you burn it literally everyone in the house that's sleeping won't hear anything ... Story I've heard is that if you burn it at the bottom of the door, that little space, as long as the [smoke] goes in and everyone in the house can actually inhale it they're gone. Then you walk in and do whatever you want to do, you can even chill and relax and walk out after, they won't hear a thing.

David also made it clear that the use of this kind of muti for crime was not restricted to the plasma gangs. Sibulelo told a story that he had heard from his aunt: 'You have to close your toilet when you are about to sleep ... Because what they do is they go into the pipes outside ... and they start burning this herb or something. It comes through and it knocks you out, they can even take your bed while you sleeping.' A number of group participants related second-hand stories about umsila wemphisi's powers. According to Thulani,

> They say they can burn it if you are sleeping, they burn it through the door ... If you inhale the slightest smoke of it, you pass out for like six to eight hours. So they can walk in and do whatever they want while you are sleeping ... The modern one I heard about but I'm not sure about it, they say even a CD, if you burn a CD someone passes out.

Another participant agreed, 'Yea vele le yeCD ngiyayicava' ['Yes I know about that CD one']. However, no one offered a theory for why a CD in particular could be used as a replacement for the substance known as hyena's tail. As with the intersection of Satanist panic and hip-hop culture mentioned briefly in Chapter 3, this fusion of forms and technologies could offer a valuable direction for future research into contemporary South African cosmologies. Interestingly, despite passing on the story as though it was common knowledge in his neighbourhood, Thulani later admitted that he had first heard of 'hyena's tail' being used for sleeping muti on the television documentary *Cutting Edge*. This transmission of ideas from media to popular culture and back illustrates one of the primary ways in which urban legends spread (Best and Horiuchi 1985, p. 490).

This series of responses highlights a strategy that township residents employed to explain, and thus to live with, a crime rate that can often seem both rampant and ignored. In crediting thieves with access to supernatural methods of home invasion, my respondents offered an explanation for their own and their communities' potential vulnerability to crime that was coherent with existing beliefs about witchcraft and danger in the township. Imbuing these criminals with occult capacities put their actions beyond the realm of 'normal' crime and normal responses to crime in a way that expressed residents' sense of powerlessness in the face of risk, and also helped them to locate these forms of danger within existing belief systems that are used to navigate precarity.

At stake here were different imaginings of the plasma gangs and of what they suggested about crime, threat and safety in Alexandra. Either plasma theft was a distressing but inevitable feature of township life, not very different from other types of risk faced by residents, or the gangs were an overdetermined symbol of the criminality of the townships. Respondents' classifications of the gangs as everyday or as exceptional crime provided them with a ethno-sociological vernacular within which to think about what crime and fear of crime meant for their daily lives. Discussing plasma gangs allowed respondents to share tales of violence, witchcraft and organised crime, to talk about how the nyaope epidemic has affected their communities and to retell stories about Alexandra that cement senses of community, albeit initiated by anxiety rather than by optimism.

The truth about (drug) crime

Throughout the media texts that I examined, the meaning and truth of the plasma gang story were constantly contested. Some news outlets offered sensationalist coverage without questioning the credibility of the story while others were sceptical or actively debunked it. *The Star* (30 August 2013), for example, published a piece claiming that several people had been killed or injured by plasma thieves. It included interviews with a woman who claimed that her sister's boyfriend had been murdered by the gang, and with the chairperson of the education committee in the provincial Gauteng Legislature, who said, 'There have been eight deaths in three months ... They don't steal (a TV) to sell it or watch it. They use it for the powder inside, but I can't confirm that.' Both of these women had appeared as guests on the 702 radio programme that broke the story the previous day. This article also named two Alexandra residents who had allegedly been killed by the plasma gang. In the first case an armed gang had broken into and looted a house; in the second a businessman had been shot in the back as he closed up his electronics store. One victim's daughter told reporters that 'they couldn't link her father's death to the gang *at the moment*' [my italics]. Despite the lack of evidence that the gangs had anything to do with these deaths, both murders appeared under the headline '"Plasma gang" believed to be behind home attacks'.

In an article titled 'Plasma gang strikes again', the *Alex News* reported that the gang were after a 'powder or gas' that they used to make drugs: 'Although no confirmation of the existence of this gang has been forthcoming from the police, the gang is said to be marauding the township and freely killing those standing between them and the TVs' (12 September 2013). The article reveals how the 'messy epistemologies' (White 2000, p. ix) of rumour, gossip and popular narrative can help people make sense of crime:

> Thabo Tshwaedi, who lives with his girlfriend and daughter in the Ladies Flats in the corner of 12th Avenue and Alfred Nzo Street, said he believed he has been the latest victim of this gang. 'I cannot outrightly say I was robbed by the so-called "Plasma Gang" but because

people are talking about this gang, I have every reason to suspect they could be the same people that robbed me,' he said. (*Alex News*, 12 September 2013)

This post hoc explanation recalls the way in which the killers of Kirsty Theologo adopted the classification of Satanism after it had been imposed by the press.

Many Twitter users agreed that the gang was both real and threatening. @Selae_T tweeted, '"Blacks" have been KILLED IN the township for their plasma's (Alex). Heard of the plasma gang?' (12 September 2013), while @KolitaLebo lamented, 'This plasma gang makes us live in fear' (14 September 2013). Some passed on tales of plasma crime: 'It's serious, my friend got shot over a plasma …' (@KGenius247, 29 August 2013); 'This Plasma Gang happening in Alex is very sad. Just on Sunday we were burying a friend who got killed during these attacks' (@madasd, 29 August 2019); 'One of my colleague was talking about that on Monday. Apparently one of his friends was murdered in his house for plasma' (@magano_a, 29 August 2013).

Other sources treated the story with suspicion. On 29 August the *New Age* newspaper ran a short article titled 'Plasma gang "a rumour": police'. It cited Lieutenant-General Mzwandile Petros of Gauteng police saying, 'There is currently no information to suggest that plasma TVs are stolen for a powder drug … Investigations have found that the plasma TV powder drug craze was a rumour circulating in Alexandra'. The *Sowetan* (30 August 2013) also quoted Petros: 'There is currently no information to suggest that plasma TVs are stolen for a powder drug … Crime intelligence information to date suggests that all crime incidents … reported were criminally motivated crimes.' Under the headline 'Cops dismiss plasma TV drug link', an article on the *Eyewitness News* website (30 August 2013) reported both police scepticism and community concerns. It began by quoting 'a former drug dealer [who] says criminals are stealing plasmas to make drugs such as nyaope, a cocktail that includes heroin and marijuana and sometimes anti-retroviral medication mixed with rat poison'. This unnamed dealer claimed, 'We use it. We started to find that inside the plasma there are chemicals.' However, the article then undermines its own source, saying, 'Many believe the gang is just an urban myth. Authorities have dismissed the claims.' On 25 September *Eyewitness News* reported that it had '[busted the] plasma powder myth'. Dr Edwin Mmutlane, a chemistry lecturer at the University of Johannesburg, took apart a plasma screen and tested the 'powder' found inside it, concluding that it had no effect as a drug: 'This stuff is magnesium oxide and when you mix it with water it forms milk of magnesia ... It's as good as inhaling dust.' Importantly, though, the article also stated that 'criminals have obviously been misinformed about the powder's benefits', suggesting that, while the plasma gang was deluded, it nonetheless existed. The TechCentral website, in a post on the same day that discussed the experiment, quoted journalist Aki Anastasiou: 'The white powder in plasma screens has no reaction to you chemically. It's not a drug. It's a rubbish story, it's a myth.'

The significance of these tussles over the meaning and existence of the plasma gangs comes into focus when we examine individual responses to the story. Sceptical approaches allowed commenters to position themselves as more knowledgeable, sophisticated and critical than those who were taken in by a 'rubbish' story. A number of tweeters agreed that the plasma gang was either made up or not a genuine threat. @Absurdities1 posted, 'How many times will @radio702 @ewn repeat the so-called "plasma gang"? Story is typical 702 all hype and hyperbole with no facts!' (29 August 2013), while @bilalb77 wrote, 'We are on the gulf of a possible world war, and yet our concerns are fuckers smoking our Tv's #plasma_gang' (29 August 2013). A poster named @jonathangmeyer wrote sarcastically about 'the ever-elusive Plasma Gang! DUN DUN DUUUUUUUUUN!' (29 August 2013). Other posters retweeted news reports calling the gang a rumour or urban legend.

While all the people that I interviewed were aware of the story, respondents approached it in different ways. None of those I spoke to within Alex itself doubted the information they had encountered about the gangs. However, attitudes were different in the focus group, which took place outside the township. Lucky, one of the last participants to speak in that group, argued that the plasma gang story was being passed around by older residents who 'don't like research into a thing, they just like believe into what they hear ... To be honest I think they are misinformed and they are scared'.

A number of those who spoke before him had made it clear that they believed the gangs were real. Once Lucky debunked the story as the beliefs of gullible older people, however, the rest of the group energetically approved of his statement that plasma gangs were 'a myth ekasi [in the township]'. In arguing that only older people living in the township believed this story, Lucky provided an opportunity for himself and his fellow respondents, all university students who had moved to the city, to lay claim to an urban and urbane sophistication. These same young people had earlier related stories about muti and local magic practices, revealing a continued engagement with township cosmologies. However, debunking or disavowing this localised urban legend allowed them to show that they had the education and savvy to avoid being taken in by what they heard. In rejecting the legend, they asserted belonging and status in the city, laying claim to a certain type of autochthonous urban modernity (Newell 2012).

Drugs, crime and TV

The third theme linked plasma gangs to existing ideas of who is responsible for crime in Alexandra. Respondents singled out a series of scapegoats who could be blamed for plasma thefts and concurrently for the lack of safety that sometimes characterises Alex life. Drug addicts, corrupt police and African foreigners were all named as culprits and causes for the apparent epidemic of plasma-related crime. This process of scapegoating reveals the way in which plasma gangs were symbolically located within wider circles of meaning.

On Twitter, many agreed that drug users posed a significant threat to their safety. @Leratopatch wrote that the gang 'r stealing TVs 2 retrieve a powder 2 use in a dangerous drug cocktail. Be warned guys!!!!' (30 August 2013). @KanyaQ_ wrote, 'The Plasma gang. They steal your plasma TVs & go make nyaope out of it. Niggas are going hard. Be careful people. #TrueStory' (31 August 2013). Similar conversations appeared elsewhere on social media. On a Facebook page devoted to the Kaya FM radio station show *At Home With Mapaseka*, one user wrote, 'I heard dat dese plasma tv's got nyaope inside so now ppl who smoke nyaope steal plasma tv's … be alert ppl' (1 November 2013). Newspaper coverage agreed that drug users were complicit in the problem of plasma gangs. *The Star* wrote, 'The theft goes on in Alex, where the community is angry about what they perceive as a new and violent crime wave … "This nyaope and whoonga has people up in arms. Community members should stay in their houses and lock their doors and gates. We don't know when this will end'" (31 August 2013).

A different picture emerged during the interviews. All of the people I spoke to acknowledged the problem of crime and safety in Alexandra, including the random violence of the nyaope gangs, which are among the most desperate and the least choosy when it comes to what to steal and whom to rob. Many of them shared stories of personal experiences with addicts. Lungile told me about a former friend whose addiction was so potent that he resorted to stealing and selling her shoes, and an acquaintance whose 'father died so he had no one. He diverted to nyaope to ease the stress'. While these stories were upsetting, many were also sympathetic to the plight of addicts. One respondent in particular, who had himself been a 'nyaope boy' and was working at the community centre as part of his recovery, made it clear that the intense demands of addiction outweigh any other considerations, and that it would not be surprising if the plasma gang stories were even worse than he had heard, given how destructive the drug is. Despite the dangerous reputation of nyaope users, some respondents took a nuanced view on their relation to the plasma gangs and their criminal scapegoating. Lucky told me, 'Everything that is happening in Alexandra or any other township where people smoke nyaope, anything that is wrong, is always blamed on the nyaope people.' David agreed that the prevalence of the plasma gang story meant that 'if you smoked nyaope you were probably a suspect'. These responses reveal a far more humane attitude to the drug crisis than was seen in the media. Residents who were personally familiar with addicts understood some of the conditions of addiction and were less likely to simply treat them as deviant folk devils or to blame them for all the ills affecting the area, even while expressing deep anxiety about the violence they were prone to.

The classification of addicts as a threat to security was tied into a demonisation of young people, particularly young men, that is common in such scares (Springhall 1998). According to Thembani, 'The first thing I can think of that produced this plasma gang is boredom. When the youth doesn't do anything ... you start looking around and start finding things to occupy that boredom.' Here the problem of plasma gangs was also a problem of the country's stratospheric rate of youth unemployment, where young men have nothing to do but take drugs and get involved in crimes.[8] Another respondent dismissed nyaope addiction as the latest teenage fad, something that young men drove each other to get involved with. Delia blamed the whole plasma gang scenario on 'peer pressure':

> The reason why I say peer pressure is because you find that one boy comes from a wealthy background and tells his friends, 'You know what? They just bought me a TV.' And his friends will say 'You know what? There's a gas or a powder inside the TV and if you smoke it you'll be living on the edge of life, and you'll forget about your worries.'

Another common element of these stories was the failure of police to protect the community. Police in South Africa are often seen to be 'ineffective and corrupt' (Baderoon 2015, p. 115), riddled with 'inefficiency, ineptitude and unwillingness ... to engage' (Comaroff and Comaroff 2016, p. 58). In one of the first tweets on the subject, the radio host John Robbie reported, 'Harry from Alex says about 8 people killed in recent attacks by plasma gang – police do not seem to care' (29 August 2013). In his YouTube video posted later that day, Robbie castigated police and politicians for their failure to stop the plasma crime wave, insisting that if the state's attitude to the drug crisis is more than just lip service it must 'go and catch the plasma gang'.[9] He used emotive words like 'ludicrous', 'ruthless', 'notorious', 'terrified' and 'mayhem' to draw on existing fears about social breakdown and state failure. This strategy seems to have been effective: soon after, a listener responded by calling police 'useless' and 'lazy' (@WinnyMelanin, 29 August 2013). The following day *The Star* again quoted the Gauteng Legislature member saying that the community was 'well aware of the gangs' and that the police were not doing enough to stop them (30 August 2013). When I asked whether police could help quell the gangs, Lungile, one of my interviewees, sniffed, 'The police? Eish, you can't take a nyaope boy to the police station ... You feel powerless, they're lazy so there's nothing they can tell you.'

Others claimed that corrupt police were actually involved with criminals. According to Fikile, 'Where I stay I've got a gang, they steal stuff, they smoke in public but the police don't do nothing ... They're scared, they don't do nothing ... the police work with them. They know, the police know, they're taking bribes.' He claimed that if he was arrested the police would steal his drugs and sell them. Other respondents speculated that the police were probably taking bribes from the gangs, which is why no one could control or resist them. In a statement that earned nods of agreement from the rest of the focus group, Thulani said, 'If we know that there's a drug dealer in our area, nobody wants to say because of their fear. If I point out that there is this drug dealer here, it will come back to me. And these people work with police, everybody knows that.' One Twitter user wrote, 'Our police suck! #sapsgang' (@neofrmthematrix, 29 August 2013). The use of the word 'gang' alongside the acronym for the South African Police Service (SAPS) creates an uneasy equivalence between law and lawlessness. Another agreed, 'Criminals get supportive from the police, they (police) even aware about drug dealers in our communities, but they don't do anything' (@tiyanindlovu, 29 August 2013).

Musila writes that 'rumour as a genre gains its legitimacy from precisely the suspect nature of officially produced truths' (2015, p. 93). In this case those officially produced truths emphasised the rule of law and the functionality of the policing system. Stories about the plasma gangs became part of a firmament of mistrust in the police, a consequence of 'postcolonial realities' that have consistently impaired 'efforts to implement a liberal, rights-based approach to enforcement' (Comaroff and Comaroff 2016, p. 57). The ubiquity, violence and weirdness of the plasma gangs are highly symbolic. As well as connoting social decay and consumption anxiety, the intensity of their affect is also related to the perceived failure of the police and thus of the state – and even, potentially, of the post-apartheid project, whose inability to create social and economic justice can be seen every day in the streets and alleyways of Alexandra.

Alongside corrupt police, another South African folk devil appeared within narratives of the plasma gangs. From popular films like *District 9* (Kapstein 2014) to the inflammatory pronouncements of the former Mayor of Johannesburg, migrants from elsewhere in Africa are frequently characterised as dangerous and undesirable.[10] Nigerians in particular have a reputation among South Africans for being rich and amoral criminal masterminds, while Zimbabweans, coming from South Africa's close neighbour and the source of the largest number of immigrants in Gauteng province, are despised as low-level criminals and job-stealers (Banda and Mawadza 2014). South African xenophobia often expands to include immigrants from the Indian subcontinent as well as South African Indians and Chinese people. These deep-seated prejudices sometimes explode into shocking instances of mob violence, stoked by politicians and other powerful figures who casually scapegoat foreigners as the source of all the country's ills. Notoriously, the first outbreak of major xenophobic violence to receive national and international news coverage began in Alexandra in 2008 (Nieftagodien 2008). The township has a history of imbrication in discourses and practices of xenophobia.[11]

According to a story in the *Saturday Star*, titled 'Xenophobia erupts over "Plasma TV" gang' (31 August 2013), locals claimed that the plasma gang was a syndicate run by Pakistanis and Somalis. The conflation of these nationalities reveals a localised iteration of global Islamophobia, part of what Gabeba Baderoon calls the 'South African experience of a local Orientalist tradition' (2015, p. 109). Earlier that week, in a 'show of anger over the [plasma gang] murders', a shop belonging to two Pakistani men had been burnt down, tyres had been set alight and rocks thrown down Alfred Nzo, one of the main streets running through Alex. These stereotypes also emerged in my interviews. According to Siphokazi, the plasma gangs were comprised of 'a set of people from outside ... Foreign people. Zimbabweans and Nigerians'. The Nigerians, he suggested, were the 'big bosses', while only the people who worked for them were actually from Alexandra. Fikile agreed that the majority of the drug trade emerged from Nigerian gangsters: 'Let me put it like this, when you can go to town right now, you'll find some Nigerians. Nigerians sell some drugs to South Africans but when you see this thing, why the police don't chase them, it's because they're scared and they have taken some bribes.'

It is important to note the spatiality of these accusations. Foreigners, particularly Nigerians, are presented not only as criminals but also as people successfully profiting from crime, who operate elsewhere or 'in town' (meaning downtown and the city centre). South Africans, both victims and gang members, often remain stuck in the township. Not only does crime pay, but it also allows other African people to transcend apartheid urban formations, which many residents of Alexandra are not able to do. The tragic logic of South African xenophobia – that 'they' have come and taken what should belong to 'us' – is enhanced, as the commodities the outsiders have claimed are not just jobs, money, homes and status but also urban mobility, the freedom to escape the economic and social constraints that tie people to the townships of their birth. Fears about the plasma gangs are overlaid with beliefs about the failure of the post-apartheid project to deliver liberation. Foreigners are conveniently, and sometimes violently, scapegoated within this narrative, which was spurred by knowledge of the many broken promises of the revolutionary era. Instead of 'great expectations and sweet dreams, "progress" evokes an insomnia full of nightmares of being "left behind"' (Bauman 2007, p. 11). In the township, residents' 'heightened anxieties about being marginalised and possibly excluded ... exacerbate existing cleavages between insiders and outsiders' (Nieftagodien and Bonner 2008, p. 418).

Ownership and display

The fourth theme that appeared is that of status and material objects. Here, my respondents discussed how they think about money, class and position in the city and how plasma TVs are related to those concerns. Many of these conversations made clear the contradiction that developed when people wanted to own and display luxury goods even though the spectacle of consumption could 'generate negative and ambivalent repercussions' (Newell 2012, p. 125).

Concerns about plasma gangs were often related to urban space, particularly to its function of flaunting socioeconomic status. One Tweeter, @drew_cfc, wrote, 'The scary thing is that the #PlasmaGang will start moving into the suburbs when their supply goes dry in Alex #murderers' (29 August 2013). It is telling here that what is defined as 'scary' is not the existence of the gangs but their potential mobility beyond class and race boundaries. This reveals the common white fear that the lawlessness associated with townships will leak out, permeate their tenuous borders and infect the more 'civilised' suburbs.

During the focus group a discussion developed around what counts as a township, in which it became clear that the localised concentration of the plasma gangs story was one of its most significant components. Sbonelo explained,

> There are different ways in which we classify a township. Where I come from is township township, hardcore township, and where Sbu comes from is Spruitview. We wouldn't classify that as a township ... That's where middle class black families live, so those are the people who are likely to have plasma TVs .... It's the perception we have in the township that people who live in Spruitview are bowling [living well] ... Where I come from when people start getting a little bit of money they want to move and go to Spruitview or Vosloorus or whatever ... There are cars everywhere, there are TVs everywhere. These criminals they know if we go to Vosloorus there is no way to hit five houses without finding a plasma TV. They know the people who have money stay there.

This description of the difference between 'actual' townships and the areas where black people move to once they are more economically stable was approved by the other participants. Sbonelo here suggested two forms of legitimacy: first, the 'hardcore', which is to say authentic, kind found in the township of Alexandra where he and the others originated from; and second, the kind displayed by people who could afford to move elsewhere and whose status was improved by the prevalence of consumer goods like cars and TVs in their neighbourhoods. (Despite these statements, when I asked Sbonelo how the lives of people in Spruitview compared with those in the still largely white suburbs of Joburg, he shook his head and said, 'There is no such thing as middle [class] black.')

Sbonelo's description suggested that plasma gangs concentrated on areas where more economically stable people live. Sandile offered an even more localised version of this class/space differential when he explained the intricacies of the township: 'Alexandra has different sections, there is River Park, there is Tsutsumani, there is Extension 7. In most cases they target River Park and far East Bank because those are expensive ... those fancy houses, yeah, those are really the most targeted.' Delia confirmed that class designations were complex within Alexandra: 'Within the township there's no one thing. Not everybody is poor in the township, there are people that are monied and choose not to move out because this is home. So they choose to stay here.' Lucky argued that the gangs were focused on Alexandra precisely because people in the township display what wealth they do have. He said, 'Around 2013 is when they were introducing these TVs around South Africa. Most people could afford to buy a plasma screen in 2013 ... They became popular, you can imagine, in Alexandra – if your house didn't have a yard, you could have 10 TVs.' Lucky's statement explains that, for people who do not have the capital to rent a larger house or to leave the township altogether, a plasma TV is an affordable 'investment', an easily readable object that illustrates the owner's status. Indeed, as Delia explained, display is part of the motivation for buying something desirable:

> Well firstly, we all like to show off, that's true. If I bought something new, I want people to see that I've purchased my new car, my new set of takkies [trainers] and so on. Within the township you find that I bought maybe a 48-inch plasma. It's installed within the house and I'll just throw the box outside the yard, then the municipality will come and do the disposal and that's when they'll see that there's a plasma in that house, they just bought it.

According to David, different TV brands hold different meanings: 'At that time it was said that they only target specific plasmas, as in your Samsungs, your LGs, not your Hisenses, your Panasonics.' Even within an urban legend about crime, the 'transformative efficacy of consumption' (Newell 2012, p. 170) is encoded in the hierarchical status of consumer goods in terms of brand, place of purchase and other markers. This brings to mind sociologist David Dickinson's (2014) descriptions of buying KFC for his township interlocutors, who always saved some of their lunch so that, returning home, they could be seen carrying the 'distinctive' red and white boxes associated with a global brand. Possession or consumption of the commodity is only part of its appeal; display and visibility are equally important components of its desirability and social purpose.

Like Twitter users who posted about the danger of buying new TVs, some of my interviewees discussed the strategies people employed to avoid being targeted by the plasma gangs. These included not owning a plasma at all, sending the item somewhere 'safe' and trying to hide its existence.

Many of my respondents explained that, once the plasma gang story began to spread, township residents became afraid to own the TVs and reverted to older, less satisfying and less impressive technology, often referred to as 'big', which here suggested ugly, unwieldy, antiquated. David told me that the plasma gang stories 'affected the whole community. At some point people didn't want to buy plasmas anymore. So everyone preferred using those old big TVs ... cause they were afraid of the break-ins that they might happen to them'. Sibulelo said, 'My aunt, she owns a big TV, and I was like aunt why don't you buy a slick TV, a nice TV, a modern TV? And she told me, "No I can't risk that, these people will find out and hurt me for this plasma TV."' Descriptions of 'big old' TVs, so different from the nice, modern, slim and slick surfaces of a desirable plasma, suggested that making the household feel safer also forced it back to an earlier, less sophisticated state. The enticing physicality of the plasma TV, its sexiness, its tactility, had to be resisted if one was to avoid harm. For people using these methods of self-protection, staying safe(er) entailed rejecting a certain type of desirable modern aesthetics.

Rather than refusing to own plasmas, some tried to safeguard their treasured objects from threat. David told me, 'At some point they tried to break into my friend's house and luckily they didn't succeed. So my friend had to take that plasma to the rural areas until the whole thing was done ... He got an old TV then. He had a boring life after that.' Again, replacing high status goods with older technology – albeit temporarily – has consequences beyond the experience of watching television, in this instance defining someone's whole life as 'boring'. A number of respondents told stories of friends or family members who hid their plasma TVs or sent them off somewhere that was seen to be safe until the danger from the gangs had passed. Many confirmed that the gangs were an urban phenomenon and that nothing like this happened in the rural areas that some of their families called home, despite living the vast majority of their lives in Alex. These sorts of crimes – involving unruly youth, drug dealers and users, foreigners, technologies and the desire for particular material objects – were imagined to be localised not just in cities but specifically in townships. Within these respondents' stories, rural areas were safer, more predictable and more manageable than the chaotic cities that are overrun with dangerous others and awash with various forms of risk.

Seeing and being seen

The final theme that emerged in both the interviews and the media material is compulsory visibility. This is an enduring feature of township life, an element of the strong sense of community that residents are justifiably proud of as well an unasked-for exposure that can make them feel less secure. This visibility has its roots as much in black South African sociality as in apartheid spatial formations. Under the rule of the white state, black people were forced into small and overcrowded areas, travel and relocation were made difficult, resources were scarce and collective sharing and organising were necessary for survival. Many townships were built in such a way as to make their inhabitants visible to the state: roads were wide enough for police and military vehicles to pass through and invasive and unattractive lighting systems were designed to allow state agents to 'keep an eye on' locations, rather than for the comfort of inhabitants. Apartheid also, notoriously, inculcated violent regimes of surveillance within townships. Both the informers who reported to security police and the vigilante gangs who 'necklaced' those suspected of informing (Gobodo-Madikizela 1999) operated within a mode of looking and being looked at. Alongside this, township visibility is informed by historical senses of community, by hybridised 'traditional' practices and by family and rural–urban networks that have persisted despite upheavals and separations of the apartheid-era homelands and migrant labour system. According to Grace Khunou,

> In the township everybody knows everybody else, where they come from, how their parents met. The city is a no man's land. Everybody has a stake in the city and can call it home. The city is for passersby. In the township, there is a strong sense of a community, of continuity and certainty. (Mbembe *et al.* 2004, p. 500)

The tensions that underlie this state of visibility were referred to numerous times by my respondents, who cited it as a primary cause for their vulnerability. Participants suggested that there are no secrets in the township, that everyone knows everything, including who owns desirable goods and who is responsible for stealing them.

According to Thembani, 'It's a very strong community, there's that kind of openness and transparency.' Thulani explained, 'It's very unlikely that you will come from a society like [ours] and not know what's going on.' Lungile told me, 'These [criminals] who break in are people who live in our community. So they know that at three o'clock I'll be going to school or the lab. That's when they come in.' The knowledge that offenders may be internal to the community is not enough to protect people. Lungile continued, 'These are people we went to school with. Obviously there's nothing you can do.' The *Saturday Star* quoted an unnamed member of the community saying, 'We know who these people are. They are the same culprits recruiting youngsters who smoke nyaope. We are informed by nyaope users that they drive Anaza taxis and are heavily armed' (30 August 2013). Criminals and dangerous people live alongside respectable families and nothing can be done to punish them for fear of reprisal. Again this reveals how one of the poles of the plasma gang myth is a lack of faith in the institutions of law, policing and the state, which fail to make life safer.

The displays of consumption that are a common part of self-presentation within a neoliberal society can also act as an attractor for crime, leaving residents stuck between the desire for safety and the desire for status. According to Sandile, 'What I've heard is that if a certain house has a satellite dish they will know okay, this is the target, there might be a plasma inside.' Thulani agreed, 'In townships they robbed a lot, because in townships it's very simple. You buy a plasma TV, they see you walking with a plasma TV on the street, so it's very simple.' Ntokozo agreed that the visibility of the TVs made one a target, which impacted on some of the forms of pleasure that they provide: 'People were still buying [plasmas] but maybe I'll buy it but I won't display it that much outside.'

Some participants blamed the generous and hospitable township culture for the rise of the plasma gangs. Sibulelo said, 'You shouldn't just allow anyone to come into your house. Because some people come into your house and look around, "Okay this one has a plasma TV," they might tell the plasma TV gangs, the people who steal.' Thulani told me, 'In the townships there's nothing to hide, everybody knows what you're doing and everybody knows what you have in your house, we have visitors, we are very open. Everybody knows everybody in the society and people tend to take advantage of that.' Delia associated this kind of crime with the expansive and generous ways in which people live, socialise and raise families:

> Within most households ... you have large amounts [of people]. Within one house you find that there's different families staying there, like my aunt, my uncle etc. Maybe my mother buys the plasma TV and my uncle's child is one of these junkies ... So when we've all gone out he sees an opportunity to steal the TV and make it look as if they broke in.

David suggested that conditions of visibility have changed since the 2013 heyday of the plasma gangs, meaning that people's consumptive practices have changed too:

> At that point people were afraid to buy plasmas, knowing that if I bought a certain thing and I was to take it back home with me then they would notice it and be like, 'Okay, here's our new target.' So right now, because no one is actually talking about this and no one has actually had to report the whole crimes, people were like, okay, no one is stealing so these people are probably gone, so let's just buy our plasmas.

What is important here is not just the display of the desirable object but also the way in which one announces its acquisition. Removing a new plasma TV from one's car or from a delivery van, carrying it home from a store or leaving its packaging on the pavement outside one's house could get the attention of criminals as well as other community members.

These responses suggest that, during the story's most powerful period, the meaning of plasma TVs within the township briefly shifted. From symbolic objects denoting status and success, they became associated with threat, something that needed to be hidden rather than exhibited. A television is fundamentally an object of visibility: it is a thing that is looked at, both for its actual purpose and for its social connotations. My respondents suggested that during the plasma gang scare that to-be-looked-at-ness became dangerous and turned in on itself, attempting to defer the gaze of the community. This is a powerful metaphor for the experience of living in a place of high risk that is both hypermodern and unstable, generous and exuberant as well as dangerous. The way that people spoke about plasma TVs, as desirable things to be hidden, sent away or avoided, shows some of the contradictions inherent in the experience of owning and displaying high status consumer objects in communities that live within a higher state of risk.

Consumption, risk and desire

This analysis of mainstream media, social media and interview material relating to the myth of the plasma gangs that was current in Alexandra township in 2013 has highlighted the connection between material objects and social anxieties for some residents of South African cities. The desire to own aspirational goods is complicated by the fear of crime, creating an affective legend in which robbery, urban witchcraft, insecurity, status and the conditions of township visibility intersect. Combined with distrust of the police, fear of foreigners and an ongoing panic about the effects on communities of rampant drug abuse, the idea that organised gangs were targeting plasma TVs in order to use them for nyaope became temporarily normalised in Alexandra. This was a rich and malleable narrative that combined many of the urban anxieties that characterise life in the township.

The plasma gang story also proved remarkably resilient to elite attempts to discredit it. While all of my interviewees agreed that plasma gangs no longer plagued Alex, many of them suggested that the gangs could now be found elsewhere in South Africa. According to Sibulelo, the gangs are at the moment 'very common' in Vosloorus. Plasma gang claims continued to appear on social media long after the main energy of the scare: on 12 October 2017 a Twitter user named @Veritas_Tattoos wrote to the then-Minister of Police, 'So what are you saying about the "Plasma Gang" in Rustenburg, that too needs an #SANDF intervention.'

The plasma gang scare is a compelling example of the power of narrative to condense and codify collective anxieties. A series of existing fears, spurred by the experiences of people living in a place that is both insecure and community-minded, both high risk and aspirational, layered on top of each other to produce a story that had a peculiar amount of social power. The fact that plasma gangs were not empirically 'real', that no mysterious powder exists inside plasma TVs that can be used to contribute to drug production, is almost beside the point. What the plasma gangs legend reveals is the way in which certain South Africans developed and transmitted stories and rumours that helped them to make sense of the world they live in. In this instance, a tale of gangster criminality, personal danger, magic, violence and fear offered a way to foreground the contradictions that come with living in the South African township, a place that both interpellates residents as aspirational neoliberal citizens and consistently imposes conditions of insecurity upon them.

Notes

1 In 2017 the media contained numerous stories of nyaope addicts 'bluetoothing': injecting themselves with the drug then drawing blood out and passing the syringe to another user, who injects it in the hopes of a secondary high. According to the Bhekisisa Centre for Health Journalism, the story developed from a misinterpreted photograph (Msomi 2017).
2 The South African Community Epidemiology Network on Drug Use (SACENDU) estimates that, for the second half of 2016, as many as 9 per cent of patients in Gauteng Province were admitted for nyaope use (cited in Mahlangu and Geyer 2018, p. 327).

3 For a thorough discussion of the township's history see Nieftagodien and Bonner (2008).

4 Other research suggests the population is closer to 500,000, including an estimated 20,000 shacks and informal homes (*Report on the Interactive Planning Workshop for Johannesburg* 2000).

5 In order to undertake this analysis I searched the SA Media Database, Google and Facebook for the term 'plasma gang'. I bounded my search by dates, starting from 15 August 2013, around the time that I had become aware of plasma gang stories in the mainstream media, to 30 August 2014. I collected 24 physical and online news articles and Facebook and messageboard posts. I then used Twitter's advanced search function to search for tweets using the phrase 'plasma gang'. I collected a corpus of 154 related tweets, many of them retweets of material posted by news sources or journalists. Tweets referred to in this section were accessed and collected on 26 September 2014 and on 20 August 2016. A few minor changes have been made for ease for reading, but for the most part tweets are quoted verbatim. Please see Appendix 3 for details of the newspaper articles referred to here.

6 To undertake these interviews, I worked with research assistants from Alex. We used snowball sampling to recruit participants. The first set of 12 respondents was comprised of university students between the ages of 19 and 23, nine male and three female, all of whom were from the township but were at that stage living in the inner city to be closer to places of study. I interviewed them on 15 April 2017 in a coffee shop in Braamfontein, Johannesburg. These were set up as individual interviews but, as the day progressed, a focus group situation developed organically. The second set of interviews took place on 24 November 2017 in an office in the Alexandra Community Centre. On this day I interviewed nine current residents of the township, two female and five male, whose ages ranged from 23 to 57. These took the form of individual interviews. All interviews were recorded and transcribed and all participants have been anonymised. Interview texts have been minimally edited for ease of reading but are generally reproduced verbatim.

7 Domestic labour is common among all racial and most class groups in South Africa. Around one in every 15 employed people in South Africa is a domestic worker (Patel 2011). Despite some legislation, domestic work remains precarious and poorly paid and leaves workers open to shocking economic and personal abuse.

8 According to Statistics South Africa, unemployment among 15–24 year olds was 55.2 per cent in the first quarter of 2019 (Statistics South

Africa 2020). Under a newly expanded definition of unemployment, and in partial reaction to the dramatic economic shrinkage caused by the pandemic, the youth jobless rate in 2021 was estimated at an astonishing and potentially destabilising 74.7 per cent (Stoddard 2021).

9 '#InMyOpinion with @702JohnRobbie on Crime in SA', accessed on 24 August 2016 and available at www.youtube.com/watch?v=ln wekMIixks.

10 In 2017 the Africa Diaspora Forum laid a claim against Johannesburg's then-mayor Herman Mashaba with the South African Human Rights Commission. The ADF argued that Mashaba's provocative rhetoric contributed to anti-African violence within Gauteng province (Mashaba to Undergo Arbitration Process 2017).

11 For a discussion of the 'profound social malaise' of xenophobia in South Africa, see Worby, Hassim and Kupe's *Go Home or Die Here* (2008).

5

Safe selves versus good selves in the suburbs

Melville is a tree-lined suburban neighbourhood in the west of Johannesburg, where homeowners vie good-naturedly over whose indigenous pavement garden is the most resplendent. They share tips for restoring the stained glass, pine flooring and pressed ceilings of their tastefully renovated 1920s houses and join groups dedicated to preserving the rare flora in the local nature reserve. They frequent their favourite restaurants, argue about new commercial developments, share annoyance about parking issues and discuss the quality of local supermarkets. They take pride in their ability to walk to and from the high street during daylight hours, an everyday experience that remains uncommon in many wealthy South African neighbourhoods. They look out for lost pets and advise each other on car mechanics, plumbers and kindergartens. Some of them belong to the local residents' association, and many are financially and emotionally invested in the ambience and reputation of the area.

Like suburban dwellers in much of the world, they also share information about crime, bills, infrastructural problems and people whose presence is seen to impact negatively on the tone of the area. Certain kinds of newcomers – particular businesses, homeowners and people who are seen to offer a contribution to the neighbourhood – are welcomed enthusiastically. Others, including precarious renters, students and business owners whose bars and nightclubs do not fit residents' ambitions for the area, are discussed with varying degrees of suspicion, while still others, defined as interlopers, provoke outrage, fear and phone calls to armed private security companies. For the middle-class, mostly white, residents who attempt to lay claim to the suburb of Melville, part of the work of community-making involves paying attention to who does and does not belong, while another part involves a collective performance of altruism that helps shape ideas about the kinds of people who live there. Notions of belonging and alien-ness, of insiders and outsiders, of appropriate and inappropriate people and behaviour, form a fundamental part of these residents' understanding of the suburb and its social meanings. These acts of collective self-definition are deeply implicated in South Africa's cultures of fear. They are intrinsically racial formations and suggest a profound anxiety around surfaces. Both the neighbourhood and the people who live within it must appear to be a certain way – clean, good – in order to remain safe, both physically and existentially, in a country that is often perceived as dangerous and hostile.

In South Africa as elsewhere, 'Suburbs are surrounded by conceptual and real barriers, both by their history and their continued development' (Durington 2009, p. 72; see also Berger and Kotkin 2018). Melville is the south-westerly point of Johannesburg's northern suburbs, which remain separated from poorer areas of the city by barriers that are both physical – steep ridges and mine dumps (Nightingale 2015, p. 230) – and less tangible. These tree-lined streets stretch between the desirable but intermittently dilapidated Parktown, the mansions on Houghton ridge, the exclusive 'villages' of Parkview and Parkhurst with their expensive high streets and well-tended green spaces, the millionaire homes and high-class malls of Melrose, Rosebank and Hyde Park, the elite enclaves and gated communities of Sandton. Other suburban areas help shape the city's character – not least the faux-Tuscan sprawl of Fourways and the rapidly gentrifying tourist magnet of Orlando in Soweto – but the leafy northern suburbs, playing host to what Joburgers are proud to call the 'largest man-made forest in the world', remain a resilient part of middle-class perceptions of the city.

This chapter discusses digital community-making in the suburb of Melville. It focuses on the narrative strategies that have emerged among certain types of residents whose social and economic privilege brings with it potent collective anxieties. These anxieties are connected to an acute consciousness of race that characterises

South Africa's emotional landscapes. I am interested in the ongoing symbols of exclusionary racialisation that drive non-legislative segregation in South African cities more than 20 years after the end of apartheid, and in the discursive mechanisms that white and middle-class people have developed to explain or deny their complicity in these symbolisations. The chapter seeks to understand oppositional forms of 'white talk' (Steyn 2005), those 'resistant white discourses' (Steyn and Foster 2008, p. 26) that enable white sense-making and self-making in South Africa, similar in operation to the ways in which narratives about the occult nature of crime help to construct shared meanings among residents of Alexandra.

In order to do this, I examine two seemingly contradictory behavioural injunctions that are expressed within online neighbourhood discourse in Melville. The first, common to wealthy areas in cities around the world, is the desire to be safe, which manifests in an often-aggressive othering of supposed outsiders. In Johannesburg the urge to be safe coheres around concern about crime and fears of vulnerability, of violence and of black (particularly male) bodies that are seen to be out of place in the suburbs and thus to pose an existential threat to the security of residents, their homes and possessions. These fears are exacerbated in multiple ways, including by one of the world's most sophisticated private security industries (Comaroff and Comaroff 2016), which benefits from the 'perception that crime is rampant' (Durington 2009, p. 76). Like the poorer residents of townships including Alexandra, suburban denizens are overwhelmingly subject to fear of crime (Lee 2011). Unlike township residents, though, those in the suburbs often communicate misplaced beliefs about white and middle-class people facing the highest levels of risk within South Africa's crime-ridden landscapes. As with white genocide conspiracy theorists, these opinions foreground their own exceptional victimhood to the exclusion of others who suffer from crime and violence, and misrecognise unfamiliar or unappealing components of the urban landscape as legitimate dangers. Joburg suburbanites engage energetically in what Sasson calls 'crime talk', one of the ways in which ordinary people 'make sense of social problems' (1995, p. 2; see also Caldeira 2000, Murray 2020). Again, we can think of this kind of talk as an ethno-sociology (Waters 1997).

Fear of crime and crime talk are not, however, the whole story of white community-making in Melville. The second injunction, which is less common in online community spaces in South Africa, is the desire to be (seen to be) good. This requires a vocal enactment of good whiteness, through which an individual can demonstrate her or his belonging within in the current 'hegemony of liberal whiteness' (Weigman 2012, p. 153).[1] Visible enactments of goodness are often aimed at poorer black women and children, who are naturalised as weak, helpless and lacking in agency. This is a local form of what Lilie Chouliaraki calls 'post-humanitarianism': apparently altruistic actions or positions that are couched in 'the language of sentimental gratitude' designed to evoke appreciation for generous benefactors (2010, p. 108), a politics of pity that is concerned with the goodness of the giver rather than with the historical and structural conditions that underlie inequality. Markus Balkenhol refers to this common trend as '"the politics of compassion"; whites as the rescuers, saviours of blacks, driven by pity and compassion' rather than solidarity or justice (quoted in Wekker 2016, p. 146).

In the context of South Africa, good whiteness is closely aligned to an idea of being liberal, an ideological position that has been the object of sharp analysis from black South African intellectuals. Particularly important here is Steve Biko, who discusses 'that bunch of do-gooders who go under all sorts of names, liberals, leftists, etc ... who argue that they are not responsible for white racism' (1988, pp. 63–64). Biko makes it clear that white South African liberalism cements rather than undoes white dominance by insisting that individual white people can elide complicity in structural racism if they decide to be 'good'. He is concerned with political liberalism, but his insights are equally applicable to contemporary white suburbanites who use the term to signal that they are 'not racist'.

Both crime talk and post-humanitarianism have performative functions. Crime talk, like other forms of white talk discussed in previous chapters, helps to construct identities and enforce social boundaries as well as cementing narratives about South Africa, Johannesburg and Melville as risky places that require vigilance and investment in security. Anxieties around crime and safety are moral and metaphorical as well as practical. Nonetheless, throughout this chapter I emphasise the performative qualities of good whiteness. The kind of humanitarianism on display in the digital community in question is framed as resistant, a liberal and even iconoclastic rebellion against the master narrative of casual racial demonisation. Posters position themselves as bravely speaking against majority opinion and as visibly taking on roles of defending the apparently defenceless. While both positions are performative, the performativity of faux-humanitarianism is of particular interest due to its hypervisibility and intentionality, which are a crucial part of its language and of the self-presentation of those who engage it.

According to Charlotte Lemanski, 'Apartheid's strongest legacy is ... not physical structure but symbolic exclusionism' (2004, p. 109). This symbolism manifests in various ways. Claims about neighbourhood character, about appropriate behaviour, about authenticity and origins, formalise an imagined community that excludes anyone who is not seen to belong to the suburb. The anxieties that underpin these attempts at communal imagining are longstanding, but have had to find new terminology in a South Africa in which outright racist speech is often (but not always) socially unacceptable. Fear of difference – which usually means racial difference – is 'not brazenly displayed, but hidden under more "acceptable" discourses' (Lemanski 2004, p. 109). These acceptable discourses invoke crime, safety and security but also moral status and ideas about whiteness and civilisation.

In order to make these arguments I examine conversations within a particular digital community. The Facebook group 'I Love Melville' (ILM) was, at the time of writing, an open group with over ten thousand members, comparatively few of whom were active posters.[2] I use posts collected from ILM to discuss the strategies that are adopted in service of the sometimes contradictory drives to be safe and to be good. I am interested in group narrative rather than in individual people's opinions or experiences, to which end I follow Sara Ahmed's suggestion of '[treating] each text as an instance in a wider intertextual web' in order to 'depersonalise the material' (2015, n.p.). This is not about how individual posters feel or what they believe, but rather about a set of collective discourses that have developed within this community. Of course ILM is not unique – other digital spaces evince the same awkward mix of behaviours – but the visibility of these conflicting narratives makes it a valuable site for research.

Unlike the previous chapter, which considered experiences that I can only approach from the outside, I write now as an insider. As well as having the social and economic privilege that characterises most urban white South Africans, I have easy access to the internet, am active in digital spaces and live in the neighbourhood under discussion. This gives me insider knowledge but also makes me complicit in the inequities that these discourses seek to mask. While I write critically about the public performances that take place on this Facebook group, I nonetheless get to enjoy the walkable streets, charming cafes and vibrant social life of the neighbourhood, maintained by the very anxieties I am concerned with here, which spur local residents to invest in 'preserving' the neighbourhood. Despite the freedoms of insider-ness, my relationship to this community is fractious. I am critical of its discourses and sensitive to its performances, particularly so as they reflect my own small daily hypocrisies back to me. This insider-outsider positionality necessitates some careful thought, not least in the methods I use here. I acknowledge my own affective intertwinings with suburban whiteness – my anger, discomfort and shame – and invoke them as elements of a textual analysis, in a way that would not be ethical in ethnography.

Melville's physical and online communities exhibit some of the features of South African whiteness that I have written about previously (for example Falkof 2015b, 2015a, 2018c) alongside a desire to claim moral approval, drawing on colonial narratives that cast white settlers as benevolent (McClintock 1995). My discussion of the suburb reveals social and spatial patterns of segregation, othering, faux-humanitarianism, racial differentiation and community-building, all drawn together into what Richard Ballard calls the right to define neighbourhood character (2005).

Leafy greens: Joburg and its suburbs

Sue Parnell and Alan Mabin write that 'the preoccupation with the genesis of urban African residential encampment has diverted attention away from the urban context of race formation and the racialisation of social relationships more generally' (1995, p. 46). Rather than thinking of South African cities as the consequences of attempts to manage naturalised and 'unassimilable' (Chambers 1997) qualities of different racial groups, we need to consider them as organic entities that actively produce race and difference (Parnell and Mabin 1995, p. 61). The contemporary production of difference in a suburb like Melville is a continuation of South Africa's long history of urban segregation, designed to, among other aims, entrench definitions of and beliefs about racial categories.

These segregationist urges drew on colonial mythology that insisted that cities naturally belonged to white people (Bickford-Smith 2016). Apartheid justified much of its most venal spatial violence by claiming that black people did not belong in urban areas and that the reserves it set aside for them were their 'natural' homes. This desire for spatial differentiation reached its apotheosis during apartheid's heyday, with the bulldozing and forced removals that ethnically cleansed some of the most vibrant, multi-racial and, yes, dangerous areas of cities (Nightingale 2015, p. 376). Awash with art and music, plugged into global flows of culture, these creative and diverse neighbourhoods threatened many of the foundational myths of the state (see, for example, Coplan 1985, Odhiambo 2006). While black South Africans were being removed from cities, white South Africans – from the elite down to barely employed 'poor whites' (Morrell 1992, Willoughby-Herard 2015) – were settling into parts of cities that had been designated for them. By the time the system collapsed in the early 1990s, South Africa's cities were doubled: urban and suburban centres that boasted world-class architecture, services, green spaces, retail, employment, education and leisure were shadowed by townships and informal settlements characterised by substandard housing, transport and other infrastructure, where large numbers of people were crammed into small areas that maintained the economies of labour needed to sustain white lives.

Johannesburg, that upstart mining town, has engaged in a project of segregation from its inception. White owners and managers in the booming mining industry invested heavily in their spatial remove from workers. The municipality 'erected compounds throughout town for its sanitation workers, construction gangs, gardeners, and maintenance crews, as well as for the "wash-boys" who worked at municipal laundry-washing facilities' (Nightingale 2015, p. 251). The city soon demarcated dedicated townships for black, Indian and coloured populations that were far away from desirable white residential neighbourhoods. These were separated by distance, by industry and by the wasteland belt of the mine dumps. The city still wears the scars of its 'fifteen-kilometre buffer ... that by the height of apartheid separated the leafy, flower-spangled neighbourhoods of white Johannesburg from Soweto and its pall of coal smoke' (Nightingale 2015, p. 233).

Under apartheid, suburbs were legally classified as whites-only zones. In terms that still resonate today, '*Suburbs* were, quite simply, white residential neighbourhoods, and *townships* or *locations* designated those neighbourhoods occupied by other groups' (Ginsburg 2011, p. 5, emphasis in original). Of course the attempt at total segregation was always doomed to fail. White 'madams' were dependent on the cheap black labour of 'maids' and 'garden boys' and black workers used these footholds in suburbia to bypass the state's system of influx control, designed to limit the number of black people in cities (Ginsburg 2011, p. 113). However, the image of suburbs as restricted enclaves of privilege has continued into the post-apartheid era. Contemporary suburbs are not formally defined by the racial identities of those who live in them but these identities continue to play a role in how suburban dwellers think of their homes, their neighbours and themselves. As I discuss elsewhere (Falkof 2015b), suburban residents have found new ways to police neighbourhood boundaries, which are now spatial, infrastructural, discursive and social rather than legislative (see also Ballard 2005, 2010). Following Doreen Massey, we can understand space here not as thing but as process, something that is created through social interactivity (1991, p. 29). Residents actively construct their suburb by developing and fortifying its immaterial boundaries.

Unlike in many global cities, Johannesburg's suburbs were not an afterthought that blossomed in the wake of so-called white flight. On the contrary, they embodied an aspirational dream from the very start of urban development. The rough, violent mining camp that was the city's original form led to an explosion of wealth and the seeds of a burgeoning metropolis. The Randlords,

Johannesburg's first elite millionaire class, quickly abandoned the swampy lowlands and began building mansions on the Parktown Ridge, which boasted the triple benefits of excellent views, physical distance from the working classes and being upwind of the fetid industrial products of the mines (Nightingale 2015, p. 229). From this impressive beginning the suburbs spread northwards, creating a landscape of Victorian homes, gardens and parks. The farmland that had been cultivated by Afrikaner settlers was quickly consumed by the suburban sprawl of the emerging middle and upper classes. The suburb of Melville was built not long after this initial expansion. It was proclaimed in 1896, just ten years after gold was first discovered on the Reef.

Melville is in some ways a liminal neighbourhood. It is located on the southern edge of the city's suburban belt, closer than most to the inner city, the central business district, Soweto and high-density edge suburbs like Bellevue, Yeoville, Berea and Hillbrow, which are considered no-go areas by most native Joburgers due to their communities of African immigrants.[3] Residents of more prestigious northerly suburbs often avoid the area, which has a reputation for crime.[4] Estate agents and property owners speak worriedly about the area going 'up' or 'down'. Melville's relative proximity to the 'coloured' township of Westbury, to 'poor white' areas like Vrededorp and Jan Hofmeyr, to the Indian communities of Fordsburg and Mayfair (now also home to a growing population of Somalis), all to its south and west, often outweighs its closeness to more reliably aspirational suburbs like Westcliff and Parkview, slightly south-east, and Emmarentia, directly north. Melville's position as a 'middle-class' area has never been fully fixed in the city's imaginary mapping; it has long been associated with poorer, working-class white communities, a reputation cemented by the hugely popular Afrikaans soap opera *7de Laan*, set around a fictionalised version of the suburb's high street.

Melville is near to Johannesburg's two major university campuses (the University of Johannesburg, within walking distance in Auckland Park, and the University of the Witwatersrand, 7 km away in Braamfontein). The area is a hub for students, featuring unethical rental practices that see crowds of young people crammed into sub-divided houses. It also boasts perfectly preserved

Victorian homes with views of the city skyline and Melville Koppies nature reserve. Swimming pools are common, as are lush gardens and private parking garages. The South African Broadcasting Corporation (SABC) headquarters and the compound of Media24, another powerful media network, are close. The suburb is home to a large number of Airbnb rentals and more traditional bed and breakfasts as well as curio sellers and businesses that advertise themselves explicitly to tourists.

Scholars who write about the city often refer to their nocturnal travels through the buzzing commercial strip of 7th Street (for example Hornberger 2008, Livermon 2008). The concentration of artists, academics and journalists living in the area has given it a reputation that continues to attract adventurous visitors. Unlike in wealthier suburbs, there are no private boom gates or gated enclaves. Melville's high street has long been famous, and at times notorious, for its nightlife: bars and restaurants come and go, crowds shift and change, residents and homeowners complain about noise and crime, retailers complain about residents blocking liquor licences. There is an ongoing tussle between stakeholders to define this neighbourhood: is it residential or retail? For families or parties? For older people or students? And, consequently, for the wealthy or the less so, the white or the black?

These two qualities – liminality and bohemianism – make Melville a powerful site of conflicting suburban anxieties around safety and morality. The neighbourhood's location and nightlife mean that it is more diverse in race and class terms than many formerly white suburbs, playing host to students, informal traders, car guards,[5] partygoers and the illicit economies that serve them, as well as to more conservative homeowners. In wealthier and more northerly suburbs, black men are usually either residents or labourers, who are easily distinguishable by their clothing and transport: the impeccable shirt, smart jeans and recent model car in the first case versus the blue overalls, outdoor work gear and creaky bicycle in the second. In Melville, however, the presence of black men whose class positions are not as easily legible to worried whites plays into the insecurity expressed by residents who post on the Facebook group, an insecurity that is exacerbated by the visibility of bodies that 'do not belong' in the suburb. Concurrently, though, many residents discuss their pride in the neighbourhood's claimed liberalism and tolerance.

White and wary in Johannesburg

Whiteness and white identities in South Africa have always been paranoid, reactive and anxious (Falkof 2015a). From stockpiling food before the 1994 elections to survivalist communities training for race war, certain groups of white people are immersed in the idea that disaster is imminent.[6] On the less extreme end of that spectrum have been communities and families who research emigrating to Perth, who 'semigrate' from Johannesburg to the Cape, whose dinner party discussions revolve around their ever-increasing sense of vulnerability and threat, neurotic iterations of white talk.

At the same time, white South Africans often make discursive claims to legitimacy, authenticity and belonging, 'the sense of being "native" that has allowed [them] strongly to defend their suburban turf in the wake of post-apartheid change' (Ballard 2005, p. 65). This sense of indigeneity stretches back to the foundational myths of the white ethnostate, which claim that white people have as much, or often more, right than black people to live, work, spend and be in the places in which they have been born or have chosen to settle. White culture is built around a powerful insistence on legitimate occupancy or co-occupancy of South African land (Steyn 2001, p. xxvi).

The often-repeated idea that white civilisation is responsible for the existence of cities is part of this narrative and negates the lives of the black migrant labourers whose bones line abandoned mine shafts and the city's subterranean architecture (Nuttall and Mbembe 2008). Claims of 'nativeness', which are 'assumed to be a fact of history ... rather than a construction of society in which dominant groups define the terms under which access to a place is granted' (Ballard 2005, p. 72), also erase indigenous African relationships to land. They do so by insisting that only those who have 'properly' worked it – which means owned, tamed, farmed, mined and built on, rather than necessarily cultivated or laboured on – can lay claim to land. Afrikaner nationalism is deeply connected to ideas about land, particularly to the farm (Devarenne 2009), while pastoral idealisations of the countryside and attachments to the idea of 'empty lands' were an important part of British colonial imaginaries (McClintock 1995). Notions of authenticity, belonging and ownership in urban environments draw on these constructions of space and underpin ideas about who does and does not belong in the city.

To summarise, whiteness in South Africa is shaped by racial paranoia and ideas about impending apocalypse, as well as by a belief in white nativeness, authenticity and belonging. These often contradictory positions inform the two injunctions that I consider in this chapter. The first underpins racially motivated concerns with security and crime while the second entrenches a sense of benevolent white belonging in the post-apartheid polis.

Achille Mbembe writes that 'most social struggles of the post-Apartheid era can be read as attempts to reconquer the right to be urban' (2008, p. 52), to carve out a legitimate place in the city that was long denied to the majority of South Africans. Beliefs about who does and does not belong in Johannesburg and its suburbs often invoke the idea of the right to the city. This idea was famously popularised by Henri Lefebvre as the 'demand … [for] a transformed and renewed access to urban life' for all (1996, p. 168). According to David Harvey,

> The right to the city is far more than the individual liberty to access urban resources: it is a right to change ourselves by changing the city. It is, moreover, a common rather than an individual right … The freedom to make and remake our cities and ourselves … is one of the most precious but neglected of our human rights. (2008, p. 23)

What happens to this right when it is selectively applied? Shannon Walsh writes that, as a consequence of wealthy suburbanites' move back into the gentrified downtown Johannesburg art quarter of Maboneng, 'the idea of a Right to the City is radically subverted from its archaic and idealist Lefebvrian conception, and is redefined within ongoing processes of capitalist accumulation and dispossession' (2013, p. 401).[7] Middle-class, largely white Melville residents' digital attempts to control and define the character of their neighbourhoods is not quite the same as the elite invasion of

Johannesburg's inner city that Walsh is concerned with. However, there are similarities, not least in the way that both groups activate a narrative of rights. People who live in the suburbs talk about the fact that they have the right to feel safe, to walk on the streets, to be free of loud music or other noise disturbances, to enjoy an environment that meets their standards of cleanliness and infrastructure. These rights are energetically asserted but their proponents fail to acknowledge that rights must accrue to *all* citizens. Thus the once-radical idea of the right to the city becomes conflated with claims to authenticity and nativeness: only those who already belong in the suburb can say that they have a right to it. Those who do not 'legitimately' live there – homeless people, car guards, even, sometimes, young black students in shared accommodation – are not afforded the same claim to rights that manifest in ILM's discursive constructions of who can and should be where. Similarly, the poorer black women and children who are the objects of residents' performances of humanitarianism are seldom discussed in terms of their rights. Rather, access to basic elements of life and dignity – food, clothing, shelter, employment, education – is treated as a privilege benevolently granted by suburban altruists.

Mark Hunter, discussing the desegregation of education in Durban after 1994, shows the way in which elite schools attempted to maintain their prestige by emphasising certain sports (mainly rugby), retaining a critical mass of white students, teaching students to speak in English-sounding accents and only accepting black pupils whose grades were high. Hunter defines this as 'white tone': the way in which formerly white institutions and spaces retain an association with the status of whiteness. He shows that 'South Africa's story is not just about class replacing race as the fundamental division in society' (2016, p. 321). The rise of the black middle class, often lauded by academics and policy-makers as a panacea for South Africa's ills, has not dislodged the prestige of white tone. Indeed, those perpetuating the esteem that white tone confers are often not white. Many suburbs, schools, restaurants and stores that have diverse clientele and communities continue to privilege styles, practices and forms of status associated with whiteness.

The I Love Melville Facebook page presents the neighbourhood as a welcoming place for all middle-class people, but also as one where behaviours associated with whiteness are expected while those associated with, for example, township or rural blackness are not acceptable.[8] The presence of non-white members of the community seldom disturbs this imaginative homogeneity, despite instances when people of colour speak back to some of the more openly racist statements on the page. Ballard writes that 'people's sense of themselves is highly dependent on their sense of place. This provides a motive as to why people might pursue strategies of boundary maintenance and attempt to regulate access to "their" space by outsiders' (2005, p. 66). In the case of ILM, the sense of self that pervades the digital community is fundamentally bound up with the idea of Melville as a 'whitely' space (Fox 2002): not necessarily one in which all people are white, but one in which membership, residency, congregation and commerce take place in modes that are familiar and comfortable to white people.

The digital community of ILM is particularly interesting given the heterogeneity of the suburb's physical community. While real life Melville often fails to match up to the ideas of its middle-class residents, the Facebook page devoted to the suburb is a haven of similarity where residents can find compatriots who agree with them about what should be done to improve and sustain the living conditions that they consider appropriate. The digital community is here the apotheosis of Benedict Anderson's imagined community (2006). Most of these people will never engage with each other on their local streets. On the Facebook page, however, all can define themselves as members of a group that has similar goals and ideas about what the neighbourhood should be. The facelessness of the digital community imparts a degree of impunity in terms of how people speak to each other and what they say. However, ILM does not claim to be anonymous. Of course Facebook's real name policy is easy enough to circumvent, but most of those posting appear to use real names or at least to give the impression of doing so.[9] Frequent posters become known to those who use the page. Local eccentrics and business owners, long-time residents, people with particular skills, those who take overt political positions, those particularly interested in or knowledgeable about wildlife, pets, local parks or other concerns, are all recognisable. This is a community not just in the sense that all members belong to it but also in the sense that there is constant negotiation and discussion, often between people who are, to some degree at least, familiar to each other. The digital community can provide a sense to residents that a physical community also exists, with all the safety and periodic irritation that can offer.

Imagined communities can provide us with an enhanced sense of selfhood and can make us feel that we belong to larger structures. This is important for middle-class white South Africans in the post-apartheid era, who often battle to self-define in the face of others' insistence that they are outsiders, colonialists, racists, settlers and monopoly capitalists. Being part of a 'liberal', 'tolerant' online community related a suburb with a reputation for open-mindedness can allow individuals to defer or negate the way in which other South Africans may classify them. Online performances of good whiteness are rewarded by other members of the digital community, who virtually cheer at displays of humanitarianism. On the other hand, imagined communities can shore up existing prejudices and positions by allowing us to associate with others who share them: it is not just what I think, but what *we* think. As Natalie Dixon explains with reference to WhatsApp use in South African suburbs,

> Information sharing in the group chat potentially generates fear and paranoia, which can be amplified by others who feel the same way. In this sense neighbours begin to feel like they are 'in this together', in a shared experience of fear of the outside world of crime and criminals … It can be argued that amidst this sense of precarity in the neighbourhood, neighbours also experience feelings of being held or contained in the safety of a collective presence (2018, p. 499)

Crime and fear of crime can 'intensify a sense of citizenship, even humanity, by playing on vectors of identification and antipathy' (Comaroff and Comaroff 2016, p. 176). Discussions about safety and security in the suburb are supported by other members of the community joining in with comments, suggestions and support whenever a resident raises a problem related to crime or outsiders, whose messy presence disturbs the image that locals wish to maintain.

In the sections that follow, I examine the way in which ILM posters share fears about risk, crime and outsiders; discuss beliefs

about their rights to the city; and engage in performances of humanitarian good whiteness.

Fear and loathing in suburbia[10]

Fear about vulnerability in Johannesburg, as in other places, often
expresses itself as fear of difference: the idea that 'we' will only
be safe if we live in a place where 'they' cannot enter. Anxiety
about the danger posed by alleged outsiders is the logic behind the
securitised spatialisation of the gated community and the mall in
north and south America (Kohn 2004, Sabatini and Salcedo 2007,
Christopherson 2008). It is the logic behind 'concerned' white
residents in US cities calling the police to report black people going
about their daily business.[11] It is the logic behind the language of
threat used in white suburban social media groups across South
Africa, where homeowners routinely post invasive and accusatory
photos of 'bravo' (black) and 'charlie' (coloured) men walking on
public streets, in a warning to neighbours to be wary that strangers
are about.[12] In South Africa, as elsewhere, 'whites have long used
fear of crime as a euphemism for fear of blacks' (Lemanski 2004,
p. 109).

The liminal suburb of Melville has its own concentration of
outsiders who can be scapegoated for a range of social ills. As
Charles Villet writes, 'Despite the fact that a substantial part (if not
a majority) of the country's population is impoverished, in South
Africa poverty is casually considered to be deviant by many suburban whites' (2018, p. 19). Comments on ILM frequently conflate
homeless people, car guards, drug users and criminals, attributing
exceptional agency to some of the most powerless people in South
African society, demonising poverty while simultaneously ignoring
its causes.

In many cases, anxiety about outsiders manifests in hyperbolic
assumptions about their links to hidden structures of power or
threat. In a post decrying the 'nuisance' of the homeless men
who crowd around a major intersection attempting to wash car
windshields for change ('Window washers'), one resident writes,
'Why must I pay for people's drug habits?' Another comments that

window washers 'are linked to smash and grab attacks'.[13] Others discuss ways to get the police to remove these men from the area. In a post on neighbourhood crime ('Pavement purse-snatchers'), residents equate homeless people and informal traders with the organised gangs who snatch cellphones and handbags from late night drinkers on the main strip. They write that 'the car guards in Melville are mostly scoundrels and thugs which bully people for tips', 'the nyaope addicts are mostly thieves … but they are on foot' and that business owners should get together to protect the area, although they may struggle to 'find honest security guards'. Another commenter writes that 'the first thing we as a community must do i [sic] get rid of these so called car guards' ('5th Avenue robbery'). When questioned on the aggressive behaviour of his employees, the owner of a local security company posts a series of pictures of weapons he claims were confiscated from car guards, and writes that '"some" of the so called car guards are part of a criminal element. They sell drugs [and] look out for car thieves … Our staff are cornered and almost physically assaulted by car guards' ('New security company').

When one resident insists that a guard at a local supermarket tried to remote jam[14] her car, others agree, commenting, 'I don't care what anybody says, these guys are spotters for criminals,' and, 'there are some that are genuine but most are spotters' ('Spar car guards'). The distinction drawn here between 'genuine' car guards and criminal spotters plays into a narrative about deserving and undeserving poor, in which car guards are automatically assumed to be complicit in criminal behaviour, meaning not only that they do not belong in the suburbs but also that ILM posters are justified in refusing to tip them.

Car guards are classified as proto-criminals even when not engaging in illegal activity. A furious resident is woken up at 6.40am on the morning of a local sports event by car guards 'whistling, shouting … [and] charging people R50 to park in front of our homes on a public road' ('Busy roads'). Here car guards take the blame for disruption and chaos rather than the people driving their cars to Melville to partake in Sunday morning leisure activities. Numerous other comments in my selected posts make the connection between homelessness, informal work and organised crime, some directly blaming these types of poor black men for robberies and other crimes in the suburb (for example '5ᵗʰ Avenue robbery', 'Crime increasing', 'Car smash').

The language that ILM users employ to discuss poor black men is embedded in colonial and apartheid stereotypes. Homeless people and car guards are described as threatening and aggressive ('Window washers', 'New security company', '5ᵗʰ Avenue robbery'). These claims draw on ideas about the inherent violence of black masculinity, so naturalised in the white imagination that they do not require explanation or justification (hooks 1992, p. 89). In some cases gender is invoked to justify racist claims, drawing on centuries of useful stereotyping in which white women have been positioned as victims of black male violence (see, for example, McCulloch 2000). Discussing the window washers on Empire Road, ILM members write that 'their strong arm tactics is too much. They seem to especially target females'; 'they intimidate females especially because they can'; 'I wish I could [argue but] being a female I just have to bite my lip and endure this nonsense'. Here white women are presented as special kinds of victims of the ever-present threat of black male violence (van der Westhuizen 2017).

ILM posters sometimes characterise groups of black men as faceless and deindividuated: 'There are so many of them, I get scared every time they all come running to my car!'; '15 of them appeared at every car, it was like an invasion' ('Window washers'); 'There are gangs of them at every robot [traffic light] these days' ('Clarens'). This characterises black people as marauding hordes rather than as humans. Terms like 'invasion' and 'gang' show how easily the black crowd is demonised and how quickly individuality is obscured. This tendency was common to colonial myths, when 'the sight of large numbers of black people ... evoked the unsettling trope of slave rebellion' (Baderoon 2015, p. 11). It also manifested frequently in apartheid-era media production (Lacey 1989) and continues to characterise news reporting in contemporary South Africa (Tolsi 2018b).

The way ILM posters speak about homeless people, informal traders and car guards brings to mind Mary Douglas' definition as dirt as 'matter out of place' (1984). In many instances, posters' anxiety and discomfort about these out-of-place people is couched within a language of hygiene, sanitation and dirt that draws on apparently scientific ideas about healthy versus unhealthy cities. A poster writes that while some homeless people have been moved on by police, 'their blankets and "living" needs are still on the pavement' ('Window washers'). The inverted commas used here suggest that this kind of living does not actually *count as* living while also classifying the few possessions poor people have as litter, waste, detritus crowding a public area. One poster refers to a pavement where some homeless men sleep as a 'proper squatter camp' ('Ocean Basket'), implying not only informal living and crime but also filth and squalor. Another writes, 'I welcome the Melville homeless community ... the pressing issues I wish we could address are the litter, and the urinating/defecting [sic] in the street' ('Clarens'). Still another argues, in a conversation about sprinklers set up outside a local building, that they are there to 'wash away more than the putrid smell of the urine marinated sidewalk' – meaning the homeless street sleepers themselves. The same poster later writes that homeless people 'are already using my pavement as an outdoor toilet', while another adds, 'They don't just sleep in front of businesses. They urinate and defecate there too. People are trying to have businesses. It's not the place for them to live' ('Sprinklers'). Still others refer to areas where homeless people sleep as 'filth', 'a mess', 'an eyesore' ('Roxy's wall'). Rather than a social problem related to historic injustice, unemployment, corruption and economic inequality, homelessness is framed as a problem of aesthetics and hygiene: it looks bad, smells bad and creates dirt and waste. As well as centralising the class position of those who live in houses in the suburb and expect their environment to be a certain way, this adds dehumanisation to the demonisation of poor and homeless people. (Here I must mention that, of course, this attitude to homeless people is far from unique to Johannesburg or South Africa.)

Importantly, though, and differently to many South African social media spaces, Melville's claimed liberalism and tolerance also appear in discussions of 'out-of-place' people. Some posters on ILM position themselves politically and morally against their neighbours. Conversations develop in which the classifications discussed above are contested – sometimes angrily – and allegations fly between members of the group, with accusations of racism and hypocrisy particularly common. ILM facilitates the scapegoating of poor black people as a response to anxieties about physical safety and neighbourhood character; it also, however, also allows residents to undertake visible performances of anti-racism in support of these same scapegoats. It is beyond the scope of this chapter to find out whether this kind of speech transmits into anti-racist action or has any effect beyond disciplining 'bad' whites online. It is likely, however, that in at least some instances it operates like the institutional anti-racism discussed by Ahmed (2004): in foregrounding the speaker's moral position, it also negates the need for her/him to actually do anything.

Sometimes the pushback from community members is comparatively gentle. One poster responds to the classification of window washers as drug users by asking, 'Are you sure they are using drugs? ... In my opinion don't make assumptions before you are 100% sure of the facts' ('Window washers'). Claims about criminal car guards are sometimes strongly contested, with posters writing, 'I think you should [make] VERY SURE that it was the car guard. They are Not all criminals'; 'But how do you know it was him'; 'My experience of the car guards has been great'; and 'Guys. Without actual proof we can't say it was definitely the car guard ... I know I would not appreciate being called a criminal' ('Spar car guards'). These responses use personal experience to claim that certain car guards are legitimate, but they do not interrogate the link that is casually made between informal work and crime. The ideological structures that underpin such assumptions remain intact despite the critique of their manifestations, meaning that these comments may impact more on the reputation of the responders than on how ILM users think about car guards as a category.

In other instances, responses to perceived racist/classist positions can be more vehement. A discussion about a tourist town that bans homeless people and car guards from its centre ('Clarens') quickly descends into outrage. Posters call this idea 'disgusting', 'absurd', 'indecent' and 'cruel'. When one commenter supports it another responds, 'Wind your neck in, and your privilege too.' A third writes, 'Even if you believe the poor should be restricted from moving or earning a living ... to say so on a public platform without shame is a f#cking travesty.' In this comment, the travesty is not the injustice of moving 'undesirables' out of towns and cities but rather the fact that such a thing has been said on the ILM forum, which suggests that contradicting the agreed-upon liberal character of the suburb poses a moral threat.

Other posters respond to the apparent menace of homeless people with suggestions for how they can be helped rather than assertions that they are dirty, dangerous and do not belong. One asks of an empty building, 'Can't all that wasted space be put to good use? Why not let the homeless who sleep outside, sleep inside?' ('Roxy's wall'). A frequent commenter suggests that local churches get involved to provide 'showers, toilets, clothes and haircuts – a one stop shop for homeless people', but another disagrees, as 'homeless can't stay [on the pavement], they need a place with a little more dignity' ('Sprinklers').

During the conversation around window washers, a commenter writes, '[We should] see if there is a place to rehabilitate them get their CV's done and try and get them proper jobs.' Another answers, 'You are speaking to the converted. CV's? It's systemic this problem and a lot of rehabilitation that needs to take place before CV's can be considered.' This soon leads to an emotional argument. The first poster is accused of '[assuming] on your moral high ground' and sarcastically told that 'perhaps as you know them so well you could facilitate shelters for them'. She replies, 'The problem with you guys is you keep on moaning about them but want other people to do the job for you so I think for once stop moaning and get out of your comfort zone and do something … instead of waiting for other people to do it' ('Window washers'). This exchange is typical of the quick escalation of tensions that characterises social media discourse. Its conflicting accusations of naivety, ignorance, hypocrisy and inaction show the shifting positions taken by members of ILM who attempt both to voice their fears about black men on the streets of the neighbourhood and to portray themselves as tolerant and progressive. In some cases it is clear that posters self-censor in an attempt to head off potential critique. One commenter writes, 'They actually ARE stealing and committing crimes … Because they are poor they resort to crime … OBVIOUSLY, other people steal too and OBVIOUSLY not all car guards/beggars do but their presence gives opportunity' ('Clarens'). Here the writer polices her own position (visible in the use of caps lock for emphasis) in an attempt to avoid being disciplined by the community, while still making a blanket statement that associates poverty with crime.

While outright accusations of racism are rare, the frequent appearance of contemporary buzzwords like 'privilege' suggests that concerns about racist speech, rather than about actual racism, underlie much of the pushback that takes place on ILM. Arguments about negative stereotypes of poor black men often devolve into opportunities for residents to display their own liberal credentials. Nonetheless, the existence of this counter-narrative illustrates the conflicting urges that characterise neighbourhood discourse within ILM: in most instances, posts that demonise poor black men are met with at least some resistance from other members.

Rights to pity or rights to the city

Another narrative that recurs within ILM focuses on the linked ideas of rights, the law and state failure. In these conversations the discomfort of middle-class residents is equated to the disintegration of the rule of law and even of the nation itself. The sense that society is at risk of collapse is seldom articulated in detail; rather, it is part of a generalised anxiety about the looming end of the world, the sense of 'rolling apocalypse' that has long characterised white South African culture (Thornton 1994, p. 14). Within this discourse the idea that 'society must be defended' (Foucault 1997) is inextricably linked to the stability of middle-class rights and privileges, and to middle-class feelings of safety and belonging. Calls for 'something to be done' reflect the anxiety of middle-class, often white, people that they are not being listened to by the ANC government.

Much like residents of Alexandra discussing the threat of plasma gangs, people who post about crime, dirt and danger often refer to the failures of the Johannesburg Metro Police Department (JMPD) or South African Police Service (SAPS). Sometimes posters complain about the ineptitude of the local Brixton Police Station. Suggestions for sorting out a robbery hotspot lead one poster to write, 'If it's the Brixton police station one would need to help that's laughable!!!!!' ('ATM robbery'). When a teenager is mugged her mother writes that she will not bother to contact the authorities: 'Feel that Brixton would be a waste of time and she does not want to endure that incompetence' ('Teen mugged'). One poster complains that nothing was done after she reported an alleged criminal's licence plate to the police ('Car smash'). In other cases posters accuse police of intentionally not doing their jobs. ILM members write comments like, '[There is] zero presence or will from SAPS or JMPD [Johannesburg Metro Police Department] to sort out the situations on weekend nights' ('New security company'). Another agrees, 'The problem is, of course, the authorities and enforcement. Unfortunately I have often seen JMPD people who prefer to sit in their car rather than enforce traffic law' ('Window washers'). Distrust of the police is common in all sorts of communities in South Africa (Comaroff and Comaroff 2016, p. 182). When it appears in a suburban context, however, this distrust sometimes draws on racist stereotypes about lazy black people, whom whites see as not only unwilling but also unable to do a decent job. Doing these jobs 'correctly' means protecting the bodies and property of white suburban residents as well as making them feel safe by shutting down the 'chaotic and aggressive' ('New security company') weekend parties on the Melville main strip.

Posters on ILM frequently discuss the disappointments of private security companies hired to patrol the neighbourhood ('New security company', '5th Avenue robbery'), in contrast to the laudatory tone that accompanies discussions of private security in other communities in South Africa (van Riet 2018a). A post about the failures of a particular company reads, 'get your act together crime has gotten worse since you guys took over and you started to take short cuts!' A commenter agrees, 'I am not using them here. They only good when they take over a suburb and then from then there service is up to shit. Sorry guys but u are useless' ('One guard per car'). Discussing a road accident, a poster asks, 'And here I thought the security company is there to look out for that kind of stuff' ('Car smash'). Site members continually question where their money goes and argue over the merits of various security companies and whether they should hire different people. Similarly to the police, the management of these companies is often characterised as incompetent and lazy. However, the tone of such accusations is different to conversations around policing: this is the outrage of badly served consumers rather than the panic that accompanies unchecked social decay. Unlike with policing, community members have some power here. They can threaten to withdraw financial resources, cancel contracts and damage reputations. They need not plead for something to be done as they themselves can do something, even if that is only to post complaints on a neighbourhood Facebook page. Discussions about security companies seldom fall within the larger narrative of the imminent collapse of society. The sense of agency that comes along with being a paying consumer forestalls anxieties about powerlessness that appear in posts about police.

No posters in my sample reject or even resist the frequent characterisations of police as inept and uncaring. As symbols of a state that is often described as corrupt and anti-white, police do not inspire performances of humanitarianism. This is not the case with guards employed by private security companies, who are always black and sometimes from elsewhere in Africa (which comes with its own sets of un-privilege). In numerous instances, posters who criticise security companies add in caveats about the danger to these workers ('5th Avenue robbery', 'Crime increasing'). Residents make comments like, 'Why is there only one guard in a car it is not safe for them or for us!', while others insist, 'You should treat the staff that work for you better! Why are all the long standing staff resigning … Pay your staff properly' ('One guard per car'). These statements again draw on the narrative of tolerant liberalism familiar within ILM; however, they do so in a way that is clearly contingent, in which the safety and wellbeing of security guards is only of interest when it impacts on the safety and wellbeing of those who pay their salaries. Middle-class white ILM members discuss security guards, their de facto employees, with similar genial concern to the domestic workers about whom they feel benevolently paternalistic (Jansen 2019), but also with an awareness that their own safety depends to some extent on the guards' treatment. There is no discussion of the overall architecture of this form of labour, and no sense that those performing it do so because of a lack of opportunity. Rather, posters advocate for employees as individuals.

As well as police and security company failures, concerns about middle-class safety as a metonym for social collapse also manifest in an overarching interest in the law. References to the law suggest that it is fact; as with the 'scientism' of hygiene mentioned above, the law is absolute and free of ideological bias or nuance. A discussion about a man who attempts to sell fireworks to a Melville resident begins with fury about the risk posed to pets ('Man selling firecrackers'). When one poster tries to resist the group outrage by suggesting that 'things are tough, I think that guy was just trying to make some cash', the conversation changes tack from a moral to a legal argument. Commenters post links to the province's fireworks law and copy and paste the relevant by-laws. They write things like, 'Doing business is one thing. DOING ILLEGAL BUSINESS IS NOT ACCEPTABLE'; 'There are lots of legal things a person can sell to make money. Things that don't injure children and animals'; 'You need a permit to sell them ... He needs to be arrested'; and 'If things are tough break the law. Have you ever thought that maybe things are tough because so many people break the law.'

Calls to the law, particularly to local by-laws, appear frequently in posts about poor black men. One poster on the window washers discussion writes, 'The problem remains, they are infringing by-laws', suggesting that the infringement of these laws is the most concerning thing about homelessness. Another says, 'Not one person mentions the by laws. But I do suppose it is because the law is a joke and not enforced ... Enforce the by laws (not only chase businesses) or change the law to allow informal trading and begging.' This post draws again on the idea of white victimhood – businesses are punished by the law but 'nuisance' beggars are not – as well as gesturing towards social collapse: the law is a joke. The idea of the law plays a dual role. It is a respected structure that ILM posters can invoke to counter the causes of anxiety but is also a cause of anxiety itself when it is seen to be precarious.

Although comparatively rare, posts do sometimes invoke the law as part of the counter-narrative of good whiteness, usually when community members post warnings about con artists, bad workers and people who are defined as dangerous, and others weigh in to criticise them. Posters are warned about the legal consequences of making such public accusations ('Bad gardener'). One commenter writes, 'Just FYI it is illegal to accuse someone of theft and slander them publically' ('Mosaic artist'). The law is usually invoked to

bolster claims about white middle-class rectitude and to demonise those who make these community members uncomfortable.
However, in certain instances the idea of the law is turned on its
head, as the outrage and entitlement of middle-class white ILM
members is classified as the object rather than the subject of law.

Crime stories also reflect residents' anxieties about the moral disintegration of communities, for example by condemning bystanders
who fail to step in and assist their fellow citizens. In a discussion
about a mugging hotspot, a commenter says, 'We came to the assistance of a young woman being scammed – everyone else and all
security looked the other way.' Others on the thread denounce
this inaction ('ATM robbery'). A different poster writes, 'People
are kak [shit]. My friend got run over on 7th in front of everybody and no one did fuckall.' Someone adds, 'The lack of concern
and assistance is shocking! A few years ago I assisted a motor-
cyclist in Albertskroon after seeing much commotion everyone
was filming as his legs were off. That should have been a criminal
offence not having assisted.' Another agrees, 'Common decency
apparently doesn't exist anymore' ('Car smash'). Arguments about
what should be done about homeless people veer from suggestions
about shelters and CVs into counter-flying accusations of inaction,
with posters aggressively asking others what they have done to
solve the problem ('Window washers', 'Clarens', 'Roxy's wall'). In
this narrative, agency and responsibility are assigned to individual
citizens, who are castigated for their failures to live up to the moral
requirements of civilised people and whose inaction is classified
as part of the social decline that characterises twenty-first-century
Johannesburg.

Nebulous fears about social collapse expressed on ILM are tied
to state and police failures, the weakness of the legal system and the
moral shortcomings of individuals. All of these issues relate to the
vexed question of rights: who has them, who deserves them and
what they are. Posters' conversations show that they believe they
deserve the right to feel safe in their cars and homes; to live in a
suburb that meets their expectations of cleanliness and environmental pleasantness; to enjoy their leisure time without being confronted
by beggars and informal workers/traders; and to be treated 'fairly',
which in practice usually means better than most South Africans,

by the state (this includes grievances about taxation and affirmative action). In some episodes this call to rights manifests directly as a claim of the right to the city: residents discuss and usually agree on what amounts to their ownership of the suburban space. Outsiders and people out-of-place – from car guards and homeless men to students and criminal gangs – are expected to behave 'properly', to meet suburban expectations. This is illustrated in a conversation about the conflict between car guards and a new security company. The company's owner tells ILM posters,

> We approach the car guards in a polite manner and with most of them they are humble and good guys to work with. Those guys are still there. We have not asked them to leave or forced them out of the area as they work with us and form part of the community ... The car guards that are decent and well-mannered are the ones that point criminals to us ... All we did was approach the guys that forced themselves onto patrons and disturbed people having lunch or dinner, and asked them to be considerate. ('New security company')

Acceptable car guards are described in terms that suggest docility and civilised behaviour – 'humble', 'good', 'decent', 'well-mannered' – in contrast to those who, in a term seamlessly if somewhat ironically borrowed from stories of gendered violence, 'force themselves' on innocent diners, whose right to enjoy the meals they are paying for is compromised by informal traders' attempts to make a living. There are elements here of the performative humanitarianism glorified on ILM, particularly in the statement that some car guards are 'members of the community', but as with the narrative around private security guards it is clear that this extension of humanity to poorer people is contingent on their value for middle-class residents.

Finally, the question of rights sometimes lends itself to a sort of *counter*-counter-narrative, in which posters blame the performed liberalism of ILM for adding to problems like crime and homelessness. This manifests firstly in an oblique dismissal of law: 'Unfortunately in South Africa criminals are not allowed to be trapped unless you apply for a court order ... unfortunately criminals have all the rights in South Africa that's why we are why [sic] we are' ('Crime increasing'). Here the idea of rights becomes something that is in itself unjust, prioritising the bad (and concurrently the poor) over those who deserve the support of the law, having earned it by being good shopping, tax-paying, worker-employing neoliberal subjects. Similarly, discussions about crime often descend into calls for the community to arm itself with everything from mace to firearms ('Window washers', 'New security company'), suggesting that the government is failing to protect residents' rights. As with the arguments around each person's responsibility to assist community members, Melville residents are also implicated in this supposed travesty of rights. Commenting on a post equating homeless people to dirt ('Ocean Basket'), one site member writes, 'The Do Gooders helping the vagrants sleeping in Main Rd are not helping the situation.' Another agrees, 'Yes, and every time anyone tries to do something about it the "Do-Gooders" get all crazy and defensive about the poor souls having nowhere else to go. It's a waste of time trying to do something about it.' The liberal tolerance that is pervasive on ILM is upended. As well as being foolish and naïve, liberal approaches actively harm the neighbourhood by ensuring that homeless people will continue to live there and passively undermine the community by ensuring that no one else can 'do something' about the apparent scourge of people as matter out of place.[15]

Performing goodness in the social media community

What makes ILM particularly interesting is the intersection of middle-class anxieties about safety and neighbourhood character, common to most visibly unequal cities, with a sometimes contradictory urge to be seen to be doing good, the 'dependence on spectacle' that is an 'important dimension of humanitarianism' (Chouliaraki 2012a, p. 2). This injunction to publically perform goodness appears most clearly in posts that discuss charity, community support and domestic labour. In these posts community members show their neighbourhood in what is imagined to be its best light: tolerant, friendly, diverse and open-minded. In most instances these performances have an overtly racial character. The person offering humanitarian speech or action is white while the object of that speech or action is black.

Chouliaraki writes that the 'relationship between humanitarianism and spectacle should be seen as characteristic of a particular conception of politics as pity' (2012a, p. 2). She is speaking about larger-scale humanitarianism, performed by distanced 'ironic spectators' (Chouliaraki 2012b) in the global north and aimed at alleviating the theoretical suffering of faceless masses in the south. However, her points are equally pertinent within the context of suburban South Africa. This type of humanitarianism is 'a politics that prioritises the moral plea to alleviate distant suffering over the re-distribution of global resources as a means for changing the conditions of suffering' (Chouliaraki 2012a, p. 2). Calls to charity and community action on ILM take the form of a similar moral plea: 'we' must help 'them' with their immediate, visible needs because it's the right thing to do. While a few posters acknowledge the structural conditions that underlie poverty, these statements are often weak and portray the posters as helpless. The site's narratives emphasise white people's individual responsibility, freely chosen, for behaving in a way that seems morally good, rather than their culpability as part of an unjust system. These narrative tropes reveal the 'inadequacy of the discourse of pity' (Chouliaraki 2010, p. 109).

Ideas about altruism and agency can be seen in the names of the charities that ILM community members discuss: Kindness like Confetti, Charity Begins with Me, Help2Read, ForGood and Charity Thursday ('Giving back'). The language used to name these organisations and events suggests the moral stance of the givers, who are kind and helpful and who do good by choice rather than by compulsion. Humanitarian action is described as individual rather than social and concurrently disavows ILM community members' relations with the colonialism and apartheid that set the stage for contemporary injustice. Chouliaraki writes that the celebrity humanitarian presides over a 'scandalous contradiction: by appearing to care for the "wretched of the earth" whilst enjoying the privilege of rare wealth, he or she glosses over the ongoing complicity of the West in a global system of injustice that reproduces the dependence of the developing world through acts of charity' (2012a, p. 4). Similarly in suburban South Africa charity can serve as a distraction, negating the need to consider the causes of inequality. Individual privilege is not threatened by acts of kindness as it would be by radical suggestions for redress like the call for white people to, both metaphorically and literally, 'give back the land' (Burnett 2018).

ILM 'do gooders' discuss helping homeless and informally employed black men, but this rarely manifests in specifics. Posters talk in vague terms about setting up shelters or assisting with job searches, or argue about what the city and other institutions should do ('Window washers', 'Sprinklers'). Calls to charity that focus on other types of people are often more detailed. Community members post information asking for aid with school literacy and old age homes ('Giving back'), with books for high school students ('School book donation') and clothes and accessories for a township school dance ('Grade 12 dance'), with supporting the financial endeavours of young people ('Siyabonga street seller'). These sorts of people are the deserving poor. They are too young or too old to be automatically classified as risks; they may be studying or working, meaning that they are trying to 'improve' themselves; they are relatable, in that they are not homeless or so poor as to be threatening; they are often female, meaning that they can bypass the threat that black men invoke in the white imagination. Here the contingent nature of post-humanitarianism can again be seen. It is applied to those who are imagined to have the potential to 'contribute' to society but not to those whose poverty and naturalised association with violence disturb the security of the givers' social order.

The performative nature of this altruistic drive is displayed in two significant ways. First, many posters argue against perceived racist speech, presenting themselves as good – here meaning politically progressive – white people. These contestations over how people speak about race and poverty often lead to arguments in which posters draw on common South African discourses to position themselves as morally superior. Second, discussions about charity and doing good often lead to congratulation that draws on 'the language of sentimental gratitude that evokes appreciation for the benefactors' (Chouliaraki 2010, p. 108). When a poster asks residents for ideas of how she can 'give back to the community', some respond, 'That's so cool!', 'What an awesome message', 'Hats off to you sister,' and 'Awesome!!' ('Giving back'). A volunteer asking for clothes and accessories for a Soweto school dance and a schoolteacher asking for books to start a classroom library garner enthusiastic support from community members, who applaud the posters and offer to donate and assist ('Grade 12 dance', 'School book donation'). This applause often includes a celebration of ILM itself, in which posters enthuse about the good things the page helps them to achieve. The spectacle of humanitarianism allows site members to collectively define the nature of their digital community, and consequently their physical neighbourhood, as performing a moral role in the 'new' neoliberal South Africa, where optional altruism stands in for social justice.

The injunction to publicly undertake goodness can also be seen in the many posts on ILM in which people discuss domestic workers and other labourers who work in their homes and gardens. The page is peppered with posts in which people ask for recommendations for workers and try to find new jobs for people they currently employ. ILM posters discussing domestic labour use a carefully benevolent tone. Site members take care to avoid problematic or ideologically loaded terminology, like the apartheid-era 'maid' (Jansen 2019, p. 13), instead employing more seemingly neutral terms like 'helper' or 'housekeeper'. These newer designations can elide the real conditions of domestic labour by making it sound like voluntary assistance or skilled household management rather than back-breaking and poorly paid work often performed by subaltern women who have little recourse to legal rights.[16]

Workers are often referred to as ladies: a 'cleaning lady' ('Bad gardener'), a 'domestic lady', a 'perfect lady' ('Dog-loving domestic'), a 'wonderful lady', an 'exceptional lady' ('Reliable domestic'). The use of lady as opposed to terms like woman or worker firstly reveals the acceptable boundaries of speech on ILM, where posters are expected to discuss working-class black women in a way that is considered polite; but secondly it suggests a collective discomfort with the realities of domestic labour, which is discursively positioned as a relationship of harmless mutual benefit despite its inherently exploitative nature. Attempts to ignore the unequal power relations that characterise this work also manifest in allusions to the familial intimacy between employer and employee (Ginsburg 2011, Jansen 2019). One poster writes, 'I am relocating to the Cape and cannot take [my domestic worker] with me' ('Reliable domestic').

The way that this is phrased suggests that the worker is a much-loved pet or possession who sadly has to be rehomed. Many commenters talk about how long they have employed their workers, mentioning time periods including 16 and 20 years ('Reliable domestic', 'Dog-loving domestic').

Site members speak about workers in ways that emphasise whether they are 'good' or not. Employers refer to their domestic workers as 'reliable and trust-worthy', someone who 'takes the initiative', 'good with kids and dogs', 'energetic and reliable' ('Dog-loving domestic'), 'hard-working, honest, trustworthy', 'hard working and very reliable' ('Reliable domestic'). The two most important traits for workers are reliability – meaning that the employer's home security is not compromised and that she or he can depend on the work being done – and working hard. Hard work is almost fetishised by site members, who use it to signal the moral respectability of their employees. One writes that he has to 'force [the domestic labourer] to stop working for lunch' ('Dog-loving domestic'). Another says of a gardener, 'I employ David on a half day basis and he never left before 4pm, because he "likes working" so we added handyman to the job description' ('Bad gardener'). ILM narratives suggest that poorly paid domestic employees, who may not have access to sick leave, pensions or other basic labour protections, work because they *like* to, rather than out of necessity. Once again this suggests an intimacy between worker and employer that ignores unequal power relations and economic status, negating the role of race, gender, poverty, migration and lack of access to education as determinants for who works in whose home, and in what ways. This allows employers to view themselves as compassionate and generous providers of wanted work rather than as complicit in an exploitative system of labour. Jacklyn Cock, in her book on domestic labour during apartheid (1989), reveals the disjuncture between how black domestic workers viewed their white employers and vice versa, with employers drawing on ideas of family and benevolent paternalism to discuss their relationships with workers who often despised them. Similarly, Rebecca Ginsburg (2011) reveals how workers' close knowledge of employers' culture, in the face of employers' ignorance about theirs, allowed them to quietly circumvent apartheid laws in creative ways.

The idea that people choose to do domestic and manual work becomes unstuck when faced with 'bad' workers. Employees who 'con' employers by claiming they work more than they do ('Bad gardener') or by not completing tasks they've been paid for ('Mosaic artist') inspire collective outrage and claims of victimhood. When a resident warns other site members about a gardener who works for less time than he is paid for ('Bad gardener'), commenters weigh in that this is 'bitterly disappointing' and advise the original poster to 'contact SAPS'. Another writes that she has clearly been 'taken advantage of', that she has a right to be 'disappointed and upset', that her 'trust' has been broken and that she should report the man to both the police and her private security company ('Bad gardener'). The language used here suggests that the poster has been mistreated in her capacity as a friend rather than as an employer. She adds, 'I am really sad that I have been taken for a ride by someone that I tried to help.' These posts evoke Chouliaraki's language of sentimental gratitude for the benefactor (2010, p. 108): the employee is expected be grateful after being given work rather than to treat it as a mutually beneficial transaction. The original poster does not discuss how much work was required for how much pay. Rather, she and her supporters are concerned with her goodness against the gardener's badness: she was trusting and generous in offering him an extra day of work, where he was conniving and dishonest in not doing as many hours as he was expected to.

A similar narrative develops around a mosaic artist who was paid to do a job and then disappeared without completing it ('Mosaic artist'). People refer to the missing man as a 'con artist' who is 'on the run after ripping off this Melville guy'. They advise the poster to contact police and the local newspaper. One commenter writes, 'Best not to help ppl. 90% time u get kicked in the face', while another is 'concerned about [the poster's] generosity and kindness being exploited'. These responses suggest that hiring an artisan to do a job is an act of altruism rather than of capitalism, and that the worker, in failing to complete the job, did not just break a contract but more importantly hurt the feelings of his employer, whose motivation in hiring him is represented as compassionate rather than pragmatic. Here performances of good whiteness intersect with the powerful sense of white victimhood and personal abuse that characterises genocide conspiracy theories. The suburban homeowner is generous and trusting but suffers at the hands of the amoral labourer who fails to live up to his responsibility to not only do but also love his work.

These two stories, of the bad gardener and the mosaic artist, also contain displays of the liberal goodness that often defines the character of ILM. In both cases, other posters weigh in to condemn social media shaming that may jeopardise the livelihoods of workers. Original posters are warned that their actions are not moral and may not even be legal. They are castigated for their lack of empathy. People query whether they have been paying the workers enough. In both instances the discussion quickly becomes a fierce argument; in the case of the mosaic artist it is so heated that the moderator closes comments. Some ILM members take the side of the original poster, insisting that there is no excuse for the artist's failure to complete the work. Others insist that the artist is a 'good guy' and a 'nice guy' who may be 'living close to the edge' or may have had some misfortune that led to his disappearance. Accusations bounce between posters; one is called 'judgemental and insufferable', another insists that 'racists be racisting'. Towards the end of the thread a further argument develops between a white man and a black woman. He writes, 'yip you should not leave your manners at the shebeen [illegal drinking den]. to u all is racist … hehe told u u on drugs. shouldn't have left ur glasses at the shebeen.' Another poster steps in to defend her: 'Manners at the shebeen? Wow. Maybe leave your mentality in apartheid. What scum.' In this post perceived racism is contrasted to the perceived stupidity of 'do gooders' who support alleged thieves. The vehemence of the argument reveals the emotional importance of these positions to the people posting about them. The anxiety about being taken for a ride, which suggests economic and even domestic vulnerability, runs headlong into the desire to appear tolerant, understanding, anti-racist and liberal.

Finally, some of the nuances of the public performance of good whiteness can be seen in the different ways in which white ILM members talk to black members who post on the site. Posters looking for domestic workers tend to garner responses from site members sharing information about their employees. The original poster usually replies with a thank you or some other acknowledgment, which may lead to a longer conversation. Sometimes, however, responses to such requests come from workers themselves, or from their friends or siblings, who use the site to look for employment. In those instances the original poster almost never acknowledges the comment. This suggests that there is something uncomfortable about workers having access to a digital community in which they are so often spoken about but so rarely speak. Workers' periodic presence lays bare the public nature of the online space, easily forgotten within the impression of community and cohesion that characterises ILM.

Such silences are in contrast to white ILM posters' responses to black people who present themselves as legitimately part of the community, and who are relatable in terms of class, education and knowledge of the social codes that are common on the page. This is evident in a post in which a black woman looks for accommodation in the suburb. She writes,

> I am a not-so-young professional, no baggage except my suitcases, and sober habits. I am generally quiet except when I speak with other Zulus on the phone. I have no pets but cats tend to like me (in our culture, that's witchcraft) and dogs too … I hope I have done well in selling myself as a dream tenant. ('Dream tenant')

Her self-deprecating joke about how 'loud' Zulus are plays subversively on white stereotypes about black people: not just that they speak loudly but that that volume is inappropriate and out of place in the suburbs, where black newcomers are expected to adopt the behavioural modes of white residents (Ballard 2010). Similarly the comment about cats being related to witchcraft 'in our culture' could be seen as a gentle lampoon of white ideas about blackness; more significantly, though, it makes clear that the intended audience for this post is *not* part of that culture, suggesting that the accommodation that this poster is looking for is owned by white people, coherent with ILM's perception of the neighbourhood character of Melville. In order to access white spaces, the poster makes herself legible to white people using wry humour and an acknowledgement of her difference. Ironically, this means that she can be accepted as one of the community as her blackness is not threatening.

This strategy is remarkably successful. Where other black posters looking for accommodation on ILM receive very few responses, this post generated 78 reactions, 69 comments and three shares. Commenters weigh in with suggestions for places to rent or friends who could be approached. Others write, 'If I had a Melville cottage you would be first tenant option,' with a heart emoji attached; 'You are so funny, you'd be a perfect tenant for anyone on here … Wishing you lots of luck. Please can you keep us updated when you find a place'; and 'You sound awesome! So love your humour – such a privilege to have people like you in Melville, on the planet … Hope you find your dream space darling.' This last comment makes it explicit that the original poster is indeed considered part of the community. She responds later in thread, saying, 'Thank you community for your heartwarming response to my plea. Please allow me time to view and deliberate with all these wonderful land-owners. Thank you one and all for being my blessers.' The references to whites as land-owners and blessers (a local term for sugar daddies) could be read as sarcastic or contentious, but they are casually passed over within a discussion in which the black speaker is classified as 'one of us'. This enthusiastic response echoes the way in which ILM posters publicly congratulate each other on acts of charity and 'giving back'. The vocal nature of reactions to the post suggests that there is something at stake for the commenters as well: being seen to be welcoming, tolerant, helpful and supportive of a black woman who can be counted as a community member is also part of the performativity of goodness that underpins recurrent narratives on ILM.

Selves and others on social media

Middle-class life in South Africa is riddled with contradictions. Citizens who live in leafy, formerly white suburbs are some of the most fortunate and well-off in the country. But despite their obvious privilege, their sense of existing under extraordinary threat is often acute. Many suburbanites live with constant anxiety about their safety and security despite their relative invulnerability when compared with residents of townships like Alexandra.

This sense of unease is tied, of course, to physical security, not surprising within South Africa's dangerous cities, but also relates to suburban senses of authenticity and to attempts to lay claim to the city in different ways. On the I Love Melville Facebook page, narratives about who fits where and how the neighbourhood works are metonymic for contestations about belonging in the twenty-first-century South African city. Outsiders, particularly black men whose homes and labour are precarious, are demonised as sources for all the ills that haunt the suburb, from crime to dirt to noise. The failings of the state and the imminent collapse of society are invoked to explain and support residents' concerns about their status and safety.

Posters on ILM also, however, use the site as a way to perform certain types of whiteness and middle class-ness that are related to tolerant liberalism. Community members can be seen to be good in ways that are fundamentally apolitical, while ignoring the historical, structural, institutional and economic conditions that underlie South Africa's high levels of inequality. These performances of tolerance, liberalism and humanitarian charity support ideas about what the neighbourhood means but also ignore the complicity of the privileged in unjust systems by allowing them to frame themselves as simply altruistic and to downplay ethical calls to justice and reparation in favour of a logic of choice and personal morality. The middle-class, largely white residents of the suburb of Melville who are active on the community Facebook page are part of tussles over meaning and rights that characterise the contemporary South African city, defined by the dual anxieties of security and belonging.

Notes

1 This good whiteness is related to the 'white innocence' that underpins Dutch culture (Wekker 2016), which casts white people as liberal, tolerant, benign, welcoming and compassionate towards negatively racialised incomers. In South Africa, of course, this collective protestation of innocence takes a different form, as white people in a post-apartheid era would struggle to claim the lack of knowledge and the personal distance from issues of race that inform white Dutch identity.

2 After a particularly fraught set of conversations about by-law infringe-
ments by local bars, the moderators set the group to closed in early 2019.
New members now have to be approved before they can read posts. All
material cited here was collected while the group was still public.

3 Directly to the south of Melville, heading in the general direction of
Soweto, one moves through Auckland Park, a once majestic suburb
featuring large homes clustered upwards on one of the city's ridges,
now increasingly given over to student housing or knocked down to
build university residences, and to Brixton, at the top of the ridge.
Brixton, too, features small Victorian houses, prized by the tight knit
community of artists and academics who inhabit its north-eastern tip.
However, rather than the artisan lattes of Melville, its high street is
a mix of cheap supermarkets, African tailors, pawn shops, bars and
second-hand stores, while its streets are criss-crossed with hawkers and
spaza shops. In this region of Johannesburg, then, Melville is the closest
obviously suburban area to the city centre.

4 Melville's reputation within the city was dramatically eroded on New
Year's Eve 2020 when it was the site of a shocking and apparently
motiveless drive-by shooting, in which three bystanders were killed.

5 Car guarding is a type of informal employment that is ubiquitous in
South African cities. Car guards, usually black men, usher drivers into
and out of parking spaces and claim to guard their vehicles against
crime on the promise of receiving small change.

6 The Suidlanders, one of the proponents of the white genocide myth,
describe themselves as 'an emergency plan initiative officially founded
in 2006 to prepare a Protestant Christian South African Minority for
a coming violent revolution ... [Constituted] for the protection of non-
combatant civilian Afrikaners (women, children, the elderly and the
non-able bodied) in the event of a civil war' (Who We Are n.d.).

7 At the time of writing, the Maboneng precinct, once considered one of
Johannesburg's tourist jewels, was in a period of flux after the development company behind it went bust (Maninjwa 2019). This has meant
a collapse of its tightly controlled security perimeter and a change in its
atmosphere as retailers, entrepreneurs and cultural industries abandon
the area to a growing concentration of late night bars. While still listed
on most travel websites as a crucial spot to visit, Maboneng is now considered edgier and more dangerous, with fewer middle-class property
owners and more cheap rents and Airbnb apartments.

8 Of course, not all people who live in the suburb consider Melville to
be a white space. The largely black student population experiences
the neighbourhood in very different ways, seen for example in a 2019

Instagram advert for a local nightclub that featured exclusively images of young black partygoers under the tagline 'We Own Melville'.

9 Although it is difficult to confirm whether Facebook identities are genuine, ILM members are censured in comment threads for using suspect names or having unreliable online histories. Intra-community policing of the 'realness' of posters suggests that members are invested in the idea that all those using ILM are authentic.

10 In order to undertake this analysis, I began by reading the archives of the ILM page. I started in September 2017 and searched through just over six months of posts, ending in March 2018. I supplemented this approach with a keyword search, looking for posts during this period that used the terms 'child', 'kid', 'school', 'charity', 'help', 'community', 'crime', 'criminal', 'homeless', 'security', 'secure', 'domestic' and 'car guard'. Posts that were selected for analysis had to relate to one of the key injunctions that make up the primary argument of this chapter and had to have a minimum of 20 comments. The finalised corpus consisted of 25 posts. The posts selected for this chapter are listed in Appendix 4 along with the shortened names that I use to discuss them. All were accessed and screengrabbed between 1 and 22 June 2018. No names or pseudonyms are used and all posts have been transcribed verbatim, barring minor edits for sense.

11 In 2018 alone, white Americans made the news after reporting black Americans to the police for using bathrooms at Starbucks, leaving Airbnb apartments, falling asleep in their dorms, unlocking their business premises, having barbecues and walking into the buildings where they live.

12 The anonymous Tumblr blog Suburban Fear (https://suburbanfear. tumblr.com/), whose tag line reads 'documenting white privilege in South Africa', collects screengrabs of conversations like these and posts them publicly. Many of the narrative themes that I discuss in the sections below recur across posts on this blog.

13 'Smash and grab' refers to a form of theft in which a car window is smashed in and the driver's phone, handbag or other visible valuable is grabbed through the broken glass.

14 Remote jamming is a form of car theft in which the signals of a security remote are jammed, leaving the car unlocked and vulnerable to theft.

15 Demonising liberal or anti-racist positions as causes of crime is relatively marginal on ILM but common in the social media groups of more conservative communities (see van Riet 2018b). This suggests again that the 'bohemian' character of the suburb has a noticeable influence on collective discourses.

16 According to the National Minimum Wage Act of 2018, domestic
    workers are entitled to R15 (about $1) per hour (National Minimum
    Wage Act 2018, p. 18). Assuming such a worker is paid for eight
    hours a day, five days a week, without deductions for food, unemploy-
    ment insurance and other sundries, that comes to a monthly income of
    R2,400 (about $166). Calculations from 2018 suggest that the gross
    living wage for a single adult for that year was over R4,000 ($277) per
    month (Living Wage Series – South Africa 2018). This does not take
    into account that many domestic workers are the sole breadwinners
    in their families, supporting children, partners, parents and other rela-
    tives, or that the cost of living is higher in Johannesburg than elsewhere
    in South Africa.

Conclusion: Risky business

I began this book by relating the multiple warnings I received from family and friends when I moved from the UK back to South Africa, which left me with confusing and upsetting feelings about risk and race. People in my life were concerned that returning home would be dangerous for my physical safety and the safety of my home and possessions, my urban mobility, my health, my financial wellbeing, the integrity of my social world. I am, however, a middle-class white academic living in the northern suburbs of Johannesburg, with a car, a permanent job and a contract with a private security company. Given these multiple privileges, it is hardly surprising that my intimates' worst fears have not come to pass. I have, like so many others, come to an accommodation with life in my anxious city, where feelings of vigilance and the awareness of persistent risk have been normalised. But while they may not have happened to me, the bad things I was warned about continue to traumatically affect others. South Africa remains an incredibly violent and unequal society, exacerbated by political corruption and infrastructural decay. These realities have important effects on local and national imaginaries. The risks that people worry about or actually face, the moral panics that express their fears about instability and vulnerability and the anxieties that are often dramatically misrecognised remain as potent as ever, impacting on everyday life in this complex, demanding place.

In a 2018 interview, the writer Sisonke Msimang says, 'In South Africa it's very easy to ... arrive at the easy conclusion. The easy conclusion is we live in a racist society and therefore it's easy to say that we are a divided country and then to accept that division.'

She goes on to make a passionate argument for the importance of complexity: 'The large seemingly intractable problems in our world are not solved with a single answer. There's always another angle' (Isama 2018). This is a place that is insecure *and* creative, violent *and* generative, conservative *and* outrageous. Its levels of fear and anxiety are part of a wider emotional topography. In an era which in the political west is marked by white supremacist massacres, expulsion of 'legitimate' immigrants and concentration camps for those deemed illegal, blatant populism, cronyism and corruption, it is no longer possible to believe in the fictions that modernity is restricted to the west or that Africa is not modern. South Africa's intricate and multiple manifestations of the culture of fear make it more, not less, important as a site for reading the contemporary world.

This book has been driven by a number of aims. Firstly, it has broadly foregrounded collective emotion as a crucial element of contemporary life, politics and narrative world-making. It has emphasised the role of fear, and its attendant features of risk, anxiety and moral panic, as some of the most significant manifestations of this emotionality. Anxiety has been posited as a nebulous and underlying trait of globalised modernity, with risk as its pervasive condition and moral panic as its repeated symptom. Secondly, it has argued for the necessity of considering emotion in, not just about, South Africa, and has shown some of the ways in which local conditions of risk and insecurity interplay with or amplify anxious global narratives. Thirdly, and most extensively, it has shown how anxiety, risk and moral panic manifested in four incidents in which they intersect with some of the most pressing issues in the country right now: racism, gender-based violence, consumption, spatial injustice, securitisation, crime.

Violence, identity, belonging

The stories in this book share a number of themes. The first is violence, which is central to so many representations and experiences of South Africa. All of these case studies are in different ways concerned with the fear or reality of violence, with actual or projected death or harm, with the vulnerability that people experience on the streets and in the buildings of our cities, with how and whether we locate ourselves as sufferers and the approaches we take to mitigate that, whether practical or emotional. Chapter 3 considers real violent crimes with real victims; Chapter 5 is concerned with the slower violence of exclusion; Chapter 4 emphasises the sometimes real, sometimes imaginary presence of bogeymen, phantoms, scapegoats; Chapter 2 shows how real violence is blended with conspiracy to become an ideological tool. Violence lurks below many South African experiences of anxiety, an ominous but nonetheless unavoidable possibility. It is ever-present; like anxiety itself, it cannot be extricated from the promises of the modern. These four stories feature violence on farms, in townships and in suburbs, aimed at women and children, at girls, at families, at black commuters and white homeowners; but these forms of violence are not the same. As the chapters in this book have revealed, there is an unbridgeable gap between the most anxious imaginings of the privileged and the grinding realities of the poor. All of these people are subject to violence, but for some the claim of victimhood requires an intentional blindness to the suffering of others.

The second theme is that of identity, particularly the intersecting matrixes of gender, class and race. The female-ness of the victims and the male-ness of the killers is a glaring absence in much of the media coverage of Satanist murders: these are quintessentially gendered crimes and their appearance in press discourse reveals the paucity of our vocabulary about gender, our inability to properly talk about what it means to be a woman or a man in South Africa today and to face (or to enact, or both) the particular kinds of violence that these positions entail. Like all South Africans, residents of Alexandra township use consumption and display to make claims about class, but this is consistently precarious, threatened not only by external infrastructures of capitalism and corruption but also by people within their community. The white genocide myth depends on the deification of whiteness as a sacrifice on the altar of the 'new', apparently non-racial, South Africa, while Melville residents' suburban anxieties swirl around both 'good' whiteness – benevolent, generous, altruistic – and the scapegoating of black masculinity as an innate threat. These episodes place people within clear frames of social identity. Like narrative, they are a powerful part of the arsenal of tools that we use to explain the world and our societies.

Third, all of these stories depend on notions of belonging and concurrently of not belonging. In each instance, the narrative in question helps to cement a group or a community, whether of anxious parents worried that their children are not safe at school; of suburban homeowners worried that homeless people will impact on their property values; of township residents afraid of certain types of crime and criminals; or of white farmers banding together in the face of a feared race war. They feature innocent protagonists and depraved villains. They depend on the creation of an inside and an outside, an us and a them, even in cases where those on the outside are ostensibly members of the community, as with 'satanic' killers and nyaope addicts believed to be part of plasma gangs. As Gabeba Baderoon writes, citing Edward Said, 'The creation of otherness is a formula for the creation of the self' (2015, p. 33). Within our cultures of fear, narrative allows us to define who we are and who we are not, and to locate others accordingly. Each statement of belonging, of naturalness, of autochthony, suggests its opposite. Those who are outside our communities have as much to do with shaping them as those who are inside.

Fear and/of failure

In South Africa, Africa and the world as a whole, it is now a cliché to say that these are anxious times indeed. Fears about safety, on both a macro and a micro level, seem to be substantiated by the news we hear about our cities, our countries and the planet in general. The proliferation of media that infuses everyday life makes it difficult to avoid the sense that we are all always at risk and that the world is shifting, inchoate, unstable. This affective intensity has only increased during the COVID-19 pandemic that has cost so many lives and altered so many others.

It may well be the case that we are all in danger, particularly as a consequence of escalating climate change, which poses an existential threat that very few humans will be able to avoid. Vaccine hesitancy is increasing, driven by anxious parents whose desire to keep their children safe leads them to conspiracy theory websites; antibiotic resistance is on the rise in the west while elsewhere governments struggle to contain new disease strains; scientists warn of an incoming age of pandemics spurred by human interventions in nature; cities plagued by drought or rising sea levels encounter new forms of precarity and crime; drone technology allows for the ever-easier murder of people in war zones and other contested areas; austerity politics block access to both basic necessities and class mobility; racist publics and the police that serve them continue to neglect and harm people of colour; immigrants and religious minorities are persecuted and killed by authoritarian states and impromptu militias; rainforests burn on the nightly news. It is no surprise that many of us live with a constant sense of insecurity.

But despite all of these frightening possibilities, humans may overall be empirically safer than we have ever been before, with data showing consistent upward mobility in the crucial areas of maternal mortality, life expectancy and access to uncontaminated water.[1] This is not to suggest that our fears are unfounded or that environmental, social and political factors do not pose a threat to different communities. The fact that global maternal mortality has lowered will be of no comfort to Dalit women in Nepal or black women in America, whose health outcomes in pregnancy and birth remain significantly lower than other women's (Chaurasiya *et al.* 2019, Racial and Ethnic Disparities Continue in Pregnancy-Related Deaths 2019). Nonetheless, when we think about risk statistics against the enormous spike in affective conditions of anxiety, what becomes clear is that we need to interrogate the *legibility* of those fears, their exaggerated presence in our daily discourse and the concurrent sense that everything is constantly getting worse.

Zygmunt Bauman writes,

> It is the people who live in the greatest comfort on record, more cossetted and pampered than any other people in history, who feel more threatened, insecure and frightened, more inclined to panic, and more passionate about everything related to security and safety than people in any other societies past and present. (2006, p. 130)

All of which said, these formulations do not quite match up to the realities of South Africa, where many people live with much higher empirical conditions of risk than in the north. Many South Africans, particularly those who are poorer and black, face daily possibilities of robbery, sexual violence, road accidents, unemployment, political coercion, power outages, incompetent healthcare and failures to enforce rights and legal protections. Even in this riskier and more uncertain place, though, the realities of danger and the way in which we communicate about it are often mismatched. The things we fear and the things that actually threaten us are not always the same in size or appearance. The allure of myth, urban legend, rumour and conspiracy theory sometimes outweighs the need to carefully manage and communicate issues of fear and danger. The particular features of moral panics and tales of risk in comparatively insecure places in South Africa are often contextually specific, but their emotional power recurs in familiar ways in all sorts of locations. Risk, anxiety and moral panic are not restricted to Africa, to the south or to the north (or to the 'south' or 'north' within individual cities and countries) but rather flow between and among locations, transmitted by elites, by popular culture, by social media and by formal and informal networks of relationality. Indeed, it is clear that the people in these stories are embedded in hypermodern cultures of fear that draw on but often misrecognise or exaggerate the realities of the risks we face. These cultures depend on media proliferation. They provide us with a collective language to discuss anxieties, insecurities, fears and threats, and are by now a common feature of the experience of late modernity.

We cannot know whether increased risk adds to increased existential fear, or whether anxiety is *empirically* higher in Johannesburg than in Cairo, New York, Shanghai or Mumbai. What we can say, however, is that there is a connection between the way people feel in different cities; nervousness, worry and insecurity are not restricted to the wealthy or the middle class, but affect us all. Concurrently, we know that the majority of public conversation about these powerful emotional conditions centralises those who have the privilege to monopolise media and political discourse. As this book has made clear, scholars of media and fear need to look beyond the wealthy (white/western) world if we are to properly understand the way in which emotion structures contemporary politics and culture. In order to think about modernity, we must become capable of recentring the old colonial map that places a shrunken Africa out of the way and at the bottom of the world. 'In the present moment, it is the Global South that affords privileged insight into the workings of the world at large' (Comaroff and Comaroff 2015, p. 1): those workings include both modernity and the culture of fear that is tied to it.

When it comes to the sources of our fears, the South Africans in these four case studies exhibit the same tendencies of deferral and misrecognition as people elsewhere, who live with lower daily experiences of risk. We are just as likely to look away from what really threatens our safety and ease in favour of an emotional overinvestment in religious, mythic, dramatic or lurid explanations for the causes of risk. Different types of people believe powerfully in different ethnosociological (Waters 1997) explanations for threatening phenomena, as we search for ways to make our worlds more explicable. Those explanations may turn out to be terrifying in themselves. But at the same time they may, by virtue of their often spectacular natures, actually allow us to defer for a little longer the realities of our fears: that the risk, crime and violence we experience are not exceptional (although they should be); that those who threaten us are not monsters, but everyday people who are more like us than we are willing to admit; and that, all too often, our suffering has no greater meaning. Like religion, nationalism and other powerful ideologies that bind people together, the culture of fear allows us to make sense of some of the otherwise overwhelming experiences that comprise contemporary life.

The case studies in this book are all built around the tendency to (sometimes intentionally) mistake what we fear, to displace conventional threats or issues with the mythic, spectacular or dramatic. For the small elite behind Afrikaner 'rights groups', the ghastly commonness of rural brutality morphs into a conspiracy theory of fictional genocidaires, recasting the deaths of white people on farms as the first wave of a looming race war. The murders of young women at the hands of young men are blamed on monstrous Satanists and never connected to endemic male violence. In Alexandra everyday property theft is rewritten as the work of sinister drug gangs with occult tendencies and disconcerting insider knowledge. Melville's nervous suburbanites turn homeless people and car guards into criminal desperadoes and emblems of the larger collapse of civilised – for which read white – society. Real deaths, real crimes, real threats and real risks become strange and fantastic. Nebulous, evasive worries about precarity, belonging and being left behind are displaced onto seemingly concrete concerns with recognisably visible folk devils at their cores.

And, of course, all four cases are suffused with misrecognitions and denials of the realities of racial apartheid and colonial history in contemporary South Africa. Wealthy white people subtly disavow their complicity in current socioeconomic injustice or explicitly reject the notion that reparation, both psychic and economic, is a necessary part of approaching the historical wounds that continue to trouble this country. Black and poor South Africans widely share stories of risk and threat, but despite many people's potent knowledges of formal apartheid and the unmissable daily experiences of racial inequity, these stories seldom foreground the structural and historical conditions that underlie them, the effects of centuries of white colonial domination that still impact so powerfully on social-spatial formation. Notwithstanding the highly attuned sense of race that has long marked South African cultures, in these instances the role of race – or more particularly the ongoing power of whiteness to terrorise and expel – remains to some extent obscured, misrecognised, vague.

As the studies in this book reveal, emotional responses to social conditions depend on the building of collective narrative, on story-making as a form of community-making. Spreading and sharing narrative seems to be crucial to our experiences of anxiety, risk and moral panic. So many of us engage in local or long distance acts of transmission, create or participate in hypothetical digital communities, pass on information that arrives without the need for verification, where a convincing meme or forwarded message bears the same heft and value as a story heard from a friend. Stories gain in importance as they gain audiences; from newspaper reports to Facebook posts to YouTube videos, shares and likes suggest not just the social currency but also the affective veracity of these narrative forms. According to Hayden White, 'Narrative might well be considered a solution to a problem of general human concern, namely ... the problem of fashioning human experience into a form assimilable to structures of meaning that are generally human' (quoted in Musila 2015, p. 5). The creating, telling and sharing of these stories of fear are intrinsically human activities, inflated to epic size and made ever more transferrable by the viral qualities of the media we share and consume so hungrily.

Of course, not all of us have access to media and the technologies that proliferate it. One of the unavoidable oversights of a book like this, whose objects are media forms and whose primary method is the analysis of media texts, is that it excludes the narratives of those who are excluded from the networked, mediatised landscape of the late modern world. A media discourse project cannot foreground the voices of people on the margins, equally subject to the emotional conditions of urban life but without access to the techniques, devices and platforms that many others use to share and spread these narratives. Future research should engage alternative methodologies to take into account the experiences of risk and anxiety of those who are most often represented as the sources for these fears for other urban dwellers.

Overwhelmingly, then, these stories of moral panic, risk and anxiety tell us something about how it feels to live in South Africa right now. They help us to understand how we use media, narrative, identity and belonging to locate ourselves in our societies, and how experiences of emotion, particularly collective and amplified emotion, shape our perceptions, our politics and our personal space. Countless numbers of such stories need to be told, from countless places. In their telling – in turning our lens onto the emotional experiences that comprise daily life in an era of late modernity, with all the insecurity, inequality, aspiration, fear and hope that that entails – we can hope to see more clearly our life worlds, our politics, our selves.

Note

1 The World Health Organization estimates that maternal mortality dropped by about 44 per cent between 1990 and 2015 (WHO 2019a), while 'global average life expectancy increased by 5.5 years between

2000 and 2016, the fastest increase since the 1960s' (WHO 2019b). While huge inequalities remain, since 1990 an estimated 6.2 billion people have had access to a water source designed to protect against contamination (WHO / Unicef 2019), the highest in human history.

Appendices

Appendix 1: 'White genocide' videos

Full name	Post details	Description & URL	Shortened name
'Unite Red October 2013 – Port Elizabeth, South Africa'	2.30 minutes, posted on 12 October 2013 by FanJan C	Homemade video of Red October protest featuring interviews with attendees. www.youtube.com/watch?v=-hK5vDgjzo	'Port Elizabeth'
'Red October, a peaceful march to the Union Buildings Pretoria'	30.53 minutes, posted on 13 October 2013 by Focus 2 Frame	Footage of main Red October march featuring Sunette Bridges' and Steve Hofmeyr's speeches and presentation of memorandum to police official. www.youtube.com/watch?v=Tz9lK9V80tQ	'Union Buildings'
'Steve Hofmeyr interview during Red October march, Pretoria'	3.03 minutes, posted on 15 October 2013 by Praag.org	Steve Hofmeyr interviewed by international media after march. www.youtube.com/watch?v=fgRdTdj76ew	'Pretoria interview'
'White plight in South Africa?'	39.30 minutes, posted on 15 October 2013 by Al Jazeera	Special on Red October featuring Sunette Bridges and Dan Roodt, among others. http://stream.aljazeera.com/story/201310152352-0023111	'The Stream'
'Judge for yourself S11E12 – The Red October campaign and white genocide'	12.24 minutes, posted on 23 October 2013 by eNCA News	Television interview with Sunette Bridges. www.youtube.com/watch?v=q9xNxWr3MfU	'eNCA interview'
'Dagbreek: Debat – Plaasmoorde'	19.15 minutes, posted on 23 October 2013 by kyknettv	Afrikaans television debate on Red October, featuring Sunette Bridges. www.youtube.com/watch?v=Cp2mOvHakA0&t=34s	'KykNet panel'

Title	Details	Description	Label
'Season 4 Episode 33: Red October'	15.19 minutes, posted on 30 October 2013 by StreetTalkSA	Footage of Cape Town march and sit-down interviews with a group of participants. www.youtube.com/watch?v=_x1kFiy94xQ&t=11s	'Street Talk'
'Mediakonferensie rakende onteiening sonder vergoeding en plaasmoorde: Ernst Roets'	16.23 minutes, posted on 20 March 2018 by AfriForum	AfriForum press conference on land expropriation, featuring Ernst Roets. www.youtube.com/watch?v=slG2JvPV4Ig&t=270s	'Land expropriation'
'Farm murders: feedback from Washington – setting the facts straight'	31.10 minutes, posted on 5 May 2018 by AfriForum	Ernst Roets' personal video response to critiques of AfriForum's US tour. www.youtube.com/watch?v=Zln7f8bgt5I&t=198s	'Washington feedback'
'MELTDOWN from South African leftists as Afriforum tours USA'	21.37 minutes, posted on 7 May 2018 by Willem Petzer	Willem Petzer's homemade video response to critiques of AfriForum's US tour. www.youtube.com/watch?v=ZiOeX8rBAr8	'Left wing meltdown'
'Ernst Roets on Fox News'	7.11 minutes, posted on 16 May 2018 by AfriForum	Ernst Roets interviewed by Tucker Carlson about farm attacks and land expropriation. www.youtube.com/watch?v=9dMYhLZb96Q&t=18s	'Fox News'

Appendix 2: 'Satanist murder' newspaper articles

Beeld

- Van Wyk, P. 'Groep snap satanisme nie, hoor hof', 20 April 2013, p. 5
- Zwecker, W. 'Kirsty: Dit voel of iets my beheer', 1 May 2013, p. 6
- Zwecker, W. 'Niemand glo dat hulle Kirsty sou offer', 30 April 2013, p. 6

Citizen

- Mashabane, P. '"Satanic" plan was to "burn, eat body"', 17 November 2011, p. 3
- Mashabane, P. '"Satanic" case may go to High Court', 2 November 2011, p. 3
- Mashabane, P. 'Satanic ritual murderers jailed for 17 years', 30 March 2012, p. 3
- Mashabane, P. 'Why choose Kirsty, asks mom', 27 October 2011, p. 6
- No author. 'Satanic panic', 21 February 2014, p. 3
- No author. 'Dobsonville murders "may not be Satanism"', 25 February 2014, p. 4
- No author. 'Movie inspired attempt to sell souls to the devil', 18 October 2013, p. 2
- No author. 'Prayers for healing at slain girls' funeral', 26 February 2016, p. 2
- No author. 'Soweto teen fit to stand trial', 18 June 2014
- No author. 'Stamp out Satanism in schools, parents plead', 24 March 2014, p. 3
- No author. 'Teen killers back in court', 11 April 2014, p. 18
- No author. 'When is enough, enough?', 28 July 2014, p. 12

Daily Dispatch

- Fuzile, B. 'Women flee murder village', 27 April 2010, p. 1

Daily News

- Kubheka, A. '"Satanic" killing case in camera', 20 March 2012, p. 5
- Serrao, A. 'Girl set alight in "satanic ritual"', 24 October 2011, p. 3

Iol

- Serra, G. 'Victim's family outraged after alleged Satanic killer gets bail', 22 June 2018. www.iol.co.za/news/south-africa/west ern-cape/victims-family-outraged-after-alleged-satanic-killer-gets-bail-15631269

New Age

- Diale, L. 'Council of Churches concerned over state of nation', 28 February 2014, p. 9
- Dube, D. 'Lungisa, wife in court', 14 April 2014, p. 3
- Madibogo, J. 'Teens in dock for suspected satanic killing', 9 April 2014, p. 6
- Nkosi, N. '"Satanists" back in court', 24 February 2014, p. 6
- Nkosi, N. '"Satanic" murders', 21 February 2014, p. 6
- Nkosi, N. 'Teen boys nabbed for "satanic" murders', 21 February 2014, p. 1
- Nkosi, N. '48 occult crime investigations on the go', 27 February 2014, p. 5
- No author. 'Satanic killer apologises', 11 October 2013, p. 3

Saturday Argus

- Du, S. 'Victim "agreed to being sacrificed"', 27 April 2013, p. 6

Saturday Star

- Bega, S. 'The devil destroyed us', 9 November 2013, p. 1
- Maphumulo, S. 'Anguish of two mothers over occult killings', 12 October 2013, p. 4

– Mokati, N. '"Satanic" murders have everyone terrified', 22 February 2014, p. 2

Sowetan

– Mazibila, S. 'Prayers to cast out Satan', 19 March 2014, p. 2
– Moeng, K. 'Satanic crimes on the rise', 27 February 2014, p. 2
– Selebi, M. 'Arrested pastor took cops to other accused in girl's killing', 7 August 2012, p. 6
– Seleka, N. 'Kill pupil murderers', 26 February 2014, p. 3

Star

– Du, S. 'I tried to protect Kirsty, court told', 22 May 2013, p. 11
– Du, S. 'Tough girl, Cleopatra, guardian angel ...', 8 November 2013, p. 8
– Germaner, S. 'Satanic ritual survivor goes home at last', 18 January 2012, p. 7
– Germaner, S. '15-year-old girl charged in Joburg satanic rite murder', 24 November 2011, p. 10
– Molosankwe, B. '"Satanic ritual" pair in court today', 25 October 2011, p. 3
– Molosankwe, B. 'Two accused in "satanic ritual" killing denied bail', 18 November 2011, p. 6
– Mooki, O. 'Four in court over girl in "satan ritual"', 26 October 2011, p. 2
– Motumi, M. 'Deadly "power" talk', 18 October 2013, p. 5
– Motumi, M. 'Justice for all', 8 November 2013, p. 1
– No author. '13-year-old girl charged with murder and rape', 2 December 2013, p. 1
– No author. 'Brake fluid not a drug, high court told in Satanism trial', 5 November 2013, p. 2
– No author. 'Rise in satanic crimes around black youth', 27 February 2014
– No author. 'The village must speak', 21 February 2014, p. 14
– No author. 'Tolerance has its limits', 28 February 2014, p. 14
– Olifant, K. 'Girls' "Satanic" end', 20 February 2014, p. 1

- Olifant, K. 'Hundreds at funeral of slain girls', 26 February 2014, p. 6
- Olifant, K. 'Satanic arrests', 21 February 2014, p. 1
- Olifant, K. 'Teens sentenced for satanic murders', 27 May 2015
- Taylor, T. 'Accused testifies in satanic killing case', 11 October 2013, p. 2

The Times

- Hosken, G. 'Satanists killing us off', 12 October 2012, p. 2
- Mailula, N. 'Devil's disciples guilty of murder', *Times*, 8 November 2013, p. 6

Witness

- Zwecker, W. '"Satan" ritual teen dies', 29 October 2011, p. 4

Appendix 3: 'plasma gang' newspaper and online articles

Alex News

- Siso, S. and Madisha, D. 'Plasma gang strikes again', 12 September 2013. http://alexnews.co.za/12746/plasma-gang-strikes-again/

Eyewitness News

- No author. 'EWN busts plasma powder myth', 25 September 2013. http://ewn.co.za/2013/09/25/plasma-gang-myth-busted
- No author. 'Cops dismiss plasma TV drug link', 30 August 2013. http://ewn.co.za/2013/08/30/police-dismiss-plasma-gang-claims

IoL

- Roane, B. 'Plasma TV powder drug craze', 29 August 2013. www.iol.co.za/news/crime-courts/plasma-tv-powder-drug-craze-1.1570154#.U_cssfmSySp

Mpumalanga News

- Nkalanga, P. 'Plasma TV gang terrorised residents', 5 September 2013. http://mpumalanganews.co.za/10017/plasma-tv-gang-terrorized-residents/

New Age

- No author. 'Plasma gang a rumour: police', 29 August 2013. www.thenewage.co.za/105892–1007–53-Plasma_gang_a_rumour_police

Saturday Star

- Mokati, N. 'Xenophobia erupts over plasma TV gang', 31 August 2013, p. 4

– Mokati, N. 'Chemicals in stolen plasma not used to make drugs', 7 September 2013, p. 8

Sowetan

– No author. 'Plasma gang "a rumour": police', 30 August 2013. www.sowetanlive.co.za/news/2013/08/30/plasma-gang-a-rumour-police

Techcentral

– Wilson, C. 'Plasma TV drugs myth busted', 25 September 2013. www.techcentral.co.za/plasma-drugs-myth-busted/43873/

The Star

– Olifant, K., Roane, B. and Liebenberg, J. '"Plasma gang" believed to be behind home attacks', 30 August 2013, p. 2

Appendix 4: posts on I Love Melville Facebook group

Original post	Date	Shortened name
'The window washers along empire [Rd] are getting a bit ridiculous. Are the metros [police] not supposed to do something about this. why should I support peoples drug habits?'	26 September 2017	'Window washers'
'Hi everyone… Our domestic lady has unfortunately left us after 3 years for a full time job. We have big shoes to fill as our 4 dogs absolutely adored her. Tasks include usual house cleaning, laundry, ironing etc. Love someone that takes initiative around the house and MUST LOVE DOGS… not just tolerate them. Please PM me only if you have someone you would highly recommend. Thank you in advance!'	27 September 2017	'Dog-loving domestic'
Link to local newspaper article: 'Business owners' talk about purse-snatching in Melville'	3 October 2017	'Pavement purse-snatchers'
'If you remember Roxies on Main Rd, well, besides all the filth outside, the wall at the side is being demolished brick by brick!'	4 October 2017	'Roxy's wall'
'Good morning. My domestic worker went back to her family in Zimbabwe. Does anyone know of a reliable, experienced and hard working domestic worker who is available 3 days a week? Thanks.'	6 October 2017	'Reliable domestic'
'My young friend Siyabonga Cyaa. Siya is a fresh entrepreneur. The boys on the ball. Dear folks of Melville please support the kid in his endeavours.' [accompanied by close-up photograph of boy]	17 October 2017	'Siyabonga street seller'

'Hi Community, I'm sure I've been too work focused in the last few days, does anyone know what the helicopters and busy roads are all about this morning? I'm on the Bamboo/Service Station side of Melville.'	22 October 2017	'Busy roads'
'I have recommended my gardener Morris, on this group. Unfortunately I have discovered he worked for only two or three hours a day on full pay. As I trusted him at my home while at the office, I am really disappointed, as he is a really good worker. I terminated his employment and he has now started phoning me and is very aggressive and threatening. Just a warning to others who might employ him. It saddens me to have to post this, as I was really impressed with his gardening skills.'	26 October 2017	'Bad gardener'
'I had lunch at Ocean Basket on Main rd. Melville today. It was like sitting in a slum looking at the view. Derelict buildings, filthy and unattractive. No wonder the manager was concerned as very view [sic] people come there anymore and they are struggling. Something needs to be done and urgently. Crime around this area has also escalated. Not pleasant as it used to be.'	2 November 2017	'Ocean Basket'
'If anyone is willing to donate any English/Afrikaans books suitable for high school learners, please let me know. I am willing to collect, even if it is just one book. Would love to start a mini library in my classroom. [smile emoji]'	7 November 2017	'School book donation'

(continued)

Original post	Date	Shortened name
'Please remove if not allowed. I know there is no Secondary School in Melville, therefor [sic] I am posting this if I may. I have been involved in the Diepdale Secondary School in Soweto since 2017. Together with my clients, we refurbished a dilapidated science laboratory. I think it is natural that after working together for more than two years, one becomes close to staff and learners; I have become very fond of the Principal, Mr Johannes Munakisi, whom I have learned to respect for so many reasons. I respect him for trying to give his learners the best, in schooling and in life. He is so passionate and committed to making their lives better. I got a call from him yesterday. The school's Grade 12 dance is on 1 December in Midrand. He wants this evening to be the best, first night of the rest of their lives. He also wants to encourage Grade 11's to work hard and look forward to an education and a Grade 12 dance where they will all shine bright! However, there are many Grade 12 learners who cannot afford beautiful clothes and accessories. We have a simple request: If anyone has any clothes they no longer use; dresses, make-up, shirts, pants, jackets, hand bags, jewellery etc, would you be willing to donate it to the school? I hope I am not breaking any rules, but I promised Mr Munakasi that I would ask. Please let know. I will arrange for a collection point and deliver any donations to the school.'	17 November 2017	'Grade 12 dance'
'Car guard at Melville Spar tried to car jam/remote jam me. Please be vigilant.'	1 December 2017	'Car guard remote'

'The driver of this car tried to sell me firecrackers at the Shell garage in Main Rd. I raised my concerns about animals and that they probably needs a permit to sell firecrackers, after which he said "animals are evil". When I called the police, he threatened that he was going to "stab" me. He managed to get away with the help of one of the petrol attendants because his car couldn't start. Garage management called CSS [private security] when I brought it to their attention. Be on the lookout, and please don't support his "business". [accompanied by photographs of face of man in car, and of petrol station worker pushing car]	31 December 2017	'Man selling firecrackers'
'Hi everyone, my daughter [teenager's name linked to Facebook profile] was violently mugged last night on 5th Avenue. Her phone & ID were stolen. We tracked the criminal from 27 Boxes to Main rd. If anyone comes across her ID- please message me. Many thanks.'	31 December 2017	'Teen mugged'
'Wouldn't it be cool if we could do the same ...?' [accompanied by photo of sign in the Free State town of Clarens, reading 'Clarens Community Notice: Central Clarens Business Area is a car washer, car guard and beggar free area. Please support this initiative']	3 January 2018	'Clarens'
'Hi i was robbed on 5th Avenue close to corner 7th. The robbers went towards 6th street and 4th avenue. If anyone find my wallet or keys in the bushes please let me know. im fine.'	11 January 2018	'5th Avenue robbery'
'It feels like crime is on the increase. 2 cars broken into last night outside [local restaurant] Perron. And again this afternoon around 3pm. ... concerned'	17 January 2018	'Crime increasing'
'To whomever drove into the back of my parked little Citroen C2 this afternoon, thank you. Thank you for breaking the boot so that I cannot open it. Thanks for the black scratches on my little car. And most importantly, thanks for not leaving your details so you could share in the cost of fixing everything! Thanks!'	18 January 2018	'Car smash'

(continued)

Original post	Date	Shortened name
'Hullo neighbours. 'Tis I. This time I seek accommodations for myself. I was happy where I am until I was burgled over the festival season. I have been burgled every year around the same time, but in different locations, for the past 3 successive years. I am a nervous wreck and pretty security conscious as a result. I was considering moving to Australia but... meh! My church is in the area so I have no intention of leaving Melville. If you have a furnished cottage/apartment below R6800pm incl water and power, please let me know. I am struggling to sleep without taking pharmaceuticals in this crime scene. PS. I am a not-so-young professional, no baggage except my suitcases, and sober habits. I am generally quiet except when I speak with other Zulus on the phone. I have no pets but cats tend to like me (in our culture, that's witchcraft) and dogs too. I am a baker so if you like cakes, we'll get on famously. I hope I have done well in selling myself as a dream tenant. Thanks!'	24 January 2018	'Dream tenant'
'Dear Melville. Did you know??? Why has [security company] CSS only got one guy in the patrol cars instead of 2? That was the big selling point when CSS 1st arrived; in that you can't drive and patrol effectively with just one guy and it is also not safe for the unit patrolling. Furthermore if there is only one guy it is now cheaper for the security company why have we not seen a discount in what we are paying, however saying that that is not the point or what we want! We want what was originally agreed to and paid for! 2 guys in a patrol car not one! We have had 1 car stolen last week And 2 cars hub caps taken within the last 2 weeks on 5th close to 9st! also a number of great proactive CSS guards have resigned due to upper management issues. This is concerning! [Name of company manager linked to Facebook page] get your act together crime has gotten worse since you guys took over and you have started to take short cuts! 1 person per car'	26 January 2018	'One guard per car'

Post	Date	Theme
'Hello fellow Melvillians, can anyone fill me in on new security company HIMA who have foot patrols on 7th and are really quite aggressive with [anyone] they deem undesirable. Who are paying for these guys? I chatted with Mohammad who drives around in a bakkie and he told me that all street guards need to bring their ID and that they will be taken to Brixton police station for fingerprints and be issued with an identity card and HIMA colours. This was 2 weeks ago and nothing has happened despite some of the car guards bringing in their ID. Sounds a bit dodgy to me.'	28 January 2018	'New security company'
'Hello guys, I am wanting to give back to the community, I just want to know from the community if there are any organisations, schools, learners, shelters or just citizens in general who need help in any way. Myself and a few other individuals are open to help or assist. Please if you know of anyone who needs help, please could you send me a personal message. Thank you so much, hope you have an awesome Thursday.'	1 February 2018	'Giving back'
'I have tried the normal things but there is no other option! This man's name is THOMAS SANTILE. He is a Mosaic Artist and we plannend [sic] to work with him, agreed on a design and also continued to work with him as soon as this 1st part was ready. Big job. We paid a deposit to buy tiles and tile cutters, cement etc. After that THOMAS disappeared and went home to see family, using our money. He worked in Melville for some time, but also disappeared without notice. He told me he worked in Sophiatown, but when I went to see him nobody knew him. Now his friends tell me he is broke, no money to buy materials, food, and again disappeared. Doesn't pick up his phone, reply to Whatsapp what he usually does..... nothing. Does anybody know where he is DON'T DO BUSINESS WITH THIS GUY and if you meet him, tell him that we are going to start legal action top get our money and pour [sic] tools back. His name THOMAS SANTILE from Zimbabwe...' [accompanied by photograph of artist posing in front of mosaic]	12 February 2018	'Mosaic artist'

(continued)

Original post	Date	Shortened name
'Please everyone be careful at this ATM near the melville spar. Just witnessed a credit card theft where the victim was almost run over by the thieves fleeing in their white audi without plates. The guys grabbed a tourist's card, jumped into their car and when he ran after them he tried to jump on the bonnet of the vehicle and he was thrown off of it. While he was not badly injured, the thieves escaped and he is understandably very upset. I also want to add that the parking guards in the lot didn't even bother to check on the man who had just been thrown off the front of a car. Luckily the centre manager went to go check on the victim as did some of the bystanders and myself, but I will never give another cent to those guys. 10111 also did a stellar job, as when I gave my phone to the victim to report the crime, they just told him to cancel his credit card and hung up. I know of another friend whose card was stolen [at] this ATM, so everyone please be wary.'	17 February 2018	'ATM robbery'
'Your opinion on the sprinkler system installed over the sidewalk next to the old Roxys rhythm bar where the majority of the Melville homeless sleep? I noticed it yesterday as I took my hound for a trot.'	10 March 2018	'Sprinklers'

Bibliography

About AfriForum [online], 2018. *AfriForum*. Available from: www.afrifo rum.co.za/about/about-afriforum/ [Accessed 29 August 2018].

Africa Check, 2018. Factsheet: South Africa's Crime Statistics for 2017/18 [online]. *Africa Check*. Available from: https://africacheck.org/factsheets/ factsheet-south-africas-crime-statistics-for-2017–18/ [Accessed 14 December 2018].

Åhäll, L., 2018. Affect as Methodology: Feminism and the Politics of Emotion. *International Political Sociology*, 12 (1), 36–52.

Ahmed, S., 2004. Declarations of Whiteness: The Non-Performativity of Anti-Racism. *Borderlands*, 3 (2), n.p.

Ahmed, S., 2014. *The Cultural Politics of Emotion*. 2nd ed. Edinburgh: Edinburgh University Press.

Ahmed, S., 2015. Against Students. *The New Inquiry* (29 June), n.p.

Alexander, M.J., 2006. *Pedagogies of Crossing: Meditations on Feminism, Sexual Politics, Memory, and the Sacred*. Durham, NC: Duke University Press.

Alexander, P., Ceruti, C., Motseke, K., Phadi, M. and Wale, K., eds., 2013. *Class in Soweto*. Scottsville, South Africa: University of Kwazulu-Natal Press.

Alexandra [online], 2016. *Statistics South Africa*. Available from: www. statssa.gov.za/?page_id=4286 [Accessed 29 November 2016].

Altheide, D.L., 2002. *Creating Fear: News and the Construction of Crisis*. New York: Aldine de Gruyter.

Altheide, D.L., 2009. Moral Panic: From Sociological Concept to Public Discourse. *Crime, Media, Culture*, 5 (1), 79–99.

Anderson, B., 2006. *Imagined Communities: Reflections on the Origin and Spread of Nationalism*. London: Verso.

Antichrist [online], n.d. *IMDB.com*. Available from: www.imdb.com/title/ tt0474549/?ref_=fn_al_tt_3 [Accessed 13 August 2015].

Apel, D., 2004. *Imagery of Lynching: Black Men, White Women, and the Mob*. New Brunswick, NJ and London: Rutgers University Press.

Arendt, H., 1963. *Eichmann in Jerusalem: A Report on the Banality of Evil*. London: Penguin.

Assouad, L., Chancel, L. and Morgan, M., 2018. Extreme Inequality: Evidence from Brazil, India, the Middle East, and South Africa. *AEA Papers and Proceedings*, 108, 119–123.

Baderoon, G., 2015. *Regarding Muslims: From Slavery to Post-Apartheid*. Johannesburg: Wits University Press.

Ballard, R., 2002. Desegregating minds: white identities and urban change in the new South Africa. PhD thesis. University of Wales, Swansea.

Ballard, R., 2003. 'The elephant in the living room': the denial of the importance of race by whites in the new South Africa. Presentation to History and African Studies Seminar, University of KwaZulu-Natal, 18 March. https://phambo.wiser.org.za/seminars/ballard/2003.html.

Ballard, R., 2005. When in Rome: Claiming the Right to Define Neighbourhood Character in South Africa's Suburbs. *Transformation: Critical Perspectives on Southern Africa*, 57 (1), 64–87.

Ballard, R., 2010. 'Slaughter in the Suburbs': Livestock Slaughter and Race in Post-Apartheid Cities. *Ethnic and Racial Studies*, 33 (6), 1069–1087.

Banda, F. and Mawadza, A., 2014. 'Foreigners are Stealing our Birth Right': Moral Panics and the Discursive Construction of Zimbabwean Immigrants in South African Media. *Discourse & Communication*, 9 (1), 47–64.

Baskin, J., 2018. Dutton's Priority Refugees. *Arena Magazine*, 154 (June), n.p.

Bauman, Z., 2005. *Liquid Life*. Cambridge and Malden, MA: Polity Press.

Bauman, Z., 2006. *Liquid Fear*. Cambridge and Malden, MA: Polity Press.

Bauman, Z., 2007. *Liquid Times: Living in an Age of Uncertainty*. Cambridge: Polity Press.

Bauman, Z. and Donskis, L., 2013. *Moral Blindness: The Loss of Sensitivity in Liquid Modernity*. Cambridge: Polity Press.

Becker, H.S., 1995. Moral Entrepreneurs: The Creation and Enforcement of Deviant Categories. *In*: N.J. Herman, ed. *Deviance: A Symbolic Interactionist Approach*. Dix Hills, NY: General Hall, 169–178.

Bell, M., 2000. American Philanthropy, the Carnegie Corporation and Poverty in South Africa. *Journal of Southern African Studies*, 26 (3), 481–504.

Benedict, H., 1992. *Virgin or Vamp: How the Press Covers Sex Crimes*. New York: Oxford University Press.

Berger, A. and Kotkin, J., eds., 2018. *Infinite Suburbia*. New York: Princeton Architectural Press.

Berns, N., 2001. Degendering the Problem and Gendering the Blame: Political Discourse on Women and Violence. *Gender & Society*, 15 (2), 262–281.

Berntzen, L.E. and Sandberg, S., 2014. The Collective Nature of Lone Wolf Terrorism: Anders Behring Breivik and the Anti-Islamic Social Movement. *Terrorism and Political Violence*, 26 (5), 759–779.

Best, J. and Horiuchi, G.T., 1985. The Razor Blade in the Apple: The Social Construction of Urban Legends. *Social Problems*, 32 (5), 488–499.

Bickford-Smith, V., 2016. *The Emergence of the South African Metropolis: Cities and Identities in the Twentieth Century*. New York: Cambridge University Press.

Biko, S., 1988. *I Write What I Like*. London: Penguin.

Bogatsu, M., 2002. 'Loxion Kulcha': Fashioning Black Youth Culture in Post-Apartheid South Africa. *English Studies in Africa*, 45 (2), 1–11.

Bond, P., 2013. Sub-imperialism as Lubricant of Neoliberalism: South African 'Deputy Sheriff' Duty within Brics. *Third World Quarterly*, 34 (2), 251–270.

Boshoff, P., 2013. The Supernatural Detective: Witchcraft Crime Narratives in the Daily Sun. *Current Writing: Text and Reception in Southern Africa*, 25 (2), 164–175.

Bourdieu, P., 1984. *Distinction: A Social Critique of the Judgement of Taste*. Cambridge, MA: Harvard University Press.

Breckenridge, K., 2014. *Biometric State: The Global Politics of Identification and Surveillance in South Africa, 1850 to the Present*. Cambridge: Cambridge University Press.

Bremner, L., 2004. *Johannesburg: One City, Colliding Worlds*. Johannesburg: STE Pub.

Bremner, L., 2010. *Writing the City into Being*. Johannesburg: Fourthwall Books.

Brodie, N., 2020. *Femicide in South Africa*. Johannesburg: Kwela Books.

Brunvand, J.H., 1981. *The Vanishing Hitchhiker: American Urban Legends and Their Meanings*. New York: WW Norton & Company.

Bueckert, M., 2018. Flight of the Boers [online]. *Africa is a Country*. Available from: https://africasacountry.com/2018/05/flight-of-the-boers [Accessed 20 June 2019].

Burger, J., 2018. *Violent Crime on Farms and Smallholdings in South Africa*. Pretoria: Institute of Security Studies, Policy Brief 115. Available from: www.africaportal.org/publications/violent-crime-farms-and-small holdings-south-africa/ [Accessed 2 March 2020].

Burnett, S., 2018. Giving back the land: whiteness and belonging in contemporary South Africa. PhD thesis. University of the Witwatersrand, Johannesburg.

Burscher, B., 2016. 'Rhino Poaching Is Out of Control!' Violence, Race and the Politics of Hysteria in Online Conservation. *Environment and Planning A*, 48 (5), 979–998.

Caldeira, T., 2000. *City of Walls: Crime, Segregation and Citizenship in São Paulo*. Berkeley, CA: University of California Press.

Calitz, W., 2014. Rhetoric in the Red October campaign. Masters dissertation. University of Oregon, Oregon.

Carter, C., 1998. When the Extraordinary Becomes Ordinary: Everyday News of Sexual Violence. *In*: C. Carter, G. Branston and S. Allen, eds. *News, Gender and Power*. London: Routledge, 219–232.

Ceruti, C., 2013. Contemporary Soweto: Dimensions of Stratification. *In*: P. Alexander, C. Ceruti, K. Motseke, M. Phadi and K. Wale, eds. *Class in Soweto*. Scottsville, South Africa: University of Kwazulu-Natal Press, 55–95.

Ceruti, C. and Phadi, M., 2013. Models, Labels and Affordability. *In*: P. Alexander, C. Ceruti, K. Motseke, M. Phadi and K. Wale, eds. *Class in Soweto*. Scottsville, South Africa: University of Kwazulu-Natal Press, 142–163.

Chambers, R., 1997. The Unexamined. *In*: M. Hill, ed. *Whiteness: A Critical Reader*. New York and London: New York University Press, 187–203.

Chaurasiya, S.P., Pravana, N.K., Khanal, V. and Giri, D., 2019. Two Thirds of the Most Disadvantaged Dalit Population of Nepal Still Do Not Deliver in Health Facilities Despite Impressive Success in Maternal Health. *PLOS ONE*, 14 (6), e0217337.

Chilemba, E.M., 2015. Evictions in South Africa During 2014: An Analytical Narrative. *ESR Review: Economic and Social Rights in South Africa*, 16 (3), 3–6.

Chouliaraki, L., 2010. Post-Humanitarianism: Humanitarian Communication Beyond a Politics of Pity. *International Journal of Cultural Studies*, 13 (2), 107–126.

Chouliaraki, L., 2012a. The Theatricality of Humanitarianism: A Critique of Celebrity Advocacy. *Communication and Critical/Cultural Studies*, 9 (1), 1–21.

Chouliaraki, L., 2012b. *The Ironic Spectator: Solidarity in the Age of Post-Humanitarianism*. Cambridge: Polity Press.

Christie, N., 1986. The Ideal Victim. *In*: E.A. Fattah, ed. *From Crime Policy to Victim Policy*. London: Macmillan, 17–30.

Christopherson, S., 2008. The Fortress City: Privatized Spaces, Consumer Citizenship. *In*: A. Amin, ed. *Post-Fordism: A Reader*. Massachusetts: Wiley-Blackwell, 409–427.

Cock, J., 1989. *Maids and Madams: Domestic Workers Under Apartheid*. Revised ed. London: The Women's Press.

Cock, J., 2001. Gun Violence and Masculinity in Contemporary South Africa. *In*: R. Morrell, ed. *Changing Men in Southern Africa*. Pietermaritzburg, South Africa: University of Natal Press, 43–55.

Cohen, S., 1972. *Folk Devils and Moral Panics: The Creation of the Mods and Rockers*. Oxford: Martin Robertson.

Cohen, S., 2013. *States of Denial: Knowing about Atrocities and Suffering*. Cambridge: Polity Press.

Comaroff, J. and Comaroff, J.L., 1999. Occult Economies and the Violence of Abstraction: Notes from the South African Postcolony. *American Ethnologist*, 26 (2), 279–303.

Comaroff, J. and Comaroff, J.L., 2015. *Theory from the South: Or, How Euro-America Is Evolving Toward Africa*. New York and Oxford: Routledge.

Comaroff, J. and Comaroff, J.L., 2016. *The Truth about Crime: Sovereignty, Knowledge, Social Order*. Johannesburg: Witwatersrand University Press.

Conway, D., 2012. *Masculinities, Militarisation and the End Conscription Campaign: War Resistance in Apartheid South Africa*. Manchester: Manchester University Press.

Coplan, D., 1985. *In Township Tonight: South Africa's Black City Music and Theatre*. Johannesburg: Ravan Press.

Cornwell, G., 1996. George Webb Hardy's the Black Peril and the Social Meaning of 'Black Peril' in Early Twentieth-century South Africa. *Journal of Southern African Studies*, 22 (3), 441–453.

Couldry, N., 2000. *The Place of Media Power: Pilgrims and Witnesses of the Media Age*. Psychology Press.

Couldry, N. and Curran, J., 2003. The Paradox of Media Power. *In*: *Contesting Media Power: Alternative Media in a Networked World*. Maryland: Rowan and Littlefield, 3–15.

Crapanzano, V., 1985. *Waiting: The Whites of South Africa*. London: Granada.

Critcher, C., 2008. Moral Panic Analysis: Past, Present and Future. *Sociology Compass*, 2 (4), 1127–1144.

Critcher, C., 2011. For a Political Economy of Moral Panics. *Crime, Media, Culture*, 7 (3), 259–275.

Cuklanz, L.M. and Moorti, S., eds., 2009. *Local Violence, Global Media: Feminist Analyses of Gendered Representations*. New York: Peter Lang.

Daniels, J., 2017. Twitter and White Supremacy: A Love Story. *DAME Magazine*, October, n.p.

David, M., Rohloff, A., Petley, J. and Hughes, J., 2011. The Idea of Moral Panic – Ten Dimensions of Dispute. *Crime, Media, Culture*, 7 (3), 215–228.

Davis, G.P. and Steslow, K., 2014. HIV Medications as Drugs of Abuse. *Current Addiction Reports*, 1 (3), 214–219.

Dawson, A., 2006. Geography of Fear: Crime and the Transformation of Public Space in South Africa. *In*: S. Low and N. Smith, eds. *The Politics of Public Space*. New York and London: Routledge, 123–142.

Debord, G., 1994. *The Society of the Spectacle*. New York: Zone Books.

Department of Community Safety, 2014. Profile of Nyaope Users and Implications for Policing [online]. *GP Community Safety*. Available from: https://gpcommunitysafety.wordpress.com/2014/07/07/profile-of-nyaope-users-and-implications-for-policing/ [Accessed 7 January 2020].

Devarenne, N., 2009. Nationalism and the Farm Novel in South Africa, 1883–2004. *Journal of Southern African Studies*, 35 (3), 627–642.

DeYoung, M., 1998. Another Look at Moral Panics: The Case of Satanic Day Care Centers. *Deviant Behavior*, 19 (3), 257–278.

Dickinson, D., 2014. *A Different Kind of Aids: Folk and Lay Theories in South African Townships*. Johannesburg: Jacana Media.

Dixon, N., 2018. Stranger-ness and Belonging in a Neighbourhood WhatsApp Group. *Open Cultural Studies*, 1 (1), 493–503.

Dosekun, S., 2017. The Risky Business of Postfeminist Beauty. *In*: A.S. Elias, R. Gill and C. Scharff, eds. *Aesthetic Labour: Rethinking Beauty Politics in Neoliberalism*. London: Springer, 167–181.

Dosekun, S. and Iqani, M., 2020. The Politics and Aesthetics of Luxury in Africa. *In*: M. Iqani and S. Dosekun, eds. *African Luxury: Aesthetics and Politics*. London: Intellect Books, 1–17.

Douglas, M., 1984. *Purity and Danger: An Analysis of the Concepts of Pollution and Taboo*. London and New York: Routledge.

Dubow, S., 2015. Racial Irredentism, Ethnogenesis, and White Supremacy in High-Apartheid South Africa. *Kronos*, 41, 236–264.

Durington, M., 2009. Suburban Fear, Media and Gated Communities in Durban, South Africa. *Home Cultures*, 6 (1), 71–88.

Dyer, R., 1997. *White*. London: Routledge.

Eisenstadt, S.N., 2000. Multiple Modernities. *Daedalus*, 129 (1), 1–29.

Ellis, S. and ter Haar, G., 2004. *Worlds of Power: Religious Thought and Political Practice in Africa*. New York: Oxford University Press.

Essa, A., 2018. South African group under fire for lobbying US for white rights. *Al-Jazeera*, 15 May.

Falkof, N., 2013. Red October [online]. *Daily Maverick*. Available from: www.dailymaverick.co.za/opinionista/2013–10–07-red-october/ [Accessed 7 September 2018].

Falkof, N., 2015a. *Satanism and Family Murder in Late Apartheid South Africa: Imagining the End of Whiteness*. London: Palgrave.

Falkof, N., 2015b. Out the Back: Race and Reinvention in Johannesburg's Garden Cottages. *International Journal of Cultural Studies*, 19 (6), 627–642.

Falkof, N., 2018a. On Moral Panic: Some Directions for Further Development. *Critical Sociology*, 46 (2), 225–239.

Falkof, N., 2018b. Sex and the Devil: Homosexuality, Satanism and Moral Panic in Late Apartheid South Africa. *Men and Masculinities*, 22 (2), 273–293.

Falkof, N., Phadke, S. and Roy, S., eds., 2022. *Intimacy & Injury: In the Wake of #MeToo in India and South Africa*. Manchester: Manchester University Press.

Falkof, N. and van Staden, C., 2020. Traversing the Anxious City. *In*: N. Falkof and C. van Staden, eds. *Anxious Joburg: The Inner Lives of a Global South City*. Johannesburg: Wits University Press, 1–18.

Feldman, A., 2003. Strange Fruit: The South African Truth Commission and the Demonic Economies of Violence. *In*: B. Kapferer, ed. *Beyond Rationalism: Rethinking Magic, Witchcraft and Sorcery*. New York and Oxford: Berghahn Books, 234–265.

Fernandes, L. and Mokwena, K., n.d. Locus of control and treatment implications for nyaope users. Presentation to Medical Research Council. Available from: www.mrc.ac.za/adarg/SACENDUpresentations/2015/LucyFernandes.pdf [Accessed 7 January 2020].

Fischer, B., McCann, B. and Auyero, J., 2014. *Cities from Scratch: Poverty and Informality in Urban Latin America*. Durham, NC: Duke University Press.

Fitzmaurice, C.J., 2015. Conspicuous Consumption and Distinction, History of. *In*: J.D. Wright, ed. *International Encyclopedia of the Social & Behavioral Sciences*. 2nd ed. Oxford: Elsevier, 695–699.

Foucault, M., 1997. *Society Must Be Defended: Lectures at the Collège de France, 1975–1976*. New York: Picador.

Fox, C., 2002. The Race to Truth: Disarticulating Critical Thinking from Whiteliness. *Pedagogy*, 2 (2), 197–212.

Frankenberg, R., 1993. *White Women, Race Matters: The Social Construction of Whiteness*. Minneapolis, MN: University of Minnesota Press.

Furedi, F., 2006. *The Culture of Fear Revisited*. London: Continuum.

Gaonkar, D.P., 2002. Toward New Imaginaries: An Introduction. *Public Culture*, 14 (1), 1–19.

Gedye, L., 2018. White genocide: how the big lie spread to the US and beyond. *Mail & Guardian*, 23 March.

Gibson, M., 2002. British Theatre and the Red Peril: The Portrayal of Communism 1917–1945. *Theatre Journal*, 54 (4), 659–661.

Giddens, A., 1991. *Modernity and Self-Identity*. Cambridge: Polity Press.

Gikandi, S., 2002. Reason, Modernity and the African Crisis. *In*: P. Probst, H. Schmidt and J.-G. Deutsch, eds. *African Modernities: Entangled Meanings in Current Debate*. Oxford: James Currey, 135–157.

Gilchrist, E., Bannister, J., Ditton, J. and Farrall, S., 1998. Women and the 'Fear of Crime': Challenging the Accepted Stereotype. *The British Journal of Criminology*, 38 (2), 283–298.

Gilchrist, K., 2010. 'Newsworthy' Victims? *Feminist Media Studies*, 10 (4), 373–390.

Giliomee, H., 2003. *The Afrikaners, Biography of a People*. London: Hurst and Company.

Ginsburg, R., 2011. *At Home with Apartheid: The Hidden Landscapes of Domestic Service in Johannesburg*. Charlottesville, VA: University of Virginia Press.

Glassner, B., 2010. *The Culture of Fear: Why Americans Are Afraid of the Wrong Things: Crime, Drugs, Minorities, Teen Moms, Killer Kids, Mutant Microbes, Plane Crashes, Road Rage, & So Much More*. New York: Basic Books.

Gobodo-Madikizela, P., 1999. Legacies of violence: an in-depth analysis of two case studies based on interviews with perpetrators of a 'necklace' murder and with Eugene De Kock. PhD thesis. University of Cape Town, Cape Town.

Gobodo-Madikizela, P., 2003. *A Human Being Died That Night: A Story of Forgiveness*. Cape Town: New Africa Books.

Goode, E. and Ben-Yehuda, N., 2009. *Moral Panics: The Social Construction of Deviance*. Oxford: Wiley-Blackwell.

Gould, C., 2018. South Africa Is At War with Itself [online]. *Institute for Security Studies Africa*. Available from: https://issafrica.org/author/chandre-gould [Accessed 16 December 2019].

Gouws, A., 2015. The Public Discourse on Rape in South Africa. *In*: M. Verwoerd and C. Lopes, eds. *Sexualized Violence in the National Debate*. Cape Town: Heinrich Boll Foundation, 66–75.

Gqola, P.D., 2009. 'The Difficult Task of Normalizing Freedom': Spectacular Masculinities, Ndebele's Literary/Cultural Commentary and Post-Apartheid Life. *English in Africa*, 36 (1), 61–76.

Gqola, P.D., 2015. *Rape: A South African Nightmare*. Johannesburg: MF Books.

Gqola, P.D., 2021. *Female Fear Factory*. Johannesburg: Melinda Ferguson Books.

Graybill, L.S., 1995. *Religion and Resistance Politics in South Africa*. Westport, CT and London: Praeger.

Grosholz, J. and Kubrin, C.E., 2007. Crime in the News: How Crimes, Offenders and Victims are Portrayed in the Media. *Journal of Criminal Justice and Popular Culture*, 14, 59–83.

Guardian, 2018. South Africa demands Peter Dutton retract 'offensive' statement on white farmer plight. *The Guardian*, 15 March.

Haider, S., 2016. The Shooting in Orlando, Terrorism or Toxic Masculinity (or Both?). *Men and Masculinities*, 19 (5), 555–565.

Halberstam, J., 1998. *Female Masculinity*. Durham, NC: Duke University Press.

Hale, C., 1996. Fear of Crime: A Review of the Literature. *International Review of Victimology*, 4 (2), 79–150.

Halim, S. and Meyers, M., 2010. News Coverage of Violence Against Muslim Women: A View from the Arabian Gulf. *Communication, Culture & Critique*, 3 (1), 85–104.

Harvey, D., 2008. The Right to the City. *New Left Review* (53), 23–40.

Hate Speech Archives [online], n.d. *AfriForum*. https://afriforum.co.za/en/tag/hate-speech/ [Accessed 29 August 2018].

Heer, B., 2017. Shopping Malls as Social Space: New Forms of Public Life in Johannesburg. *In*: O. Moreillon, A. Muller and L. Stiebel, eds. *Cities in Flux*. Zürich: Lit Verlag, 101–121.

Hirsch, V., 2016. Interview with Valerie Hirsch. Skype.

Hjelm, T., Bogdan, H., Dyrendal, A. and Petersen, J.A., 2009. Nordic Satanism and Satanism Scares: The Dark Side of the Secular Welfare State. *Social Compass*, 56 (4), 515–529.

Hook, D., 2007. *Foucault, Psychology and the Analytics of Power*. Basingstoke: Palgrave Macmillan.

hooks, bell, 1992. *Black Looks: Race and Representation*. Boston, MA: South End Press.

hooks, bell, 1995. *Killing Rage: Ending Racism*. New York: Henry Holt.

Hornberger, J., 2008. Nocturnal Johannesburg. *In*: S. Nuttall and A. Mbembe, eds. *Johannesburg: The Elusive Metropolis*. Durham, NC: Duke University Press.

Howard, J.A., 1984. The 'Normal' Victim: The Effects of Gender Stereotypes on Reactions to Victims. *Social Psychology Quarterly*, 47 (3), 270–281.

Hsu, L.-Y., 2014. Ketamine Use in Taiwan: Moral Panic, Civilizing Processes, and Democratization. *International Journal of Drug Policy*, 25 (4), 819–822.

Hunter, M., 2016. The Race for Education: Class, White Tone, and Desegregated Schooling in South Africa. *Journal of Historical Sociology*, 29 (3), 319–358.

Hyslop, J., 2003. The White Poor at the End of Apartheid: The Collapse of the Myth of Afrikaner Community. *Intinerario*, 27, 226–242.

Institute for Security Studies, 2015. Factsheet: South Africa's Official Crime Statistics for 2013/14 [online]. *Africa Check*. Available from: http://afri cacheck.org/factsheets/factsheet-south-africas-official-crime-statistics-for-201314/ [Accessed 8 May 2015].

Iqani, M., 2015a. *Consumption, Media and the Global South: Aspiration Contested*. London: Palgrave.

Iqani, M., 2015b. 'The Consummate Material Girl?' *Feminist Media Studies*, 15 (5), 779–793.

Iqani, M., 2015c. A New Class for a New South Africa? The Discursive Construction of the 'Black Middle Class' in Post-Apartheid Media. *Journal of Consumer Culture*, 17 (1), 105–121.

Isama, A., 2018. In Conversation: Sisonke Msimang Wants Young South Africans To Always Ask, 'And Then What?' [online]. *OkayAfrica*. Available from: www.okayafrica.com/in-conversation-sisonke-msimang-always-another-country/ [Accessed 16 September 2019].

Jackson, P., 2015. 'White Genocide': Post-war Fascism and the Ideological Value of Evoking Existential Conflicts. *In*: C. Carmichael and R.C. Maguire, eds. *The Routledge History of Genocide*. Abingdon: Routledge, 207–226.

Jansen, E., 2019. *Like Family*. Johannesburg: Wits University Press.

Jason Hickel, 2015. *Democracy as Death: The Moral Order of Anti-Liberal Politics in South Africa*. California: University of California Press.

Johnson, J., 2018. The Self-radicalization of White Men: 'Fake News' and the Affective Networking of Paranoia. *Communication, Culture & Critique*, 11 (1), 100–115.

Kapstein, H., 2014. The Hysterics of District 9. *ESC: English Studies in Canada*, 40 (1), 155–175.

Keegan, T., 2001. Gender, Degeneration and Sexual Danger: Imagining Race and Class in South Africa, ca.1912. *Journal of Southern African Studies*, 27 (3), 459–477.

Klein, D.R., 2006. Negotiating femininity, ethnicity and history: representations of Ruth First in South African struggle narratives. PhD thesis. University of Cape Town, Cape Town.

Kohn, M., 2004. *Brave New Neighborhoods: The Privatization of Public Space*. New York: Taylor and Francis.

Kruger, C., 2017. (Dis)-empowered whiteness: an ethnography of the King Edward Park. PhD thesis. University of the Witwatersrand, Johannesburg.

La Fontaine, J., 1998. Ritual and Satanic Abuse in England. *In*: N. Scheper-Hughes and C. Sargent, eds. *The Cultural Politics of Childhood*. Berkeley, CA: University of California Press, 277–294.

Lacey, M., 1989. 'Platskiet-politiek': The Role of the Union Defence Force (UDF) 1910–1924. *In*: J. Cock and L. Nathan, eds. *War and*

Society: The Militarisation of South Africa. Cape Town: David Philip, 28–39.

Lamb, S. and Snodgrass, L., 2013. Growing Up with Normalised Violence: Narratives of South African Youth. *Commonwealth Youth and Development*, 11 (1), 4–21.

Lee, M., 2011. *Inventing Fear of Crime: Criminology and the Politics of Anxiety*. 3rd ed. Oxford and New York: Routledge.

Lefebvre, H., 1996. *Writings on Cities*. Minneapolis: Wiley-Blackwell.

Lemanski, C., 2004. A New Apartheid? The Spatial Implications of Fear of Crime in Cape Town, South Africa. *Environment and Urbanization*, 16 (2), 101–112.

Ligthelm, A.A., 2008. The Impact of Shopping Mall Development on Small Township Retailers. *South African Journal of Economic and Management Sciences*, 11 (1), 37–53.

Linnemann, T., 2010. Mad Men, Meth Moms, Moral Panic: Gendering Meth Crimes in the Midwest. *Critical Criminology*, 18 (2), 95–110.

Livermon, X., 2008. Sounds in the City. *In*: S. Nuttall and A. Mbembe, eds. *Johannesburg: The Elusive Metropolis*. Durham, NC: Duke University Press, 271–284.

Living Wage Series – South Africa [online], 2018. *WageIndicator.org*. Available from: https://wageindicator.org/salary/living-wage/south-africa-living-wage-series-january-2018 [Accessed 13 January 2020].

Lux, J. and Jordan, J.D., 2019. Alt-Right 'Cultural Purity', Ideology and Mainstream Social Policy Discourse: Towards a Political Anthropology of 'Mainstremeist' Ideology. *Social Policy Review 31: Analysis and Debate in Social Policy, 2019*, 151–176.

McCauley, C., Moskalenko, S. and Van Son, B., 2013. Characteristics of Lone-Wolf Violent Offenders: A Comparison of Assassins and School Attackers. *Perspectives on Terrorism*, 7 (1), 4–24.

McClintock, A., 1995. *Imperial Leather: Race, Gender and Sexuality in the Imperial Conquest*. London and New York: Routledge.

McCombs, M., 2002. The agenda-setting role of the mass media in the shaping of public opinion. Presented at the Mass Media Economics 2002 Conference, London School of Economics. Available from: http://sticerd.lse.ac.uk/dps/extra/McCombs.pdf.

McCracken, G.D., 1990. *Culture and Consumption: New Approaches to the Symbolic Character of Consumer Goods and Activities*. Bloomington, IN: Indiana University Press.

McCulloch, J., 2000. *Black Peril, White Virtue: Sexual Crime in Southern Rhodesia, 1902–1935*. Bloomington, IN: Indiana University Press.

McRobbie, A., 2009. *The Aftermath of Feminism: Gender, Culture and Social Change*. London: Sage.

Magubane, Z., 2004. The Revolution Betrayed? Globalization, Neoliberalism, and the Post-Apartheid State. *South Atlantic Quarterly*, 103 (4), 657–671.

Mahlangu, S. and Geyer, S., 2018. The Aftercare Needs of Nyaope Users: Implications for Aftercare and Reintegration Services. *Social Work*, 54, 327–345.

Malan, R., 1991. *My Traitor's Heart*. London: Vintage.

Maldonado-Torres, N., 2007. On the Coloniality of Being. *Cultural Studies*, 21 (2–3), 240–270.

Maninjwa, S., 2019. Joburg gentrification dream Maboneng goes up in smoke. Here's what went wrong. *BizNews.com*.

Manzo, K. and McGowan, P., 1992. Afrikaner Fears and the Politics of Despair: Understanding Change in South Africa. *International Studies Quarterly*, 36 (1), 1–24.

Mashaba to Undergo Arbitration Process [online], 2017. *South African Human Rights Commission*. Available from: www.sahrc.org.za/index.php/sahrc-media/news/item/955-mashaba-to-undergo-arbitration-process [Accessed 2 November 2018].

Massey, D., 1991. A Global Sense of Place. *Marxism Today*, 38, 24–29.

Mathews, S., Jewkes, R. and Abrahams, N.I., 2011. 'I Had a Hard Life': Exploring Childhood Adversity in the Shaping of Masculinities among Men Who Killed an Intimate Partner in South Africa. *British Journal of Criminology*, 51 (6), 960–977.

Matthews, S., Abrahams, N., Martin, L.J., Vetten, L., Van der Merwe, L. and Jewkes, R., 2004. *Every Six Hours a Woman is Killed by Her Intimate Partner*. Cape Town: Medical Research Council, Policy Briefs.

Mbembe, A., 2008. Aesthetics of Superfluity. *In*: S. Nuttall and A. Mbembe, eds. *Johannesburg: The Elusive Metropolis*. Durham, NC: Duke University Press, 37–67.

Mbembe, A., 2012. Theory from the Antipodes [online]. *Johannesburg Workshop in Theory and Criticism*. Available from: www.jwtc.org.za/salon_volume_5/achille_mbembe.htm [Accessed 18 September 2019].

Mbembe, A., Dlamini, N. and Khunou, G., 2004. Soweto Now. *Public Culture*, 16 (3), 499–506.

Mbembe, A. and Nuttall, S., 2004. Writing the World from an African Metropolis. *Public Culture*, 16 (3), 347–372.

Mbembe, A. and Nuttall, S., 2008. Afropolis. *In*: S. Nuttall and A. Mbembe, eds. *Johannesburg: The Elusive Metropolis*. Durham, NC: Duke University Press, 1–35.

Meyers, M., 1994. News of Battering. *Journal of Communication*, 44 (2), 47–63.

Meyers, M., 1997. *News Coverage of Violence against Women: Engendering Blame*. Thousand Oaks, CA and London: Sage.

Meyers, M., 2004a. African American Women and Violence: Gender, Race, and Class in the News. *Critical Studies in Media Communication*, 21 (2), 95–118.

Meyers, M., 2004b. Crack Mothers in the News: A Narrative of Paternalistic Racism. *Journal of Communication Inquiry*, 28 (3), 194–216.

Mhlambi, I.J., 2016. Embodied Discordance: Vernacular Idioms in Winnie: The Opera. *African Studies*, 75 (1), 48–73.

Miller, D., 2005. Consumption as the Vanguard of History. *In*: D. Miller, ed. *Acknowledging Consumption*. London and New York: Routledge, 1–52.

Mokoena, H., 2017. The Rickshaw Puller and the Zulu Policeman: Zulu Men, Work, and Clothing in Colonial Natal. *Critical Arts*, 31 (3), 123–141.

Mokwena, K. and Morojele, N., 2014. Unemployment and Unfavourable Social Environment as Contributory Factors to Nyaope Use in Three Provinces of South Africa. *African Journal for Physical Health Education, Recreation and Dance*, 20 (Supplement 1), 374–384.

Mondon, A. and Winter, A., 2020. *Reactionary Democracy: How Racism and the Populist Far Right Became Mainstream*. London: Verso Books.

Morrell, R., 1992. *White but Poor: Essays on the History of Poor Whites in Southern Africa, 1880–1940*. Pretoria: University of South Africa.

Morris, C.E., 2002. Pink Herring and the Fourth Persona: J. Edgar Hoover's Sex Crime Panic. *Quarterly Journal of Speech*, 88 (2), 228–244.

Moses, A.D., 2019. 'White Genocide' and the Ethics of Public Analysis. *Journal of Genocide Research*, 21 (2), 201–213.

Mosse, G.L., 1999. *The Fascist Revolution: Toward a General Theory of Fascism*. New York: Howard Fertig.

Mosselson, A., 2020. Inner-city Anxieties: Fear of Crime, Getting By and Disconnected Urban Lives. *In*: N. Falkof and C. van Staden, eds. *Anxious Joburg: The Inner Lives of a Global South City*. Johannesburg: Wits University Press, 241–264.

Mpalirwa, D., 2015. 'Asking for it': evaluating the framing of the sexual violence epidemic in South Africa. Presentation at University of Toronto. Available from: https://tspace.library.utoronto.ca/bitstream/1807/67804/1/2015_kiessling.pdf.

Msimang, S., 2018. Writer Sisonke Msimang on the positive power of South Africa's anger. *Financial Times*, 6 December.

Msomi, N., 2017. 'Bluetoothing': The Drug Myth that Fooled a Nation? *Bhekisisa*, 15 February. Available from: https://bhekisisa.org/article/2017-02-15-00-bluetooth-the-myth-that-fooled-a-nation/.

Murray, M.J., 2011. *City of Extremes: The Spatial Politics of Johannesburg*. Durham, NC: Duke University Press.

Murray, M.J., 2020. *Panic City: Crime and the Fear Industries in Johannesburg*. California: Stanford University Press.

Musila, G., 2015. *A Death Retold in Truth and Rumour: Kenya, Britain and the Julie Ward Murder*. Suffolk: James Currey.

Mutula, S.M., 2005. Peculiarities of the Digital Divide in Sub-Saharan Africa. *Program*, 39 (2), 122–138.

Mythen, G. and Walklate, S., 2006. Communicating the Terrorist Risk: Harnessing a Culture of Fear? *Crime, Media, Culture*, 2 (2), 123–142.

National Minimum Wage Act, 2018.

Newell, S., 2012. *The Modernity Bluff: Crime, Consumption and Citizenship in Côte d'Ivoire*. Chicago, IL: University of Chicago Press.

Nieftagodien, N., 2008. Xenophobia in Alexandra. In: E. Worby, S. Hassim and T. Kupe, eds. *Go Home or Die Here: Violence, Xenophobia and the Reinvention of Difference in South Africa*. Johannesburg: Wits University Press, 65–78.

Nieftagodien, N. and Bonner, P., 2008. *Alexandra: A History*. Johannesburg: Wits University Press.

Nightingale, C.H., 2015. *Segregation: A Global History of Divided Cities*. Chicago, IL: University of Chicago Press.

Nixon, R., 1994. *Homelands, Harlem, and Hollywood: South African Culture and the World Beyond*. New York and London: Routledge.

Nolan, L.B., 2015. Slum Definitions in Urban India: Implications for the Measurement of Health Inequalities. *Population and Development Review*, 41 (1), 59–84.

Nuttall, S., 2004. Girl Bodies. *Social Text*, 22 (1(78)), 17–33.

Nuttall, S. and Mbembe, A., eds., 2008. *Johannesburg: The Elusive Metropolis*. Durham, NC: Duke University Press.

Nuttall, S. and Michael, C.-A., 2000. *Senses of Culture: South African Culture Studies*. Oxford: Oxford University Press.

Odhiambo, T., 2006. Inventing Africa in the Twentieth Century: Cultural Imagination, Politics and Transnationalism in Drum Magazine. *African Studies*, 65 (2), 157–174.

Odugbemi, J., Rammala, O. and Wa Kamonji, W., 2019. There is no Africa in African studies. *The Mail & Guardian*, 16 August, n.p.

Onslow, S., 2012. White Power, Black Nationalism and External Intervention. In: S. Onslow, ed. *Cold War in Southern Africa: White Power, Black Liberation*. London and New York: Routledge, 9–34.

Pantucci, R., 2011. What Have We Learned about Lone Wolves from Anders Behring Breivik? *Perspectives on Terrorism*, 5 (5–6), 27–42.

Parenzee, P. and Smythe, D., 2003. *Domestic Violence and Development: Looking at the Farming Context*. Cape Town: Institute of Criminology, University of Cape Town.

Parnell, S. and Mabin, A., 1995. Rethinking Urban South Africa. *Journal of Southern African Studies*, 21 (1), 39–61.

Patel, S., 2011. Domestic Workers Summit Presentation. Presentation to COSATU. Available from: www.cosatu.org.za/docs/misc/2011/dwsum mitpresentation.pdf.

Pogue, J., 2019. The Myth of White Genocide [online]. *Pulitzer Center.* Available from: https://pulitzercenter.org/reporting/myth-white-genocide [Accessed 2 March 2020].

Posel, D., 1989. A Battlefield of Perceptions: State Discourses on Political Violence, 1985–1988. *In*: J. Cock and L. Nathan, eds. *War and Society: The Militarisation of South Africa*. Cape Town: David Philip, 262–274.

Posel, D., 2010. Races to Consume: Revisiting South Africa's History of Race, Consumption and the Struggle for Freedom. *Ethnic and Racial Studies*, 33 (2), 157–175.

Racial and Ethnic Disparities Continue in Pregnancy-Related Deaths [online], 2019. *Center for Disease Control.* Available from: www. cdc.gov/media/releases/2019/p0905-racial-ethnic-disparities-pregnancy-deaths.html [Accessed 16 January 2020].

Ramaga, P.V., 1992. Relativity of the Minority Concept. *Human Rights Quarterly*, 14 (1), 104–119.

Ramutsindela, M., 2002. 'Second Time Around': Squatter Removals in a Democratic South Africa. *GeoJournal*, 57 (1/2), 49–56.

Ranstorp, M., 2013. 'Lone Wolf Terrorism'. The Case of Anders Breivik. *S&F Sicherheit und Frieden*, 31 (2), 87–92.

Ratele, K., 2016. *Liberating Masculinities*. Cape Town: HSRC Press.

Red October [online], 2014. Available from: http://redoctober.co.za/ [Accessed 20 May 2014].

Reiger, K. and Dempsey, R., 2006. Performing Birth in a Culture of Fear: An Embodied Crisis of Late Modernity. *Health Sociology Review*, 15 (4), 364–373.

Rentschler, C.A., 2015. Distributed Activism: Domestic Violence and Feminist Media Infrastructure in the Fax Age. *Communication, Culture & Critique*, 8 (2), 182–198.

Report on the Interactive Planning Workshop for Johannesburg, 2000. Greater Johannesburg Metropolitan Council.

Richardson, J., 2006. *Analysing Newspapers: An Approach from Critical Discourse Analysis*. New York: Palgrave.

Richardson, J.T., Best, J. and Bromley, D.G., eds., 1991. *The Satanism Scare*. New York: Aldine de Gruyter.

van Riet, G., 2018a. One trek laer: the laager as infrastructure in the reiteration of onslaught in 21st century Potchefstroom. Conference presentation, '(Re)imagining Liberations', University of the Witwatersrand, 6 August.

van Riet, G., 2018b. Personal communication with Gideon van Riet.

Rinelli, L. and Opondo, S.O., 2013. Affective Economies: Eastleigh's Metalogistics, Urban Anxieties and the Mapping of Diasporic City Life. *African and Black Diaspora: An International Journal*, 6 (2), 236–250.

Roberts, B., 2010. Fear Factor: Perceptions of Safety in South Africa. In: B. Roberts, M. wa Kivilu and Y.D. Davids, eds. *South African Social Attitudes Second Report: Reflections on the Age of Hope*. Pretoria: HSRC Press, 250–275.

Rousseau, J., 2013. Occult crime unit is offensive to common sense and morality [online]. *GroundUp*. Available from: www.groundup.org.za/article/occult-crime-unit-offensive-common-sense-and-morality/.

Roy, S., 2008. The Grey Zone: The 'Ordinary' Violence of Extraordinary Times. *Journal of the Royal Anthropological Institute*, 14 (2), 316–333.

Sabatini, F. and Salcedo, R., 2007. Gated Communities and the Poor in Santiago, Chile: Functional and Symbolic Integration in a Context of Aggressive Capitalist Colonization of Lower-class Areas. *Housing Policy Debate*, 18 (3), 577–606.

Sasson, T., 1995. *Crime Talk: How Citizens Construct a Social Problem*. New York: Aldine de Gruyter.

Scheper-Hughes, N., 1992. *Death Without Weeping: The Violence of Everyday Life in Brazil*. California: University of California Press.

Sebro, T.H., 2013. Terrorism in Norway: Of Trolls and Other Monsters. *Tani Sebro, PhD*. Available from: https://tanisebro.com/2013/07/26/terrorism-in-norway-of-trolls-and-other-monsters/.

Sentence imposed on Vicki Momberg confirms double standards in South Africa regarding race, 2018 [online]. *AfriForum*. Available from: https://afriforum.co.za/en/sentence-imposed-vicki-momberg-confirms-double-standards-south-africa-regarding-race/ [Accessed 29 August 2018].

Showalter, E., 1997. *Hystories: Hysterical Epidemics and Modern Culture*. New York: Picador.

Sibanda-Moyo, N., Khonje, E. and Brobbey, M.K., 2017. *Violence Against Women in South Africa: A Country in Crisis 2017*. Johannesburg: Centre for the Study of Violence and Reconciliation.

Sibembe, Y. and Simelane, B.C., 2019. Alexandra Renewal Project: search for the missing R1.6bn [online]. *Daily Maverick*. Available from: www.dailymaverick.co.za/article/2019-04-12-alexandra-renewal-project-search-for-the-missing-r1-6bn/ [Accessed 9 January 2020].

Silber, G. and Geffen, N., 2016. Race, Class and Violent Crime in South Africa: Dispelling the 'Huntley Thesis'. *SA Crime Quarterly*, 30, 35–43.

Simone, A., 2004. *For the City Yet to Come: Changing African Life in Four Cities*. Durham, NC: Duke University Press.

Simone, A., 2008. People as Infrastructure: Intersecting Fragments in Johannesburg. *In*: S. Nuttall and A. Mbembe, eds. *Johannesburg: The Elusive Metropolis*. Durham, NC: Duke University Press, 68–90.

Skogan, W.G., 1995. Crime and the Racial Fears of White Americans. *The ANNALS of the American Academy of Political and Social Science*, 539 (1), 59–71.

Smit, A., 2016. Reading South African Bridal Television: Consumption, Fantasy and Judgement. *Communicatio*, 42 (4), 63–78.

Soyinka, W., 2007. *Climate of Fear: The Quest for Dignity in a Dehumanized World*. London: Random House.

Special Committee of Inquiry into Farm Attacks, 2003. *Report of the Committee of Inquiry Into Farm Attacks*. South Africa.

Spinks, C., 2001. A New Apartheid? Urban Spatiality, (Fear of) Crime and Segregation in Cape Town, South Africa. *In: Working Paper Series*. London: Development Studies Institute, London School of Economic and Political Science.

Springhall, J., 1998. *Youth, Popular Culture and Moral Panics: Penny Gaffs to Gangsta-Rap, 1830–1996*. Basingstoke: Macmillan.

van Staden, C., 2015. Chewing on Japan: Consumption, Diplomacy and Kenny Kunene's Nyotaimori Scandal. *Critical Arts*, 29 (2), 107–125.

van Staden, C., 2020. We Are All in This Together: Global Citizen, Violence and Anxiety in Johannesburg. *In*: N. Falkof and C. van Staden, eds. *Anxious Joburg: The Inner Lives of a Global South City*. Johannesburg: Wits University Press, 23–44.

Statistics South Africa, 2017. *Living Conditions of Households in South Africa 2014/15*. Pretoria: Statistics South Africa.

Statistics South Africa, 2019. Inequality trends in South Africa: A multi-dimensional diagnostic of inequality [online]. *Statistics South Africa*. Available from: www.statssa.gov.za/?p=12744 [Accessed 27 November 2019].

Statistics South Africa, 2020. Youth graduate unemployment rate increases in Q1: 2019 [online]. *Statistics South Africa*. Available from: www. statssa.gov.za/?p=12121 [Accessed 4 March 2020].

Steinberg, J., 2002. *Midlands*. Johannesburg; Cape Town: Jonathan Ball Publishers.

Steyn, M., 2001. *Whiteness Just Isn't What It Used to Be: White Identity in a Changing South Africa*. New York: State University of New York Press.

Steyn, M., 2004. Rehabilitating a Whiteness Disgraced: Afrikaner White Talk in Post-Apartheid South Africa. *Communication Quarterly*, 52 (2), 143–169.

Steyn, M., 2005. White Talk. *In*: A.J. López, ed. *Postcolonial Whiteness: A Critical Reader on Race and Empire*. Albany, NY: State University of New York Press, 119–136.

Steyn, M. and Foster, D., 2008. Repertoires for Talking White: Resistant Whiteness in Post-Apartheid South Africa. *Ethnic and Racial Studies*, 31 (1), 25–51.

Stoddard, E., 2021. Business Maverick: first-quarter unemployment rate hits record high of 43.2%, youth jobless rate 74.7% [online]. *Daily Maverick*. Available from: www.dailymaverick.co.za/article/2021–06–01-first-quarter-unemployment-rate-hits-record-high-of-43–2-youth-jobless-rate-74–7/ [Accessed 7 July 2021].

Stoler, A.L., 2010. *Carnal Knowledge and Imperial Power: Race and the Intimate in Colonial Rule*. Berkeley, CA: University of California Press.

Suarez, E. and Gadalla, T.M., 2010. Stop Blaming the Victim: A Meta-Analysis on Rape Myths. *Journal of Interpersonal Violence*, 25 (11), 2010–2035.

Swanson, M.W., 1977. The Sanitation Syndrome: Bubonic Plague and Urban Native Policy in the Cape Colony, 1900–1909. *Journal of African History*, 18 (3), 387–410.

Taylor, A., 2018. Australia looks into resettling white South African farmers who say they are persecuted. *Washington Post*, 16 March.

Teppo, A., 2004. *The Making of a Good White: A Historical Ethnography of the Rehabilitation of Poor Whites in a Suburb of Cape Town*. Helsinki: Helsinki University Press.

The 'Poor-White' Problem in South Africa, 1933. *British Medical Journal*, 2 (3,788), 296–297.

Theodosiou, P. and Sinclair, H., 2018. Dutton's white South African farmers claim 'breathtakingly hypocritical': HRW [online]. *SBS News*. Available from: www.sbs.com.au/news/dutton-s-white-south-african-farmers-claim-breathtakingly-hypocritical-hrw [Accessed 29 August 2018].

Thomas, L.E., 1999. *Under the Canopy: Ritual Process and Spiritual Resilience in South Africa*. Columbia, SC: University of South Carolina Press.

Thompson, A., 2003. Tiffany, Friend of People of Color: White Investments in Antiracism. *International Journal of Qualitative Studies in Education*, 16 (1), 7–29.

Thompson, L., 1985. *The Political Mythology of Apartheid*. New Haven, CT and London: Yale University Press.

Thornton, R., 1994. South Africa: Countries, Boundaries, Enemies and Friends. *Anthropology Today*, 10 (6), 7–15.

du Toit, L., 2014. Shifting Meanings of Postconflict Sexual Violence in South Africa. *Signs*, 40 (1), 101–123.

Tolsi, N., 2018a. The rainbow beauty of Hashim Amla [online]. *Cricket Monthly*. Available from: www.thecricketmonthly.com/story/1131324/ the-rainbow-beauty-of-hashim-amla [Accessed 6 December 2018].

Tolsi, N., 2018b. Starting the Fire: The 2018 Ruth First Memorial Lecture. Available from: http://journalism.co.za/wp-content/uploads/2018/10/ Ruth-First-Memorial-Lecture-by-Niren-Tolsin-full-speech-2018.pdf.

Ullmann, C., 2005. Black peril, white fear – representations of violence and race in South Africa's English press, 1976–2002, and their influence on public opinion. PhD thesis. Universität zu Köln, Köln.

Üstüner, T. and Holt, D.B., 2010. Toward a Theory of Status Consumption in Less Industrialized Countries. *Journal of Consumer Research*, 37 (1), 37–56.

Vahed, G., 2015. Migrants, Drugs and Xenophobia: The Case of Whoonga Park in Durban. *The Oriental Anthropologist*, 15 (2), 261–282.

Valji, N., Harris, B. and Simpson, G., 2004. Crime, Security and Fear of the Other [online]. *Centre for the Study of Violence and Reconciliation*. Available from: www.csvr.org.za/media-articles/latest-csvr-in-the-media/2099-crime-security-and-fear-of-the-other [Accessed 5 December 2017].

Vetten, L., 2005. Addressing domestic violence in South Africa: reflections on strategy and practice. Presented at the Expert Group Meeting on 'Violence against women: good practices in combating and eliminating violence against women', United Nations Division for the Advancement of Women, Vienna, 17–20 May.

Victor, J.S., 1991. The Dynamics of Rumor-Panics about Satanic Cults. *In*: J.T. Richardson, J. Best and D.G. Bromley, eds. *The Satanism Scare*. New York: Aldine de Gruyter, 221–236.

Villet, C., 2018. South Africa as Postcolonial Heterotopia: The Racialized Experience of Place and Space. *Foucault Studies*, 24, 12–33.

de Vries, F., 2008. Megamalls, Generic City. *In*: S. Nuttall and A. Mbembe, eds. *Johannesburg: The Elusive Metropolis*. Durham, NC: Duke University Press, 297–306.

Wainaina, B., 2006. How to Write about Africa. *Granta Magazine*, 92, n.p.

Walby, K. and Spencer, D., 2011. How Emotions Matter to Moral Panics. *In*: S.P. Hier, ed. *Moral Panic and the Politics of Anxiety*. London: Routledge, 104–116.

Waldron, D., 2005. Role-Playing Games and the Christian Right: Community Formation in Response to a Moral Panic. *The Journal of Religion and Popular Culture*, 9 (1), 3–3.

Walsh, J., 2019. A conspiracy: How the far-right fan the flames of south africa's farm murders [online]. *The New European*. Available from: www.theneweuropean.co.uk/top-stories/how-far-right-fan-flames-south-africa-farm-murders-1-6193577 [Accessed 15 August 2019].

Walsh, S., 2013. 'We Won't Move': The Suburbs Take Back the Centre in Urban Johannesburg. *City*, 17 (3), 400–408.

Wambugu, J.N., 2005. When Tables Turn: Discursive Constructions of Whites as Victims of Affirmative Action in Post-Apartheid South Africa. *Psychology in Society*, 31, 57–70.

Wasserman, H., 2009. Learning a New Language: Culture, Ideology and Economics in Afrikaans Media After Apartheid. *International Journal of Cultural Studies*, 12 (1), 61–80.

Waters, A.M., 1997. Conspiracy Theories as Ethnosociologies: Explanation and Intention in African American Political Culture. *Journal of Black Studies*, 28 (1), 112–125.

Weigman, R., 2012. *Object Lessons*. Durham, NC: Duke University Press.

Wekker, G., 2016. *White Innocence: Paradoxes of Colonialism and Race*. Durham, NC: Duke University Press.

van der Westhuizen, C., 2007. *White Power and the Rise and Fall of the National Party*. Cape Town: Zebra Press.

van der Westhuizen, C., 2017. *Sitting Pretty: White Afrikaans Women in Postapartheid South Africa*. Durban: UKZN Press.

White, L., 2000. *Speaking with Vampires: Rumor and History in Colonial Africa*. Berkeley, CA: University of California Press.

WHO, 2019a. Maternal Mortality [online]. Available from: www.who.int/news-room/fact-sheets/detail/maternal-mortality [Accessed 16 September 2019].

WHO, 2019b. Life Expectancy [online]. Available from: www.who.int/gho/mortality_burden_disease/life_tables/situation_trends_text/en/ [Accessed 16 September 2019].

WHO / Unicef, 2019. Updated Estimates Available for Household Drinking Water, Sanitation and Hygiene [online]. *World Health Organization/ Unicef Joint Monitoring Programme*. Available from: https://washdata.org/ [Accessed 16 September 2019].

Who We Are [online], n.d. *Suidlanders*. Available from: https://suidlanders.org/who-we-are/.

Wilkinson, K., 2017. Why calculating a farm murder rate in SA is near impossible [online]. *Africa Check*. Available from: https://africacheck.org/2017/05/08/analysis-calculating-farm-murder-rate-sa-near-impossible/ [Accessed 28 August 2018].

Willoughby-Herard, T., 2015. *Waste of a White Skin: The Carnegie Corporation and the Racial Logic of White Vulnerability*. Oakland, CA: UCLA Press.

Witz, L., 2003. *Apartheid's Festival: Contesting South Africa's National Pasts*. Bloomington, IN: Indiana University Press.

Worby, E., Hassim, S. and Kupe, T., eds., 2008. *Go Home or Die Here: Violence, Xenophobia and the Reinvention of Difference in South Africa.* Johannesburg: Wits University Press.

Wright, L., 1994. *Remembering Satan.* London: Serpent's Tail.

Index

240 *Index*

discourse (*cont.*)
  press 87, 193
  progressive 72
  white 36, 47–48, 153
Dixon, Natalie 165
Dobsonville 78, 98–109, 121
domestic employees *see* labour:
  domestic
Dosekun, Simidele 39, 117, 121
Douglas, Mary 168
drugs 21, 109, 167
  addicts 114–115, 128, 135–136
  dealers 5, 32, 126, 128, 138, 144
  nyaope 32, 114–115, 117, 124,
    126, 128, 131, 133, 1357,
    145, 147–148, 167, 194
  users 32, 115–116, 127, 135–136,
    166, 170
du Plessis, Elmien 71–72
Durington, Matthew 122, 152–153
Dutton, Peter 41–42, 50–51

Economic Freedom Fighters 67, 104
  see also Malema, Julius
emigration 63, 66
ethnosociologies 15–16, 82, 117,
  131, 153, 197
Eyewitness News 126, 133–134

Facebook 32, 39, 48, 51, 122, 126,
  135, 149, 155–156, 160, 163–
  164, 174, 187, 189, 198
farm murders 29, 36–40, 49, 62,
  70–71, 74n11, 76n22
  see also Roets, Ernst
farmers 35, 38, 41, 50, 58, 60–61,
  63, 66, 72–74, 194
  see also boer
Feldman, Allen 88, 95
femicide 30, 37, 61, 87, 94, 99
  see also violence against women
feminist 14, 56–57, 69, 83, 111n2
folk devils 15, 32, 69–72, 99, 136,
  138, 198
  see also Cohen, Stanley

Fox News 41, 51, 58, 62, 65,
  67, 71
Freedom Front Plus 38

Gaonkar, Dilip 22
gated communities 18, 122, 152, 160
gay men 21, 69
Gedye, Lloyd 38, 51, 73
gender-based violence *see* femicide;
  rape; violence against women
genocide 39
  see also white: genocide
Gikandi, Simon 9, 22
Ginsburg, Rebecca 158, 181–182
global
  media 9, 10, 22, 24, 70
  north 27, 179
  order 17, 24
  south 6, 7, 10, 18, 19, 27–28,
    34n6, 116, 120, 197
globalisation 10, 11, 12, 20, 86, 115,
  118, 192
Gobodo-Madikizela, Pumla 88, 144
good whiteness 154–155, 166, 175,
  183–184, 187
Goode, Erich 12
Gouws, Amanda 94
government 5, 38–39, 46, 67, 74–75
Gqola, Pumla Dineo 23, 36, 79, 95,
  110–111, 111n2

Halberstam, Jack 27
Harvey, David 162
hate speech 53, 67–68, 76
Hickel, Jason 129
hip-hop 96, 131
HIV 3, 115
Hofmeyr, Steve 40–41, 52, 57–58,
  61, 64, 67–68
homelessness 3, 163, 166–171,
  175–178, 194, 198
Hook, Derek 29
hooks, bell 36, 168
housekeeper 129, 181
  see also labour: domestic

EU authorised representative for GPSR:
Easy Access System Europe, Mustamäe tee 50,
10621 Tallinn, Estonia
gpsr.requests@easproject.com

www.ingramcontent.com/pod-product-compliance
Lightning Source LLC
Chambersburg PA
CBHW071017280326
41935CB00011B/1392